Angles of Vision

Angles of Vision

How to Understand Social Problems

Leonard Beeghley
University of Florida

Westview Press
A Member of Perseus Books, L.L.C.

Copyright © 1999 by Leonard Beeghley

Published in 1999 in the United States of America by Westview Press, 5500 Central Avenue, Boulder, Colorado 80301-2877, and in the United Kingdom by Westview Press, 12 Hid's Copse Road, Cumnor Hill, Oxford OX2 9JJ

Library of Congress Cataloging-in-Publication Data
Beeghley, Leonard.
 Angles of vision : how to understand social problems / Leonard
Beeghley.
   p.   cm.
 Includes bibliographical references and index.
 ISBN 0-8133-2948-5 (hc.).—ISBN 0-8133-2949-3 (pbk.)
 1. Social problems.   I. Title.
HN17.5.B374   1999
361.1—dc21   98-13958
                                                                                                        CIP

The paper used in this publication meets the requirements of the American National Standard for Permanence of Paper for Printed Library Materials Z39.48-1984.

10   9   8   7   6   5   4   3   2   1

For EHB,
who faces the world with a smile

Contents

Tables and Figures

Preface

In his essay "Sociology's Critical Irony," Joseph Gusfield tells an anecdote about four professors who come across a human body at the base of a bridge (1990:37). The physicist examines the body as matter that has been in motion from the bridge. The biologist examines it to determine if it is still alive. The psychologist speculates about the possibility of suicidal motives. The sociologist examines the pockets to find out what groups the person belonged to. All these angles of vision are useful; each can lead to valuable knowledge. But Gusfield's point, if I read him correctly, is that sociological explanations tend to focus on the context in which behavior occurs. For example, at the individual level, sociologists want to know how people are affected by and affect groups. At the structural level, sociologists want to know why so few or so many individuals are like the unfortunate person at the base of the bridge. The distinction is crucial.

In this book, I try to explain clearly and concisely the origin and nature of selected social problems, with an emphasis on distinguishing between individual and structural angles of vision. In so doing, I have tried to give readers a sense of real people struggling in a context of vast historical changes that have increased their range of choices. I argue that the key to understanding social problems involves looking at the social structure. The reason for this emphasis is that knowing why individuals with certain characteristics act as they do explains little about how the social structure encourages or discourages such behaviors. As will become clear, there is nothing vague about structural explanations; it can be shown how and why specific variables affect rates of behavior.

The book is addressed to the beginning student and also the general reader. As a look at the table of contents reveals, the book is relatively brief. My goal is not complete coverage of topics dealt with in social problems courses. It is, rather, to present a strategy for understanding such issues.

There are advantages to a brief book. It seems to me that the large coffee-table-style texts produced today are often confusing. The (frequently irrelevant) pictures, marginalia, boxes, inserts, and other trappings make it hard to find the running text and hard to follow the author's theme. So I have omitted any "filler" material and tried to write a book that is interesting and provocative, that stimulates readers to think for themselves.

My hope is that the brevity of this book will lead readers to look at some of the original sources. A few are sociological classics. By "classic," I mean a book or article that remains stimulating, no matter when it was written. Some obvious examples come to mind: *Rules of the Sociological Method* by Emile Durkheim (1895; considered in Chapter 1) and "The Web of Group Affiliations" by Georg Simmel (1908; considered in Chapter 10). Other original sources are more recent but engaging and insightful, worth readers' time. Some examples are *The Social Meaning of Money* by Viviana Zelizer (1994; considered in Chapter 3) and *Crime and the American Dream* by Steven Messner and Richard Rosenfeld (1997; considered in Chapter 7). I have suggested items that are worth reading by citing the author's name and the title in the text rather than relegating them to the references.

This book has other advantages as well, which can again be contrasted with the coffee-table-style texts. Those books tend to introduce the discipline in terms of mutually competing assumptions made by "functionalists," "conflict theorists," "symbolic interactionists," and so on. This strategy is misbegotten and misleading. It is misbegotten because it orients the analysis to the intellectual turf wars that so debilitate the discipline. In contrast, I have focused on American society and its comparison to other Western nations rather than on sociologists. More seriously, the strategy of presenting sociology according to its practitioners' assumptions is misleading because it implies that findings depend on assumptions. Nothing could be further from the truth. No science assumes; it hypothesizes, discovers, explains. For example, physiologists would never "interpret" the spleen based on competing assumptions about its nature or impact; they would look and then try to explain. So do sociologists—in practice. In order to suggest this fact, I have made a point of stating hypotheses and empirical generalizations in covariance form. This pedagogical device helps readers see how a change in one phenomenon is associated with change in another. The issues considered in this book (and in social problems courses) are serious. Their political and moral implications are profound. I am convinced that sociology can (and should) inform public debate. It can do so, however, only when its empirical basis is clear.

Leonard Beeghley

Acknowledgments

Several persons read various chapters of this book in manuscript form and made suggestions. Among them are the following:

Betty Alt, University of Southern Colorado
Patricia Atchinson, Colorado State University
Chet Ballard, Valdosta State University
Lori Brown, Meredith College
Christopher Chan, Florida State University
Tom Cook, Wayne State College
Terry Danner, Saint Leo College
Bob Granfield, University of Denver
Beth Hess, County College of Morris

All too often, I find myself being an intellectual pilgrim: looking into new areas of specialization. My colleagues at the University of Florida graciously tolerate this habit, often consenting to read and comment on what I write. This is so even though they sometimes disagree with me. For this book, the following individuals were especially helpful: Ronald Akers, Stan Albrecht, Anthony LaGreca, Lonn Lanza-Kaduce, Terry Mills, John Scanzoni, Karen Seccombe, and Eleanor Stoller.

Finally, I would like to thank the staff at Westview Press, especially Adina Popescu, the sociology editor, and Lisa Wigutoff, the project editor, for all their kindness and help. Alice Colwell did a marvelous job of copyediting the manuscript.

I am most grateful to all those named here. Obviously, any mistakes that remain are mine.

L. B.

1 The Study of Social Problems

Outline of Chapter 1

I. Defining Social Problems
   A. The Extent of Harm
   B. Identification and Political Recognition
   C. Need for Improvement

II. Understanding Social Problems
   A. Identifying the Facts
      1. The Dimensions of Social Problems
      2. Consequences of Social Problems
   B. Explaining the Facts
      1. Individuals and Social Problems
      2. Social Structure and Social Problems
   C. Exploring the Implications

The subjects covered in this book are familiar, almost too familiar. Everyone has attitudes about abortion, poverty, drugs, and all the other issues dealt with here. Yet precisely because these topics are so familiar, they are often not understood. This lack of insight occurs mainly because conventional interpretations of events are so easily accepted; they are common sense. But relying on explanations that seem obvious usually does not get us very far. The problem, as Randall Collins observes, is that for each commonsense interpretation there usually exists an opposing view that is equally commonsensical to those who believe it (1992:87). Such differences are difficult to reconcile without evidence and a framework for asking questions about that evidence. This book analyzes selected social problems. Its purpose is to help you view familiar subjects in new ways.

Most people realize in their everyday lives that familiar subjects have several aspects, not all of which are readily apparent. This is certainly so in financial dealings. To take a trite example, most people learn not to accept a telephone company's presentation at face value, since actual long distance charges are often significantly higher than customers were led to believe when they signed up for the service. Yet this insight also applies to more serious issues, such as intimate relationships. At some point, each of my children has ended a statement with "and that's the truth." Alas, it sometimes turned out that important elements of "the truth" had been omitted. In daily life, then, most people try to pierce through the conventional explanations offered by children, spouses, salesclerks, and others in order to find the nonobvious elements of their presentation.

Sociologists do the same thing, using a social scientific angle of vision. As one of the founders of sociology, Emile Durkheim, remarked, a science of society sometimes causes people "to see things in a different way from the ordinary, for the purpose of any science is to make discoveries, and all such discoveries more or less upset accepted opinions" (1895:31). For example, some people see the problem of abortion as simple: It is murder. For others, the problem is equally simple: Restrictions on abortion deny women the right to control their fertility and, hence, keep them unequal to men. Note that both positions are moral stances and each seems like common sense to its adherents. There must be some underlying issues that are not obvious. Our challenge, in daily living and in social science, is to figure out what they are, to avoid being deceived by familiarity.

Sociology offers one way of overcoming this difficulty. Phrased formally, *sociology* can be defined as a systematic attempt at seeing social life as clearly as possible, understanding its various dimensions, and doing so without being swayed by one's personal hopes and fears. Although this is a complex task and not every sociological analysis leads to clarity or insight, sociology at its best employs a debunking orientation that takes observers beyond common sense, that upsets accepted wisdom. Its message, as Peter Berger comments, is that things are not what they seem.[1]

As I later explain, data in the form of systematic observations are necessary in order either to confirm or get past what seems like common sense. They indicate how often a harmful condition occurs and its consequences. Data usually lead to questions. One of my goals in this book is to teach you that the answers to questions depend on your angle of vision.

In order to illustrate how important the angle of vision is, imagine you are taking a course in art history and must do research on one of the paintings by the Dutch impressionist Vincent van Gogh, perhaps *Café Terrace at Night* (completed in 1888). As shown on the cover of this book, the painting depicts a modest establishment visited by ordinary citizens in the evenings, where they eat, drink, and socialize. Yet like much great art, this piece can be understood from several points of view, not all of them obvious.

One angle of vision would involve using a spectroscope to analyze the chemical composition of the paint, as van Gogh's work is characterized by bright colors. Another approach would be to use a magnifying glass to examine the artist's brush technique, since van Gogh used heavy, slashing strokes. A third perspective would be to look closely at it from a short distance to see how the images fit together. Finally, you might move several feet away to get an overall view. These last two steps are important because, as with many impressionist works, what viewers see changes at varying distances. Each of these angles of vision provides different yet complementary information. Each level of analysis is valid. And combining them leads to greater insight about the painting.

In this book, I emphasize two angles of vision—individual and structural—that, taken together, provide a more complete view of the problems facing our society. For example, one factor that helps to explain why individuals use drugs is the stress caused by unemployment, an individual issue. Yet as I argue, this information says little about why so many people ingest harmful substances. To deal with this problem it is necessary to look at structural factors. It turns out that all affluent societies display relatively high levels of drug use, so there must be something about affluent social structures that leads lots of people to "do drugs." Considered jointly, then, these two angles of vision, which I explain in more detail in a few moments, provide complementary ways of understanding.

Right now, however, a definition of social problems is necessary. The process of defining our topic not only illustrates the importance of viewing familiar subjects in new ways, it also suggests some fundamental characteristics of the United States.

Defining Social Problems

Defining social problems might seem straightforward. Everybody knows what they are. Indeed, the table of contents of this book provides a list of well-known subjects: ill health, gender inequality, and so on. But definition by example constitutes a poor tactic because it does not indicate why some issues become problematic while others do not. This fact is important because, perhaps surprisingly, not all harmful conditions are recognized as social problems.

Consider the harm caused by drug and automobile use. In 1995 almost 12,000 persons died from drug-related causes, only some of which involved illegal substances (NCHS, 1996b:22). Illicit drugs, like heroin and cocaine, are associated with crimes costing millions of dollars each year. Basing their judgments on such evidence, many people conclude that drugs constitute a major problem in the United States. This seems like common sense. Yet automobiles pose greater risks and costs than drugs. In 1995 about 42,000 persons died in automobile accidents and countless more were injured. Motor vehicle mishaps, in fact, are the leading cause of death in the population under 35 years of age. Further, property damage from these collisions totals billions of dollars each year. In addition, auto use creates air pollution, resulting in discomfort and illness for millions of people. Finally, automobile use contributes to the greenhouse effect, atmospheric warming, which may produce significant economic dislocation in the future. These differences mean that cars are inherently more harmful to human life than drugs. After all, people are three times more likely to die from using cars as drugs. Perhaps we ought to "just say no" to automobile use? This seems like common sense (!?).

My point, of course, is that a little data can turn "common sense" on its head. It is clear that the issues labeled "social problems" have hidden dimensions that go beyond a simple calculation of harm. As observers, we need guidelines to help us understand why such things as drug and auto use are evaluated differently. A definition of social problems provides such direction.

Here is the definition used in this book: A *social problem* is a harmful condition identified by a significant number of people and recognized politically as needing improvement. According to this definition, social problems have three aspects that should be discussed. (1) An objective part shows the extent of harm. (2) A subjective component indicates that a harmful condition has been identified and political debate ensued. And (3) an optimistic aspect suggests that people believe the condition can be improved.[2]

The Extent of Harm

Harm comes in many forms. People can be physically hurt, they can lose money or power, their moral values can be offended, or the environment in which they live can be degraded. In every case, however, harm must be a factual situation whose dimensions can be accurately described. Those asserting that either drugs or cars constitute a social problem must show the extent of drug and automobile use and its consequences. Ideally, as I later emphasize, such a description would examine both historical and international data because they help to place an issue into perspective. For example, reporting how drug use varies over time and from one nation to another leads to greater understanding.

Moreover, such information helps to show the harm caused by both drugs and policies designed to cope with them. Without gathering data that are as objective as possible (a demanding task), it is hard to assess the seriousness of a social problem. It is also difficult to identify the hidden factors involved.

Nonetheless, merely showing the existence of harm is not sufficient, as the different evaluations of automobile and drug use reveal. No matter how objective the data, some conditions that produce relatively little harm are defined as social problems while others that produce far more death, destruction, and cost are not treated in this way. Additional information is obviously needed.

Identification and Political Recognition

The recognition of social problems requires a subjective assessment by a "significant number" of people (Fuller and Myers, 1941). There has been considerable controversy in sociology as to how many persons are "significant," and it is easy to see why this question seems difficult to resolve. Does it take a majority of the population? An intense minority? A single powerful person? An expert or group of experts? In fact, there are occasions when each of these entities succeeds in claiming that a harmful condition constitutes a social problem. Thus, the answer has less to do with the absolute number of people who assert a condition is harmful than their influence in society.

The process of identifying a social problem typically involves feedback between the public and *opinion leaders,* those who bring issues to people's attention and teach them where their interests lie (Katz and Lazarsfeld, 1955). Most individuals use family and friends as their primary opinion leaders simply because of their emotional ties to them and the frequency of talking with them. But more distant opinion leaders exist as well. Some of them are politicians, such as the president, governors, members of Congress, and state legislators. Others are political activists concerned about specific issues. Still others are moral entrepreneurs, such as clergy, who want public policy to reflect a specific ethical position (Becker, 1963). Finally, some are idea brokers, such as professors, journalists, and experts in think tanks (Smith, 1991). These categories are not mutually exclusive; some opinion leaders fall into more than one. Their common characteristic is an active attempt at identifying social problems. In so doing, they place issues before the public, which responds (or not).

Here is an example of how the feedback between ordinary people and opinion leaders works. In 1962 a journalist named Michael Harrington wrote a book about the poor, *The Other America,* that sold well and also came to the attention of President John Kennedy. Many of the insights in this book were rather new and startling at the time because even though poverty was widespread, it was not considered a social problem. The issues Harrington raised were debated within the administration, and shortly after Kennedy's death, President Lyndon Johnson declared a War on Poverty. Moreover, during this same period many poor persons were demonstrating dissatisfaction—sometimes in unruly fashion—with their situation in life. As a result, then, of actions by an idea broker, the public's purchasing and reading the book, attention from politicians, and protests by impoverished persons, a harmful condition that most people (the nonpoor) had ignored was transformed into a social problem that remains vexing today. The issue was framed and political debate ensued in a complex interaction among opinion leaders and the public.[3]

Politics, at least in democratic societies, is a competitive process in which individuals and groups vie to get the attention of decisionmakers and ordinary citizens. The task, as C. Wright Mills phrased it in *The Sociological Imagination* (1959:8), is to transform the harm experienced by individuals as private troubles into public issues, into social problems that can be improved. Once this process is understood, it becomes clear that social problems change over time as political issues change.

Sometimes a condition accepted as right at one time becomes unacceptable and hence harmful later on. For example, the inequality that is intrinsic to traditional marriages (in which the husband is employed outside the home while the wife works inside) was considered by both men and women as natural just a few years ago, which meant that gender inequality was not deemed harmful. But times change, and this phenomenon is now considered a social problem because it restricts both women's and men's choices.

Sometimes a condition defined as harmful at one time becomes acceptable later on. For example, the acceptability of suicide among older persons appears to be increasing in the context of an aging population. This change indicates a rising concern about the current tendency to extend life without regard to its quality.

Note, however, that data were implicit in the examples used above. People claiming that gender inequality is a social problem point to the facts, such as income differences, marital roles, and the like. On this basis, they argue that such variations ought to be reduced. So there is always an interplay between the facts and subjective interpretation.

This interaction has important implications for understanding social problems. On the one hand, people select from reality certain issues to notice (drugs, for example), while ignoring others (cars). As a famous sociological aphorism states: If individuals define their situations as real, then they are real in their consequences. The authors of this statement, William I. Thomas and Dorothy Swaine Thomas, meant that there is a subjective component to human life that must always be taken into account (1928:272). On the other hand, the facts, the extent of harm as verified by observation, constitute a necessary counterpoint to people's subjective sense. The facts are vital because, in Robert K. Merton's words, "if people do not define real situations as real, they are nonetheless real in their consequences" (1976:22). Put differently, what you do not know can indeed hurt you. This is why I emphasize the importance of determining the amount of harm a condition produces. The definition of social problems, then, rests on these twin poles: data and their subjective interpretation. Then the possibility of improvement arises.

But the social world is rather obdurate, filled with competing interest groups. A problem for one group is often a solution for another group. But we are incurable optimists.

Need for Improvement

The pervasiveness of social problems reflects hope for the future, a sense that our lives can be improved. All notions of improving society are based on values, since there is no other way of evaluating social life. At least two principles underlie the desire for improvement: the belief in progress and the conviction that each individual has dignity and worth. These values, elements of faith, really, have been fundamental to Western culture for two millennia (Nisbet, 1969; Berger, 1992). Although often unrecognized, actions taken in terms of these values have had a double impact over time: They lead to the solution of some problems and the creation of others.

"Progress," an old commercial stated, "is our most important product." This could be the American motto. The notion of progress is a metaphor, of course, a way of talking about improving our lives. Consider how much better off we are today than in the past, simply as a result of technological advances. Improvements in nutrition, hygiene, and prenatal care mean that nearly all babies now survive. Children mature faster, grow larger, and are generally healthier. They have healthy (and straight!) teeth. Pregnancy can be controlled. For most persons, work is far less physically demanding. Many people live into old age. Most are now well educated. The home has become a place of relative luxury, filled with items that did not exist a century ago: plastic goods, gas and electric stoves, refrigerators, telephones, televisions, VCRs, computers, and bathrooms. Almost every adult now owns a car. More generally, improvements in transportation and communication have made the entire world seem smaller, more accessible. These examples show clearly that social life in the United States is far different today than it was just a short time ago. Indeed, it makes little sense to speak of fully modern societies before the latter part of the nineteenth century.

This 200-year process constitutes one of the greatest revolutions in history, nearly as significant as the emergence of agriculture and the development of the first civilizations. The basis for this revolution has been the growth of scientific knowledge, which leads to technological advances (Rosenberg and Birdzell, 1990). Science is a peculiar way of understanding the world. It emphasizes that each event has a cause, which can be discovered and verified by observation. Science and scientific ways of thinking have become embedded in Western culture. The widespread application of scientific knowledge to the practical problems human beings face has transformed our world over the past several centuries and made human beings less subject to the caprice of nature. As a result, we have choices today undreamed of in the past. Indeed, the story of the past two centuries is one of increasing choice in human affairs. The fact of choice indicates greater control over the dimensions of life: social, biological, and environmental. Everything is affected.

Some of these choices reflect trivial, albeit costly, changes in lifestyle. When I was a child, one purchased an inexpensive pair of "tennis shoes" and used them for every sport. Today I go into a store and the clerk asks if I walk, jog, play basketball, play racquetball, or play softball. I say yes and walk out with five pairs of shoes and a huge hole in my wallet.

Many of the choices stemming from progress, however, have significant political and moral implications and produce new social problems. For example, when it was shown that chlorine kills the cholera bacillus, chlorine was introduced into public water supplies beginning in 1908 (Page, 1987). One result of this change (along with other advances in sanitation and nutrition) is that people now live into old age. Yet such progress has led to difficulties never before seen in history. How are elderly people to be cared for? How are they to be supported economically? Note that these unresolved questions stem from a positive good: We now have the ability to delay death. Moral dilemmas follow. Who should choose the time and circumstances of death? In particular, when, if ever, is suicide among the aged justified? And how about assisted suicide? The salience of these questions indicates that scientific progress permits—even encourages—behaviors that were either impossible or immoral a few years ago.

Many people find it difficult to accept the idea that social problems constitute the paradoxical results of progress. The conventional assumption is that they represent the breakdown of society, not its advancement. "Decline," in fact, is a word often used in connection with commonsense interpretations of social problems. Yet few people would give up the technological advances described above that are the fruits of scientific progress. They do not want to go back to a preindustrial and rural lifestyle. Living rustically may be fun on vacation, but after a few days nearly everyone wants to use indoor plumbing. Although it sounds odd, the hidden reality is that the old verities people believe in and act on—among them a belief in hard work, acquisition of wealth, individualism, and scientific advance—frequently cause the very situations they define as problems.

The desire to improve people's lives leads to social problems in another way as well, through the increasing recognition that all human beings have dignity and worth. Historically, a process of value generalization has occurred in modern societies as this ethical principle has been applied to wider segments of the population. For example, problems like gender inequality reflect a recognition that people should not be discriminated against on the basis of their physical characteristics. And the situation is, in fact, somewhat better now than in the past: Discrimination has declined, and people's lives have improved.

Yet these (limited) improvements divide U.S. society, mainly, I think, because it is so much easier to imagine "the way we were" than to cope with change—even desired change. We hear, then, of the decline of the nuclear family and morality since, say, the 1950s. If mothers would just stay home and have lots of babies, if parents would just stay together, and if teenagers would just stay out of each other's arms, it is said, problems of the family would disappear. Such pleas cast a soft glow on reality and ignore certain ugly facts: among others, that in the 1950s women usually could not develop their nonreproductive abilities and many who found themselves pregnant resorted to dangerous and illegal methods to control their fertility. Although appeals to a mythical past soothe the psyche, they do not work in practice because they do not reflect these unpleasant realities.

Modernity has changed the family. A century ago it was a center for productive activity, and spouses were economically dependent on one another. In this historical context, the limits on women and men seemed (to most) part of the natural order. In order to return to the way we were, the United States would merely have to go back to a relatively preindustrial and rural lifestyle. My use of the word "merely" in this context is sarcasm, of course, since almost no one really wants to return to the past. Once again, the values we hold frequently lead us to see harmful conditions that become social problems, such as gender inequality.

The subjects dealt with in this book are familiar. Newspapers and television report on them each day, often without much depth or insight. The reason for this superficial quality is that the mass media typically provide only a snapshot of the situation. They offer a dramatic depiction of what is happening right now. Although such reports are useful, they often feature commonsense interpretations and much metaphorical hand-wringing. One (albeit not the only) way to attain greater insight is to study social problems sociologically.

Understanding Social Problems

We live in an uneasy time. People see changing morality about life and death, and feel adrift. They see families breaking up and worry about the future. Whites see periodic uprisings by African Americans and become afraid. Men see women demanding equality and (try to suppress) panic. In short, people sense that older ways of thinking and feeling are no longer useful. But in the face of unease, they cling to common sense. And common sense does not provide understanding. So they cling all the more. This is because ordinary people live in a private orbit composed of family, neighborhood, religion, and job. Thus circumscribed, they remain only dimly aware of the intricate ties between their own lives and the larger world. They fail to connect what happens to them with the course of history. Yet this is precisely the task if understanding is to occur. As C. Wright Mills put it, people must learn "to grasp history and biography and the relations between the two within society" (1959:4). Achieving such insight requires an intellectual framework. To see how important this is, imagine trying to put together a jigsaw puzzle without the aid of the picture on the box or the edge pieces. In this section, I introduce a framework for understanding social problems that I go on to use in each of the following chapters. My hope is to stimulate greater awareness of the sources of unease in the face of change.[4]

Identifying the Facts

It is essential to begin with data. In so doing, you should remember that all knowledge is based on comparison. It is not possible to understand any phenomenon—a tree, a car, an individual, a society—without comparing it in some fashion with another. In each chapter, I make such comparisons along two axes: the extent of a problem, which is to say how often it occurs, and how harmful it is, which is to say its consequences.[5]

The Dimensions of Social Problems.   Sociology at its best looks at the data along two dimensions: historical and international (Kohn, 1987). Historical data reveal how much change has occurred over time within one society, such as the United States. In general, I extend the analysis in each chapter back 100–200 years, or as far as plausible data are available.

This is a particularly useful period to examine, since it marks the transition to modernity. International data indicate the extent to which harmful conditions in one country occur at similar rates in others. I usually restrict international comparisons to Western industrial societies. Since these nations share a common cultural heritage and display advanced economies, their similarities and differences regarding the issues dealt with in this book can be especially revealing.

Information like this leads to productive questions, the key to understanding. For example, if the rate of poverty in the United States was high in the past (and it was) but is much lower now, one asks what has changed. Individual motives? Perhaps. But if the rate of poverty in this country is much higher than in Western Europe, one immediately wonders if barriers to opportunity have been imposed that keep large numbers of people impoverished. The strategy, then, is to look for explanatory factors that differ historically and internationally and appear logically related to poverty. Science, it seems to me, is simply the art of asking questions. The idea is that there are no secrets. The facts of nature, social life, even people's unconscious motives can be discovered if one asks the right questions. In sociology, historical and international data provide an empirical basis for such queries. They lead to greater understanding.

Max Weber pioneered use of such data in his studies of the relationship between religion and the origin of capitalism (1905, 1913, 1917, 1920). Weber wanted to understand why capitalism as an economic system arose in Western Europe and ushered in modern life. Thus, he performed a "logical experiment" by systematically comparing various Western nations in the seventeenth and eighteenth centuries with India and China at the same time and found that what distinguished Europe (and the United States) from these other nations was not the level of technology, a free labor force, or a variety of other factors. Rather, the West became unique because of the rise of the culture of capitalism as an unintended consequence of the Protestant Reformation (see Turner, Beeghley, and Powers, 1995). The term "culture of capitalism" refers to a set of values that support and justify making money. What happened was that behaviors undertaken for purely religious reasons, such as hard work aimed at acquiring wealth, were transformed over time into secular cultural values. These ethical standards in turn helped to usher in a new kind of society, one never before seen in history.

Weber's work is significant for two reasons. First, his research strategy can be used with other topics, such as the social problems considered in this book. As is typical, he began by identifying the facts and then attempted to explain them. Second, the culture of capitalism, capitalist economies, and scientific progress are linked (Rosenberg and Birdzell,

1990; Berger, 1986). One result is the revolutionary technological advances cited earlier, along with a cornucopia of consumer products. Enjoying these fruits of science requires a profit-based mechanism for production and distribution. Capitalist economies in turn depend upon a set of historically new cultural values that first appeared in the Western world a few hundred years ago. Another result has been the social problems considered in this book. Progress, you should recall, produces both benefit and harm.

I want to pause here for a moment and return to van Gogh's *Café Terrace at Night*. Imagine that as part of your research project you need to know more about its significance; after all, no painting exists in isolation. Such curiosity, I submit, must necessarily involve historical and international comparisons. In a short life (he died at age 37), van Gogh produced more than 800 works, which means it would be useful to place *Café Terrace at Night* into the context of his other paintings. Moreover, the impressionist movement of which van Gogh was a part developed at a crucial point in history, the latter years of the nineteenth century, which marks the transition to modernity. So it would be useful to understand how van Gogh was influenced by other Dutch painters (e.g., Rembrandt) who came before him as well as artists from other societies. For example, he admired romantic painters of an earlier era, such as the French master Eugène Delacroix, for their use of color. He also imitated certain aspects of Japanese art. Thus, although van Gogh's works usually depict ordinary scenes in "modern" (nineteenth-century) life, they do so with spectacular hues and shades characteristic of a previous era and with techniques borrowed from the Far East. Thus, in assessing the significance of van Gogh's work, your research strategy would mimic (loosely) Max Weber's "logical experiment."

I try to do the same thing in this book. In addition to considering the historical and international dimensions of social problems, however, it is also useful to know how much harm occurs.

Consequences of Social Problems. As the definition of the term "social problem" emphasizes, the claim that an issue constitutes a social problem is always based on an assessment of its harmful consequences. This is another way of comparing, of course. The sources of harm can be values, the impact of public policies regulating behavior, or the negative effects of positive changes, among other factors.

Some social problems carry harmful consequences because of the values people hold. Thus, because we value life we try to postpone death and have become pretty good at it. Success in the form of an aging population, however, creates economic problems (paying for income support and medical treatment) and moral dilemmas (suicide and assisted suicide among the elderly).

Some social problems occur because people have competing values. Abortion is an obvious example. Other social problems have harmful consequences because of public policies. For example, by keeping such drugs as alcohol and tobacco legal, government policy produces high use rates, along with high medical costs, deaths, accidents, and other problems. Alternatively, keeping such drugs as marijuana and heroin illegal directs people to the more dangerous legal substances and produces crime, violence, and neighborhood destruction. As you might guess, there are no easy answers to this issue; every policy alternative has, as it were, a down side.

Finally, historical changes sometimes have unintended harmful consequences that become social problems. As I mentioned earlier, although industrialization and capitalism led to a society of plenty, one side effect has been a rising divorce rate.

Although one could describe other types of harm, my intent here has been to provide a sense of the possibilities. Thus, by this point in each of the following chapters two types of information will be available: the historical and international dimensions of the issue and some of its harmful consequences. The next goal is to attempt an explanation.

Explaining the Facts

Understanding social problems requires a method, by which I mean a strategy for explanation rather than a statistical technique. As noted earlier, my approach is to distinguish between social psychological explanations of why individuals act and structural explanations of why rates of behavior vary. Each angle of vision refers to a complementary level of analysis. The point to remember is that the explanatory variables at each level differ.

Individuals and Social Problems.   The initial task is to understand why individuals act. Why does a person use drugs? Being unemployed and having friends who use drugs are typical explanations. These variables are social psychological in origin or impact; *social psychology* focuses on how people act, interact, influence groups to which they belong, and are influenced by groups. Put differently, social psychology is the study of how individuals react to their experiences with one another. As the drug example implies, individuals make decisions (although not always consciously) in light of their personal experiences.

The term *socialization* describes these experiences. It refers to the lifelong process by which individuals learn norms and values, internalize motives and needs, develop intellectual and social skills, and enact roles in everyday life (Brim, 1966). In plainer language, socialization refers to the process of growing up, with the addendum that it continues throughout life. In effect, each individual's personal experiences form a sort of prism through which she or he channels behavior.

Four basic principles shape this prism, at least initially. First, childhood interactions are usually more influential on individuals than later experiences. Second, interaction in primary groups (such as family and faith groups) is usually more influential than interaction in secondary groups (such as schools and work groups). Third, interaction with people who are emotionally significant (such as parents and friends) is usually more influential than interaction with ordinary persons. Fourth, long-term interaction is usually more influential than short-term interaction.[6]

Knowledge of these principles helps observers understand how individuals' backgrounds lead them to act as they do. People's biographies are composed of family, friends, and enemies. They also comprise the schools attended, the books read, and even the television programs watched. If people adhere to a religious faith, join a Scout troop, attend parties, or belong to a gang, these experiences, too, become part of the socialization process. Eventually, most persons enter an occupational group, identify with a political party, and have other experiences by which they learn what is expected (norms and values), develop personality characteristics (internal motives and needs), and understand how to act (knowledge and skills). These are the elements of socialization as defined above. Note the active verbs: People attend, join, enter, and so on; they choose, even at rather young ages. Socialization is not a passive but an interactive process.

This element of choice is important because, as I mentioned earlier, socialization continues throughout people's lives. In effect, the prism through which individuals channel their behavior is not cut once, in childhood, say, and left that way forever. Rather, people periodically re-cut their own prism—that is, they change their behavior—in light of new experiences. For example, regardless of family background, when people obtain jobs that require self-direction they become more intellectually flexible themselves and come to value this trait in others as well (Kohn and Schooler, 1983). Similarly, when people change faith groups they often alter their behavior. The Southern Baptist, say, who becomes an Episcopalian (it happens), is more likely to drink; the Episcopalian who becomes a Southern Baptist (it also happens) is less likely to drink (Beeghley, Bock, and Cochran, 1990). Thus, as individuals move through life they adopt a variety of *reference groups* along the way (Merton and Rossi, 1968). The term refers to collectivities of people whose values, tastes, and patterns of action become significant in the development of one's own attitudes and behavior.

Taken together, knowing how individuals are socialized and their choice of reference groups leads to understanding. We see why people perform the harmful acts considered in this book.

A qualifying note: Other ways of understanding individuals exist. One of the most important is to look for the unconscious motives and drives underlying human behavior (Turner, 1988). This task is difficult because everyone exposed to modern technology becomes accustomed to the use of reason and to pragmatic approaches to daily life. Yet, as Daniel Goleman observes in *Emotional Intelligence,* behind the utility of logic lies the reality of emotions, many of which we are unaware (1995). Although such data are very hard to obtain, I refer to them periodically.

Although knowledge of why individuals act is useful, it fails to take us beyond people's private orbits. In fact, I would like to make a surprising claim: Individuals are neither the cause of nor the solution to social problems. This idea contradicts common sense and is, hence, difficult for many people to accept. Such difficulty is probably due to certain unique aspects of U.S. history. Our Puritan heritage emphasizes an individual's personal relationship to God (Weber, 1905). In addition, the rugged lifestyle of the frontier, as reality and myth, teaches that individuals must be self-reliant to survive (Turner, 1920). These and other factors have produced in most people a preference for seeing individuals as both initiating and solving social problems.

The association may surprise you, but this preference is epitomized in the Star Wars movies. As you may remember, near the end of the last episode Luke and Darth Vader are finally fighting it out and, not surprisingly, Darth seems to be winning. Luke entreats Darth to find the goodness still inside him. The issue, which has been building up through three feature-length films, is whether Darth has the fortitude to surmount the enticements of the emperor, who embodies evil (or the devil, depending on your religious beliefs). In the end, Darth Vader masters his personal flaws, kills the emperor, and as the picture concludes, returns to life as Luke's father and joins Obiwan Kenobi and Yoda in what appears to be heaven. (Note the triune image.) As a result, the empire is overthrown, the people are saved, and viewers feel good. They feel good because the movie celebrates the triumph of individuals over great odds. Good vanquishes evil. Individuals, people in the United States believe, carry within themselves all the strength and aptitude necessary to succeed. As with Luke (and Darth Vader), they simply have to work at it. Such faith may be why public policies in this country so often demand heroism by impoverished or troubled persons. Subsequent chapters of this book reveal the ill-advised nature of such standards, since few possess Luke Skywalker's or Darth Vader's fortitude. These are fictional heroes. More serious for my purpose, this emphasis on individuals sometimes blinds observers to the larger reality within which individuals act. Most of the time, I argue, changing individual's actions will not alter the social context (or structure) producing a high rate of such behavior. In order to understand why so many harmful acts occur, the angle of vision must be shifted. In terms of the metaphor used earlier, viewers must move away from the painting to get an overall view of it.

Social Structure and Social Problems. The next explanatory task is to understand the factors influencing rates of behavior. Why has the abortion rate risen so much over time? Why is the U.S. rate so much higher than in Britain or France? The answers to such queries must be structural. *Social structure* refers to the networks of relationships and values connecting people to one another and to the society.

A structural analysis always focuses on how networks of relationships or values (or both) promote or discourage action. For example, every Western nation displays a long-term rise in abortion. This fact suggests that common structural changes have occurred in all of them that produce this phenomenon, such as changes in family structure and industrialization. These concepts (to be defined later) refer to networks of interaction. The U.S. abortion rate, however, is much higher than in Western Europe. This fact implies that significant structural differences exist in this country compared to others.

The abortion rate example illustrates an essential explanatory principle: The variables explaining individual behavior and rates of behavior differ. The contrast between an individual and structural level of analysis can be illustrated by the questions posed. Thus, observers can study poverty by asking why individuals become poor, and the answer will always focus on their personal experiences. One person lacks an education; another loses his or her job; still another obtains a divorce and, without skills, becomes impoverished. These results, which are correct, tell us about individual travails. But—and this is the key point—they say nothing about why the rate of poverty is so high. To deal with that question, observers must shift the level of analysis (adopt a different angle of vision). The issue then becomes how the social structure promotes or discourages behavior. For example, macroeconomic policy determines the number of jobs that are available: When they are restricted to keep inflation low, the poverty rate goes up. A structural analysis always explains why so many (or so few) act or display some attribute, such as poverty. The result, I would like to suggest, enables observers "to grasp history and biography and the relations between the two within society" (Mills, 1959:4). It allows observers to understand the big picture.

Obtaining such understanding is a little like looking at a house rather than the individuals in it. A house, with its arrangement of rooms, doors, windows, electrical outlets, and other characteristics, influences rates of behavior. Most people, for example, will go in and out through the doors. In fact, most will use the front door, fewer the back. Once in a while, however, someone (a teenager seeking to evade parents, a burglar) will use a window as a means of entry and exit. And it is possible to imagine using a sledgehammer to force an opening through a wall, although that would be rare. Thus, the house sets the context in which action occurs. Even without any knowledge of which individuals go through which doors or their motives, it is still useful to study how the house influences rates of this and other behaviors. But people can and do remodel the houses in which they live: They move a door; add rooms; build a pool. These changes, of course, alter rates of behavior. Moreover, houses vary from one neighborhood to another—in size, say—and this difference influences rates of behavior as well. Just as people build houses and sometimes remodel them, human beings increasingly control the social structure in which they live. They pass laws, for example, or invent new technology or transform the workplace. In each case, the "social house" is changed, and so are the choices the inhabitants face.

The house metaphor suggests two characteristics of social structures that I want to make explicit.

The first is that they exist externally to individuals and influence their range of choices. This insight is most often associated with Emile Durkheim, although it is not unique to his work. In *Rules of the Sociological Method*, he simply said: "Social facts are things" (1895:60). The aphorism means that, like houses, social structures have an objective existence. They are real. A person cannot make them disappear through an act of imagination. Thus, changes in "things" sometimes encourage new behaviors by widening the range of choices. For example, advances in medical technology made abortion a safe procedure during the latter part of the nineteenth century. As a result of this new choice (along with other changes), an increase in the abortion rate occurred, especially among middle-class women. In contrast, changes in "things" sometimes discourage behaviors by narrowing the range of choices. For example, the passage of laws making abortion illegal in most states around the turn of the century made it harder for women to terminate pregnancy. A choice that had been briefly available thus became far more difficult. Now it is not possible to tell, with this information, which individuals obtained an abortion and which gave birth; these choices are based on people's personal experiences. But it is possible to state that the rate of abortion reflects the impact of advances in medical technology and legal changes, along with other structural factors. So people can rail against "things," like laws, but their separate (or emergent) existence cannot be denied. Durkheim emphasized this separateness in the other part of his dictum. The phrase "social facts" indicates, as he put it, that society constitutes a reality at its own level, which cannot be reduced to the sum of its parts—individuals. He meant that social structures comprise a separate class of objects which must be explained in their own terms (at their own level), independently of the variables associated with individual behavior.

Durkheim provided an example of the distinction between the social and individual levels of analysis in his book *Suicide* (1897). He studied a very private behavior and showed that structural phenomena existing externally to individuals guide them and affect the rate of suicide within a society. Thus, when the bonds binding individuals to the society are strong—as among employed, married people with children who regularly attend church—the suicide rate will be low. But guidance is not force, and individuals' personal experiences vary. Some suicides do occur among people like this. In contrast, people whose ties to the society are limited take their own lives at a higher rate. Adolescents and aged people fall into this category. As the chapters in this book suggest, Durkheim's idea can be applied to many issues.[7]

With this example, Durkheim suggested that social structures, such as laws and the economy (to be defined later), constitute independent explanatory variables that decisively influence rates of behavior. This line of reasoning means that the rate of any behavior reflects the organization of a society, not individual experiences, and that its explanation requires a focus on the social structure.

The second characteristic of social structures is that, like houses, they can be changed. For example, although divorce was plausible in the nineteenth century, it was difficult. Hence, when marriages broke down the spouses usually remained together in their pain (and sometimes abuse). A few dissolved their marriages informally as one partner fled to the frontier. But economic dependence and legal restrictions kept divorce from being a realistic choice for most people. Today the situation is much different. The frontier no longer exists because people filled it up; that option is closed. Changes people made in both the economy and law, however, have opened other doors, and couples who have developed irreconcilable differences can now divorce. My point is paradoxical: On the one hand, individual men and women did not decide their range of choices for themselves; rather, it was given by the fact of living in a particular place at a particular point in history. The average couple in an unhappy marriage does not determine what their alternatives are. Instead, the social structure does, in the form of territorial expansion, economic development, and laws. So the rate of some behaviors—staying in broken marriages, fleeing to the frontier—declined. And the rate of another behavior—divorce—rose. On the other hand, people changed the options available to themselves, leading to new rates of behavior. This is because, as mentioned earlier, people can now influence their environment, which means they have choices undreamed of in the past. Human beings, depending on their social class, institutional location, and other factors, increasingly determine the choices available in a society (Beeghley, 1996a, 1996b). This ability, which is an altogether new phenomenon in history, places a premium on making wise decisions based on knowledge. It also creates social problems, of course, as people come to grips with the changes they have made. Most of the time, these changes are actively desired; they are defined as progress. This is because they signify improvement in the human condition.

But what are we to do? In terms of the metaphor used above, how are we to remodel or rebuild the house? This is, after all, the key question. It is now time to make connections and assess alternatives.

Exploring the Implications

A concluding section ought to offer some closure. The facts, let us suppose, are plain. The explanation, let us suppose further, is logical and makes sense. On that basis, each chapter ends with a brief description of the implications that follow. I try to identify the issues we (as a society) need to discuss and to suggest the nature of the choices we face.

In making choices based on (inevitably imperfect) knowledge, there is no guarantee that things will get better (Rule, 1978). In fact, attempts at solutions sometimes make the situation worse, creating new and different problems (Sieber, 1981; Tenner, 1996). Because of such possibilities, some people flee from choice, flee from change. After all, it is often easier to imagine things going on in the same way than to imagine change. This reaction has been perennial since the latter years of the nineteenth century. For example, some observers have argued that van Gogh's *Café Terrace at Night* expresses his fear about social instability in the modern world via the emphasis on the uneven cobblestones outside the cafe and the Roman architecture across from it (Welsh-Ovcharov, 1974). Whether this interpretation is correct or not, we do indeed live in an uneasy time, full of disconcerting changes. Alas, appeals to the past will not work. In modern societies, the one thing we cannot do is choose to be people who do not have choices.

Notes

1. The definition of *sociology* paraphrases that given in Peter Berger's *Facing Up to Modernity* (1977:vii). The last line of the paragraph is taken from his *Invitation to Sociology* (1963:23).

2. This and the following paragraphs draw on my essay defining "social problems" (Beeghley, 1993).

3. In *Constructing Social Problems,* Malcolm Spector and John Kitsuse show how this process occurs (1987).

4. Some of the phrasing in this paragraph draws on C. Wright Mills, *The Sociological Imagination* (1959:1–8).

5. The remainder of this chapter draws on and reprints material from my *What Does Your Wife Do? Gender and the Transformation of Family Life* (Beeghley, 1996b:4–13).

6. These principles are rarely stated formally. I first did so in "Religious Change and Alcohol Use: An Application of Reference Group and Socialization Theory" (Beeghley, Bock, and Cochran, 1990).

7. I have simplified Durkheim's analysis for presentation here. See Turner, Beeghley, and Powers, *The Emergence of Sociological Theory* (1995).

Recommended Reading

Durkheim, Emile. *Rules of the Sociological Method* (New York: Free Press, 1982; original 1895).

Kohn, Melvin. "Cross-National Research as an Analytic Strategy." *American Sociological Review* 52(1987):713–31.

Lemert, Charles. *Social Things: An Introduction to the Sociological Life* (New York: Rowman & Littlefield, 1997).

Mills, C. Wright. *The Sociological Imagination* (New York: Oxford University Press, 1959).

Spector, Malcolm, and John I. Kitsuse. *Constructing Social Problems* (New York: Aldine de Gruyter, 1987).

Weber, Max. *The Protestant Ethic and the Spirit of Capitalism* (New York: Scribners, 1958; original 1905).

2 *Abortion*

Outline of Chapter 2

I. Dimensions of Abortion
   A. Historical Dimensions
   B. International Dimensions

II. Consequences of Abortion

III. Individuals and Abortion
   A. Personal Characteristics
      1. Age
      2. Marital Status
      3. Social Class
   B. Personal Experiences
      1. Educational and Occupational Aspirations
      2. Religiosity
      3. Parental and Peer Influences
   C.   The Timing of Abortion

IV. Social Structure and Abortion
   A. The Long-Term Rise in the Abortion Rate
      1. Changes in Family Structure
      2. Industrialization
      3. Advances in Medical Technology
      4. The Rise of Feminism
      5. Legal Changes
   B. Abortion in the United States and Other Nations

V. Implications

In Greek mythology, Atlas was condemned to support the world on his shoulders. Today, the womb is like the body's Atlas. It bears the weight of both future generations and bitter social conflict.[1]

On a commonsense level, this conflict is about the status of the embryo developing inside the womb: Is it a person or a potential person? If the embryo is assumed to be a person, then abortion is murder. But if the embryo is assumed to be a potential person, then abortion is a woman's right to control her fertility. Each stance reflects an unverifiable assumption about when human life begins—an issue that cannot be resolved. This fact heightens the conflict because activists ("pro-choice" and "pro-life") believe they are defending a moral position.

In considering the morality of abortion, however, you should recall that subjects have several aspects to them, some not obvious. In this case, the conflict over abortion is also about men's and women's relationship to each other and their activities outside the family. It is also, in short, about whether women and men should be equal. Thus, the moral conflict over what is inside the womb symbolizes social relationships outside of it.[2]

Those seeing themselves as "pro-life" not only have a moral stance, they are also defending traditional relations between men and women (Beeghley, 1996b). From this point of view, wives ought to stay home as breadservers while husbands ought to earn a living as breadwinners. The "pro-life" logic is as follows: Sexual intercourse should be restricted to marriage and serve mainly as a means of procreation. Divorce should be limited. Abortion and birth control should be illegal. And since pregnancy can occur at any time, women's educational and occupational ambitions should take a backseat to their primary tasks as wives and mothers. Taken together, these issues comprise a coherent package suggesting how men and women are to organize their lives together.

In contrast, those seeing themselves as "pro-choice" not only have a moral stance, they are also defending egalitarian relations between women and men. From this point of view, both wives and husbands can be breadservers and breadwinners. Again, logical implications follow: Sexual intercourse can occur prior to marriage (at least among adults), since its purpose can be pleasure as well as procreation. Divorce should be available when marriages break down. Birth control and abortion should be legal so that if the former fails, women can control their fertility. This position means that women and men can plan the birth of their children, fitting them into their educational and occupational ambitions. Again, these issues comprise a coherent package; but in this case the ties between men and women differ—they are equals.

Most people find themselves in the middle on these issues. About 83 percent of the public believes that abortion should be legal in some or all circumstances (Moore et al., 1996). But this assent is ambivalent because many people are divided within themselves about both the morality of abortion and the underlying implications for family life and equality. As I show just below, their attitudes about abortion often become less ambivalent when an unwanted pregnancy occurs. This willingness to obtain an abortion, I suggest, reflects the increasing choices people have in modern societies. In order to see how this change came about, it is necessary to begin with a solid empirical foundation.

Dimensions of Abortion

Consider the following situation: Maria is 17 years old and a good student. She wants to go to college and perhaps become a physician. An active Roman Catholic, she has been raised by loving parents. Maria is pregnant. Her parents do not like her 18-year-old boyfriend, who has dropped out of school and is working as a mechanic. Now consider some possible outcomes: (1) Maria knows it will hurt her parents but cannot lie. When she tells them, her mother screams, "How could you do this? You're a slut!" As Maria is leaving, her father intervenes to stop her. "He just said he loved me," Maria reports, "and that we would figure it out." As a family, and despite their religious faith, they decide on an abortion. "I'm too young to have a baby. My future is in front of me," Maria says. (2) Knowing her parents' attitudes, Maria and her boyfriend borrow $200 from various friends. She skips school one day, and they go together to a clinic where she has an abortion. (3) After telling her parents, Maria and her family consult their priest. Together, they decide that Maria will have the child and that she will live at home and attend the local junior college. The boyfriend is informed of this decision and told he must help support the child.

Now construct your own vignettes. Vary the family attributes, the age of the girl or woman, her aspirations, and the conditions under which she became pregnant. In each instance you will find that an unintended or unwanted pregnancy is often a tragedy. This has been so throughout history. Desperate women have sought abortions.

Historical Dimensions

To varying degrees, women have always tried to control their fertility. After all, women, not men, undergo the danger of pregnancy, and death during this period is very common in all preindustrial societies. Without reliable methods of birth control, women have turned to abortions.[3] As indicated in Chapter 1, I am restricting the analysis presented here to the past two centuries or so. This period not only marks the transition to modernity, it is also a time frame for which scholars have assembled reasonable estimates of the abortion rate.

TABLE 2.1   Estimates of the Abortion Rate Prior to 1970

	Rate per 100 Live Births
1800–1850	3–4
1850–1900	16–20
1900–1930	25–33
1930–1940	60–100
1945–1970	25–33

SOURCES: Mohr (1978); Francome (1986); Rongy (1933); Taussig (1936).

Table 2.1 summarizes what is known about past rates. Few laws regulated abortion during the first half of the nineteenth century. Prior to quickening (the first movement of the developing embryo), women considered themselves to be carrying inert nonbeings. According to James C. Mohr in *Abortion in America,* about three to four abortions occurred per every 100 live births (1978). It appears that most of those terminating pregnancy were single women avoiding the stigma of bearing an illegitimate child. But regardless of motive, abortion was a private, not a public, issue.

The rate increased sharply after 1850, however, to about sixteen to twenty per 100 live births. Most observers believe these data are conservative, that at least 20 percent of all pregnancies were terminated during this period (Francome, 1986). The presence of children in families indirectly indicates how often abortion was occurring. Between 1860 and 1900, the number of children less than 5 years old per 100 women of childbearing age fell from eighty-nine to sixty-four, or 27 percent (USBC, 1975:54). Abortion helped produce this decline in fertility.

Abortion became a public issue at this time (Mohr, 1978). This recognition occurred not only because the number rose but also because those who terminated pregnancy changed: Married women, especially middle- and upper-class Protestants, started to obtain most abortions. In addition, physicians mounted an extensive campaign against this practice (Starr, 1982). They seized on abortion as part of a drive to professionalize and eliminate so-called irregular (especially female) practitioners from the market (Luker, 1984). The medical profession made rather contradictory arguments. On the one hand, it claimed that abortion is murder. On the other, it claimed that only a doctor can competently decide if an abortion is necessary. In effect, the physicians' goal was to regulate abortions, not eliminate them. They succeeded.[4]

By 1890 every state had made abortion illegal (Mohr, 1978). Most, however, included a "therapeutic exception" allowing physicians to terminate pregnancy when in their judgment the life of the mother was threatened. In this context, the issue disappeared from public debate, again becoming a private matter. Thus, an unintended pregnancy gave a woman three choices: (1) She could give birth. (2) She could persuade a family (or friendly) doctor of the need for a legal abortion. (3) She could obtain an illegal abortion. The situation remained like this for about seventy years.

As Table 2.1 shows, the abortion rate increased to about twenty-five to thirty-three per 100 live births during the early years of the twentieth century. It became much higher during the Great Depression, however, possibly equal to the birthrate—that is, one abortion for every live birth (Rongy, 1933). Although other estimates are lower, all observers concur that it was very high (Taussig, 1936). Finally, the rate declined after World War II, back to twenty-five to thirty-three for the years 1945–1970.

Since they were illegal during this period, the estimates in Table 2.1 reflect both therapeutic and criminal abortions. Many of the latter were performed by those whom Carole Joffe calls "doctors of conscience" (1995). Other criminal abortions were performed by competent laywomen; for example, in *The Abortionist: One Woman Against the Law*, Ricky Solinger describes a person who performed about 40,000 abortions with no deaths over a fifty-year period (1994). Many criminal abortions, however, were performed in unsanitary settings by individuals with little or no training. It has been estimated that 1,000–5,000 women died each year between 1945 and 1962 as a result of illegal abortions (Tietze, 1948; Leavy and Kummer, 1962). Countless more were injured, often for life.

Better data are available since 1973, the year of *Roe vs. Wade*. Table 2.2 shows an abortion rate of sixteen per 1,000 women age 15 to 44. (Note that the unit of measure in Table 2.2 differs from that used in Table 2.1.) After legalization, the rate rose to twenty-nine, remained stable for about a decade, and fell recently. This decline reflects the impact of restrictions on abortion (about which more later).

In 1995 about 1.2 million abortions occurred. From 1973 to 1995, there were more than 32 million abortions. By extrapolation, about 43 percent of women will have at least one abortion by the time they are 45 years old (AGI, 1997:1). These numbers imply that everyone knows a woman who has had an abortion. They also suggest that people often lose their ambivalence when faced with an unwanted pregnancy. But these numbers are extremely high, much higher than in other nations.

International Dimensions

Table 2.3 displays the abortion rate among women in the prime childbearing years in six nations. Thus, the U.S. level is twenty-eight per 1,000

TABLE 2.2   The Abortion Rate, 1973–1995

	Rate per 1,000 Women, Age 15–44
1973	16
1975	22
1980	29
1985	28
1990	27
1995	20

SOURCES: AGI (1997:4); Lewin (1997).

TABLE 2.3   The Abortion Rate, Selected Nations, Mid-1980s

	Rate per 1,000 Women, Age 15–44
United States	28
Sweden	20
United Kingdom	14
France	13
West Germany	7
Netherlands	6

SOURCE: Henshaw (1990:78).

women, whereas that for Sweden is twenty, for the United Kingdom fourteen, and so on. The Netherlands reports the lowest level, only six. In considering these data, you should remember that abortion is legal in all the societies shown in the table. The low rate in other nations suggests they have strategies for preventing it.

I would like to conclude this section by commenting on the use of quantitative (or numerical) data. You will notice throughout this book that I rely heavily on this kind of information. Although some readers are put off by such data, I would like to persuade you of their usefulness. People believe the abortion rate is, say, too high. Is the perception accurate? Quantitative observations answer that initial question. But, and this is important, the numbers do not end the analysis; they begin it. As the great economist Joseph Schumpeter noted, "We need statistics not only for explaining things but also in order to know precisely what there is to explain" (1954:14). This is why in Chapter 1 I distinguished between discovering the facts and explaining them.

Nonetheless, you need to carefully evaluate quantitative data. Sometimes people (whether scholars, activists, or politicians) use numbers to defend a position rather than to explain reality. This is a little like using a lamppost for support rather than light—it is not the purpose. Cynicism, in the form of a questioning stance, will often pay off. Assuming, however, that the facts above are reasonably accurate, it is time to explore their consequences.

Consequences of Abortion

In order to place the consequences of abortion in perspective, it is useful to begin with the Supreme Court's decision in *Roe vs. Wade.* Justice Harry Blackmun, writing for the Court, pointed out that abortion embodies three conflicting rights. First, citizens have a right to privacy. Second, pregnant women have a right to have their health protected. Third, the developing embryo has a right to life. To balance these opposing rights, Justice Blackmun divided the gestation period into thirds. During the first twelve weeks, women have an unconditional right to an abortion. Under the right to privacy, women ought to be able to control what happens to their own bodies. During weeks thirteen through twenty-four, states can impose reasonable medical standards but cannot prevent abortions. The logic is that this requirement protects maternal health, since illegal abortions maimed and killed many women in the past. During weeks twenty-five through thirty-six, states can regulate and indeed prevent abortion, unless it is necessary to save the mother's life. Here, possible survival outside the womb obligates the state to protect developing life. Thus, *Roe* invalidated all state laws preventing abortions.

Subsequent decisions limited the scope of *Roe*. In 1992 the Court held in *Planned Parenthood vs. Casey* that states may regulate abortion throughout pregnancy as long as they do not impose an "undue burden" on women. It thus upheld a twenty-four-hour waiting period and a requirement of parental consent for teenagers seeking abortions. These limits have reduced the abortion rate and increased the birthrate. For example, when Mississippi imposed a waiting period, it prevented 11–13 percent of women who would have had abortions from so doing. Those most affected were poor and had less than a high school education (Joyce et al., 1997).

In this context, I want to return to 17-year-old Maria, who found herself pregnant a few pages ago. The "pro-life" position is simple: Abortion is murder. From this angle, there are 1.4 million murders each year, and "pro-life" activists want to save these unborn children. Their argument is that women's primary responsibility in life is to bear and raise children. They believe that mothers and fathers will learn to love their children. Their logic implies that women's reproductive abilities are more important than other aspirations. So the "pro-life" position would be that Maria and her boyfriend should have their child.

Starting from a different angle of vision, the "pro-choice" argument is equally simple: Adolescents and young women who become pregnant often suffer long-term tragic consequences if they bear children. People like Maria, for example, are more likely to: die in childbirth, bear more children soon, have higher total fertility, display lower educational attainment, earn less, become poor, receive public assistance, abuse and neglect their children, marry young, and obtain a divorce. For many, then, giving birth is a tragedy. It transforms their lives.[5] This is also true for the children born to people like Maria: They are more likely to display low birth weight and long-term health problems, die in the first year of life, and suffer abuse and neglect.[6] The "pro-choice" logic implies that women of all ages should be able to balance their reproductive abilities with other aspirations and abilities. So their position would be that Maria, her boyfriend, and her parents should consider their options very carefully.

One way to think about the "pro-life" and "pro-choice" positions is to compare the experiences of young women who bear children with those who obtain abortions. In *Adolescent Mothers in Later Life*, Frank Furstenberg and colleagues show that teenagers who bear children often do all right over the long run (1987:158). Even though they do "not understand how they were able to get through those difficult years" after their children's birth, they usually graduate from high school and hold a stable job. More generally, when matched groups of pregnant teenagers are compared, those who obtain an abortion do better in school, are more likely to graduate, and are less likely to become pregnant again than those who bear children (Zabin and Hayward, 1993). Thus, depending on people's values, the consequences of abortion are negative, a high rate of murder, or—on balance—positive, the prevention of unwanted children and the human tragedy that often results.

The data presented so far lead to a simple question: Why do some individuals rather than others obtain abortions? After all, individuals make choices in this world, some wise and others unwise.

Individuals and Abortion

When a woman becomes pregnant, she has a profound choice to make: whether to have a baby. This is an easy decision when the pregnancy is desired, and positive outcomes usually result. When it is not desired, however, the choice becomes far more difficult. Despite stereotypes, the decision to terminate a pregnancy is rarely made lightly; an unexpected, unwanted pregnancy places ordinary people in a terrible dilemma. Remember, a single mistake in forty years (the average length of time a woman is capable of conception) can lead to this situation, resulting in a path of pain that sometimes takes an individual to an abortion clinic.

In describing the factors leading to an abortion, I assume (1) that the couple either did not use birth control or it did not work properly and (2) the pregnancy is unintended. All the findings reported in this section are empirical generalizations.

Personal Characteristics

Age. *The younger a woman is when she becomes pregnant, the more likely she will obtain an abortion.* Thus, adolescents and young adults are twice as likely to procure abortions as older women (Henshaw and Kost, 1996). Overall, those less than 30 years old obtain the most abortions, 87 percent. These data are why so many of the examples used here refer to young people. By most standards, they are not ready to parent because their socialization into adult roles remains incomplete. In addition, they often cannot support themselves and a child.

Marital Status. *Single women who become pregnant are more likely to obtain an abortion than married women.* Unmarried women obtain 82 percent of all abortions (Henshaw and Kost, 1996). A correlation exists, of course, among youth, marital status, and abortion. Whether young or not, many single women view themselves as incapable of providing for a baby. They have ambitions and careers; an accidental pregnancy (remember, one mistake in forty years) can transform their lives.

Social Class. The term *social class* refers to people's location in the stratification structure, as shown by their jobs, income, and education. The relationship between social class and abortion is curvilinear in the shape of an upside-down bowl: *Poorly and highly educated women who become pregnant are less likely to obtain abortions.* Women with less than a high school degree procure 22 percent of all abortions, those with a high school degree and some college 64 percent, and those with a college degree 14 percent (Henshaw and Kost, 1996). This pattern occurs because poorly educated women have less access to effective birth control or abortion, whereas well-educated women have greater access to the most effective methods of birth control.

Personal Experiences

Educational and Occupational Aspirations. *The greater her aspirations, the more likely a woman will obtain an abortion if she becomes pregnant* (Hayes, 1987). Put bluntly, people with ambition want to control the timing of their fertility. A birth would be transformative, influencing every aspect of their lives: their ability to stay in school, remain on the job, obtain a promotion.

Religiosity. *The less the religiosity, the more likely a woman will obtain an abortion if she becomes pregnant.* Women reporting no religious identity are four times more likely to terminate a pregnancy than those reporting some identity (Henshaw and Kost, 1996). All religions teach that human life is sacred, so people who are active religiously tend to avoid abortions, regardless of faith.

Parental and Peer Influences. *The more supportive a woman's mother and friends are of an abortion, the more likely she will obtain one if she becomes pregnant* (Hayes, 1987). These people constitute reference groups whose members are emotionally significant in a woman's life. Their opinions count. They also tend to be the ones whom a woman will consult in an emergency. And an unwanted pregnancy is an emergency. The earlier in the pregnancy an abortion occurs, the safer it is.

The Timing of Abortion

Most abortions occur early, 89 percent in the first twelve weeks (AGI, 1997:4). In addition, virtually all of them happen prior to twenty-one weeks, well before viability. Although medical advances now allow many premature babies to live, an impenetrable barrier exists: lung development. Lungs cannot function prior to twenty-four or twenty-five weeks, even with the help of a respirator (Hoekelman et al., 1987).

The controversy over late abortions (less than 1 percent) should be considered in light of these facts. The main reason women give for delaying abortion is that they failed to recognize they were pregnant (AGI, 1997:2). Denial is a powerful motive, especially among young persons. In addition, nearly half of all abortions after fifteen weeks of gestation occur because the women had problems getting to an abortion clinic or getting the money for the procedure. Consider Maria. Assume for a moment that she is afraid to tell her parents and lives in one of the thirty-nine counties in California without an abortion provider. How is she going to get to a clinic? This is a common problem, since only 16 percent of U.S. counties have abortion services available (Henshaw and Van Vort, 1994:105). Only one clinic exists in South Dakota. Assume that Maria is poor and most of her friends are poor. Where is she going to get the money? Assume Maria lives in Pennsylvania; only 30 percent of counties have abortion providers, and the state requires parental permission for adolescents like her to obtain an abortion. What is she to do? The

Supreme Court has ruled that such restrictions do not constitute an undue burden, and twenty-six states now enforce such laws (AGI, 1997:3). In Mississippi there was about a 20 percent increase in second-trimester abortions after passage of restrictions like these (Kolbert and Miller, 1994). Two conclusions emerge. First, late abortions can be prevented. Second, legal restrictions will produce more late abortions and more births to mothers who are themselves children.

Despite the controversy over late abortions, most of those terminating pregnancy are young, single, or believe they cannot properly care for a child. And they secure an abortion early in the pregnancy. These individual dilemmas, however, say nothing about the structural factors producing a high rate of abortion. After all, people make choices in a social context.

Social Structure and Abortion

Let us review the situation. It is known that the abortion rate rose over time. It increased initially during the second half of the nineteenth century to about sixteen to twenty per 100 live births. It went up once again after 1900, to about twenty-five to thirty-three and remained in that range until the 1970s. The much higher level during the depression was clearly an aberration, and I shall set it aside. Finally, the rate rose again after legalization to about twenty-eight or twenty-nine per 1,000 women of childbearing age (again, note the change in unit of measure). Although the rate has declined recently because of legal restrictions on access, I focus on why it rose over the long term and why the U.S. level is so much higher than in other societies.

Before doing so, however, I want to remind you that the goal in a structural analysis is to explain why a rate has changed, not why individuals act. In terms of the metaphor used in Chapter 1, abortion can be seen as like a door that people installed in our (society's) house. Although this door has been locked and unlocked at various times, its existence coupled with the desire to control fertility has meant that people wanted to go through it. And indeed they have done so—either legally or not. Why?

The Long-Term Rise in the Abortion Rate

My hypothesis is this: *The long-term rise in the abortion rate reflects (1) changes in family structure, (2) industrialization, (3) advances in medical technology, (4) the rise of feminism, and (5) legal changes.* I use the word "hypothesis" here in order to emphasize that the explanation is tentative. One of the paradoxes of sociology is that the more important issues are frequently not susceptible to precise measurement. As a result, it is often necessary to use what Seymour Martin Lipset, with a bow to Max Weber, calls the "method of dialogue" (1968:51). Thus, a logical hypothesis is advanced along with evidence supporting it. Others think about the issue, publish their interpretations, debate ensues, and—over the long run—knowledge grows. This process implies that social scientific explanations are always probabilistic (Lieberson, 1992). This in turn means that absolute certainty is impossible, in sociology as in other arenas of life.

Changes in Family Structure. The family in Western European societies has become conjugal over the past 400 years; that is, it comprises a husband, wife, and their immediate children; it lives in relative privacy, separately from other kin, and is child centered. A paradox results: As children became central to family life, the importance of fertility control and hence the rate of abortion increased as well. In order to understand this seeming contradiction, some background is necessary.

"There was no place for childhood in the medieval world," Philippe Ariès observes in *Centuries of Childhood* (1962:33). Family life was lived in public, and personal privacy was unknown. Children and adults, masters and servants, all lived on top of one another. Houses were open to callers at any time. Rooms had no specific function; people slept, ate, and talked in any of them. Individualism, in the modern sense of people's recognition of their uniqueness, of their personal interests, of their existence apart from family or society, hardly existed. Childhood as a distinct period of life was not recognized; after the age of 6 or 7, children were viewed as "little adults" and became no different from adults in terms of dress, daily activities, or other traits. This is the reason a boy could masquerade as a woman in Shakespeare's plays and have audiences believe the performance. The actors were adults, aged 10 to 15. It was indeed a different world then.

In this context, the birth of a child did not carry much significance. "Childhood," Ariès comments, "passed quickly and was just as quickly forgotten" (1962:34). He quotes a typical sentiment: "I have lost two or three children in their infancy, not without regret, but without great sorrow." Such attitudes appear shocking to modern sensibilities. Yet they reflect the experiences of people who regularly lost children. Hence, parents delayed becoming attached to the young until they assumed the obligations of adulthood. In such a context, abortion rarely became an issue.

According to Ariès, this context began changing in the sixteenth century. Over time, the structure of houses changed, with rooms set aside for sleeping, seeing visitors, and the like; and norms about visiting became more restrictive. These alterations indicate not only that family life was becoming more private but that personal privacy was becoming valued. In addition, values of individualism and equality were emerging. These changes occurred first among the upper classes, spreading slowly to the others, and were first applied to men. Thus, instead of the first-born male inheriting family property, all male children came to be treated equally. Furthermore, boys began to be educated outside the home. It is significant that boys (not girls) by this time wore clothes that distinguished them from adults. Slowly, the relationship between parents and children came to have emotional depth. In this environment, couples began limiting fertility.[7]

So the birthrate began falling, first in Europe and then in the United States. In 1800 there were 275 live births for every 1,000 white women, age 15 to 44, a figure that declined to 65 by 1995 (USBC, 1975:49; NCHS, 1996b:8). Among African Americans (for whom data do not go so far back in time), the rate declined from 138 in 1920 to 72 in 1995. Among Hispanics the rate was 104 in 1995, which probably represents a long-term decline. The birthrate fell for two reasons. First, initially in Europe and later in the eastern part of the United States, fertile land became occupied. As a result, men and women delayed marriage until the former could acquire land, the means to support a family (Easterlin, 1976). This delay reduced the number of years during which women could bear children and so reduced their fertility. Second, of greater importance, the rise of the conjugal family meant that husbands, wives, and children lived rather privately, nurturing one another. In this context, children are valued for their own sake. Most people see these changes as progress.

Yet according to Carl Degler in *At Odds: Women and the Family in America from the Revolution to the Present,* this change implied that the number of children had to be reduced if parents, especially mothers, were to attend to the needs of each (1980:201). It is hard to nurture large numbers of little ones. Further, as the number of children fell, norms about proper care became stricter, a result that enhanced the child-centered nature of families. These attitudes grew widespread in the latter part of the nineteenth century.

This process continued into the twentieth century. Viviana Zelizer, for example, notes that whereas the loss of a child to accident or disease had been a routine matter in the past, it has now become a tragedy (1985). She also describes the conflicts over child labor, children's insurance, and wrongful death litigation during the early 1900s; they indicate, she argues, the increasing importance of childhood as a special time. Children became "priceless," an intrinsic value, and as a result couples wanted fewer children in order to nurture them properly.

Although less frequent intercourse, male withdrawal, douches, and (in the second half of the nineteenth century) condoms were effective in reducing fertility, the falling birthrate could not have occurred without abortion. It appears that the average married couple in the nineteenth century had three to six fewer children than they would have had without practicing birth control (Sanderson, 1979). Two or three of these pregnancies were ended by abortion.

Here is an apocryphal example. In *Little House on the Prairie* and subsequent books, Laura Ingalls Wilder described her life growing up in the Midwest in the last years of the nineteenth century (1953). Her parents had only three children instead of the eight to ten that would have been typical earlier in the century. Thus, the Ingalls family fits the scenario described above statistically in that Ma and Pa Ingalls limited their fertility. Although Laura is silent about how this was accomplished, it is probable that the couple practiced birth control; it is also possible that Ma Ingalls had an abortion. Remember, contraception was less effective then, and it only takes one failure for conception to occur.

In sum, the family changed: Couples now want fewer children. The new value can be simply stated: Creating a child is one of the noblest expressions of a woman and man. And to give it all the care, attention, and education possible helps to realize that expression. So the birthrate dropped, and an increase in the rate of abortion constituted one mechanism producing this decline. Couples can control fertility and have fewer children. This change represents increasing choice in human affairs. After all, couples today can, if they wish, have many children. In this context, the changing nature of family life dovetailed with the transformation of the economy.

Industrialization. Prior to the nineteenth century, societies barely produced enough so that everyone could survive. Most people subsisted by means of hard manual labor, scratching a living from the soil. In this context, children were economically valuable; phrased crudely, they produced more than they cost. From the age of 5 or 6, a child labored as a "little adult." In addition, children were like pension plans are today: a means for parents' security in old age. Hence, an incentive existed to have many children. This situation remains characteristic of developing societies today and resembled the United States in the first half of the nineteenth century. In that context, the abortion rate was relatively low.

Industrialization changed social life forever. The term refers to the transformation of the economy as new forms of energy were substituted for muscle power, leading to advances in productivity. Now this definition, while accurate, is also narrow; as a historical phenomenon industrialization is linked to a number of other changes. First, it is linked to the rise of capitalism as it reached a critical stage in the nineteenth century (Berger, 1986). Second, it is linked to the rise of work-centered values associated with the Protestant Reformation (Weber, 1905). Third, it is linked to the application of science to problems of economic production; the significance of this connection has increased in importance over time (Kuznets, 1985). Fourth, it is linked to the value placed on personal freedom that arose in the West in the eighteenth century (Lenski, 1966). Finally, it is linked to increasing life expectancy and the improvement in the education of the labor force (McKeown, 1976). These factors coalesced over several centuries to produce an engine for economic growth and transformation. I use the term "industrialization" to summarize this fundamental historical change.

One result is that industrial societies can, if they choose, ensure that everyone survives, indeed prospers. Further, the available amenities have grown much wider, ranging from housing to VCRs. Another result, which I intend to emphasize, has been that the occupational structure changed. In 1870, for example, the vast majority of people still worked either on farms (53 percent) or in blue-collar jobs doing manual labor (29 percent) (USBC, 1975:139). Most of the latter lived in cities and received cash wages. Their jobs involved physically arduous tasks. In addition, a small middle class had formed: About 19 percent of the population worked in white-collar jobs doing nonmanual labor.[8]

In this context, the working and middle classes faced rather different situations. The working class continued to need child labor, since children (those aged 6 to 14 years) often brought in 30–40 percent of family income (Zelizer, 1985:58). Historically, such individuals had always labored on farms, and many continued doing so in the late nineteenth century. Thus, many families had little motivation to control fertility, and their abortion rates remained low.

The new middle class, however, found itself in a different environment. Upwardly mobile, often working in occupations that had not existed previously, husbands now earned a "family wage"; that is, they could support their wives and children without requiring them to work for pay. This situation, of course, presupposed that families were relatively small. As always, most housework remained labor intensive. In this context, middle-class families wished to limit their number of children. Although contraception, as described earlier, worked reasonably well, many middle-class women resorted to abortion during this period (Mohr, 1978; Sanderson, 1979). Overall, then, the abortion rate rose.

With the passage of time, the occupational structure has changed as the size of the middle class increased. Few people work on farms today; rather, 39 percent are engaged in blue-collar and 58 percent in white-collar occupations (USBC, 1996d:405). This transformation carries important implications: Families in industrial societies do not require many children. Hence, the value placed on fertility control has risen, as has the abortion rate. Like the changes in family life, industrialization represents an increase in both choice and control in human affairs. After all, anyone can choose to live "rustically"—without running water or electricity, for example—but few do. If the impact of industrialization is "added" (in a conceptual way) to the change in the family, it becomes easier to understand why the rate of abortion rose.

One last note: Recall from Table 2.3 that abortion rates are much lower in other industrial societies than in the United States. This fact means that although increases in abortion are correlated with changes in the family and industrialization, they are not inevitable. I come back to this issue in a later section. In the meantime, it is necessary to describe the impact of increasing scientific knowledge.

Advances in Medical Technology.   During the first half of the nineteenth century, women who had stopped menstruating knew they might be pregnant. Given this possibility, those seeking an abortion faced limited and hazardous choices (Mohr, 1978). One strategy was to swallow a noxious (often poisonous) herb or potion in order to produce indigestion. The idea was that violent sickness would dislodge the fertilized egg, a tactic that occasionally worked. A second strategy required jumping, falling, or in some way physically injuring oneself. The idea here was to remove the developing embryo by force, a risky but sometimes effective tactic. A third strategy involved internal douching with vinegar, hot water, or wine. If forced into the uterus after cervical dilation, these substances could in fact cause an abortion. Finally, the developing embryo could be surgically removed. Trained physicians had the knowledge and tools necessary to perform this procedure, and by the standards of the time, it was relatively safe—probably no more dangerous than giving birth (Mohr, 1978:18). Alas, physicians knew nothing about bacteria, hence, the risk of infection was great. Because of the danger, most who found themselves pregnant had their babies. Abortion, although a choice, was rare.

The development of rubber condoms after 1860 changed this situation dramatically. As with many forms of progress, however, its impact was paradoxical. On the one hand, those wishing to prevent pregnancy had another option. On the other hand, when populations unfamiliar with birth control begin using new methods the abortion rate always goes up because they typically use such methods ineffectively (Tietze and Henshaw, 1986). The U.S. experience in the latter part of the nineteenth and early twentieth centuries illustrates this phenomenon.

In a context of changes in family values and industrialization, people wanted more than ever to reduce their fertility; thus, the need for abortion rose just when physicians learned to perform the operation safely. This advance was mainly due to knowledge about bacteria. As antisepsis (keeping the operating area sterile) became more widespread, abortion became a safe, practical surgical procedure. Over time, then, medical advances meant that abortion became safer than childbirth. That has been the situation throughout most of the twentieth century. This combination of factors widened people's choices, and the rate of abortion rose. At the same time, feminism, too, rose.

The Rise of Feminism. The term "feminism" refers to an ideology of equality between women and men and the social movement supporting that goal. This development has taken a long time, about two centuries, and it is linked to the variables described earlier. After all, a dominant value in Western history has been the recognition of the dignity of every human individual. One aspect of this value is to free people from dependence on others.

Ariès, you recall, described how the rise in individualism affected family life. In this context, men began seeing themselves as individuals much sooner than women. During the seventeenth and eighteenth centuries, few women could imagine themselves existing separately from their husbands and children. The notion of equal rights was absurd. Women bore children and cared for husbands; their reproductive ability defined the limits of their lives.

Degler argues that the following factors, taken cumulatively, produced a rise in individualism among women (1980:189). First, the Protestant Reformation encouraged each person, male and female, to develop a special relationship to God. Second, the Enlightenment emphasized the importance of scientific knowledge to understanding human affairs, an orientation suggesting that anyone, females as well as males, can use reason. Third, the attack on slavery implied that human beings of both genders ought to be free to pursue their goals. Fourth, the early economists seeking to understand capitalism emphasized the social benefits that follow from individual ambition. And fifth, the "Declaration of the Rights of Man," passed during the first heady days of the French Revolution, explicitly included women in its demand for equal rights. One result of all these events is that some women began to see themselves as individuals. They began to see themselves in nonreproductive activities. They began to see themselves as having rights. These advances required limiting fertility.

The feminist movement reflects this recognition. Its "official" origin is usually described as the Seneca Falls convention of 1848 (DuBois, 1978). This meeting of about 300 people issued a declaration of the rights of women against the oppression of men, outlining in scathing prose all the elements necessary for the equality of women: the right to vote, to obtain a job, to regulate fertility, and the like. Because I do not have the space to describe the history of the feminist movement here, I must skip to the situation in the 1960s.

During this decade, feminism flowered into a coherent movement for equal rights and many women began making a revolutionary claim: No man, especially a physician, can make an "objective" decision about abortion; only a woman is entitled to weigh the competing interests involved. One of Kristin Luker's respondents describes the situation this way (1984:97):

> When we talk about women's rights, we can get all the rights in the world—the right to vote, the right to go to school—and none of them means a dog-gone thing if we don't own the flesh we stand in, if we can't control what happens to us, if the whole course of our lives can be changed by somebody else that can get us pregnant by accident, or by deceit, or by force. So I consider the right to an elective abortion, whether you dream of doing it or not, is the cornerstone of the women's movement.

Thus, in Luker's words, women "who valued motherhood, but valued it on their own terms," began claiming abortion as a right. They argued that it was "the right to be treated as individuals rather than as potential mothers." They argued further that without the right to an abortion, all other rights are illusions because a woman's plans or aspirations based on the notion of equal rights may be destroyed at any time if she cannot control her fertility.

Not everyone agreed with these ideas. Certainly, those opposed to abortion did not (and do not). Yet new ideas and values are like railroad switches; they redirect human behavior to new tracks, new directions (Weber, 1922). The linkage of women's rights and the ability to control fertility is one of those ideas. Fundamental values, in this case about equality, are applied to new situations, such as the relationship between men and women. When coupled with the changes described earlier—in the family, economy, and medicine—feminism provided a powerful justification for abortion as a fundamental right. In that context, *Roe vs. Wade* occurred.

Legal Changes.   Laws regulate behavior; they constitute codified norms. By dictating which choices will be proscribed, laws encourage some actions and discourage others. I noted earlier that physicians (who were mostly male) pressed for laws regulating abortion during the nineteenth century as part of their drive to seize control of medical treatment. Physicians, however, were not alone; several religious groups and even some feminists of the period also supported laws to prevent abortion (Mohr, 1978). Their success meant that the rate was lower than it would otherwise have been. It is probable that the difficulty of obtaining an abortion increased as social class declined; that is, poor women had more trouble getting an abortion than anyone else. If true, this is one reason why lower-class women displayed greater fertility.

As described earlier, the legal status of abortion began changing in the 1960s. The most important event, of course, was *Roe vs. Wade* in 1973. Based on this decision, women can now seek an abortion legally, subject to limits imposed by each state.

The cumulative impact of the changes outlined in this section produced a long-term rise in abortions in the United States. This increase, however, constituted a side effect of the desire for small families. People have come to value children and childhood, which requires limiting births. Children are no longer productive; with industrialization, the skills demanded of workers require extensive and costly training. Hence, an incentive to have fewer children now exists. The ability to perform surgery allows physicians safely to save lives. All of these advances (note the word) are desirable, and few people want to give them up. Yet fertility control follows inexorably from them. And in the United States (unlike other nations), that means a high rate of abortion. Surprisingly, the feminist movement was slow to see the connection between the independence of women and their right to abortion. Further, even given this recognition, not everyone sees feminism as progress. It does follow, however, from the other changes described above. In this context, legal changes made safe abortions available to women. In sum, the abortion rate increased in response to historical developments. In a sense, it is built into the social structure.

Yet the changes described here also occurred in Western Europe. The abortion rate, however, is far lower in all those societies. Why? What factors produce this difference?

Abortion in the United States and Other Nations

Let us compare the U.S. abortion rate to that of the Netherlands. These two nations display the highest and the lowest rates of abortion among Western nations (see Table 2.3).

The major difference between the two countries lies in the use of contraception. The relationship between contraception and abortion is straightforward: *The greater the use of one of the highly effective methods of contraception in a society, the lower the rate of abortion.* For example, in the United States only about 37 percent of adult women use one of the effective forms of contraception, and as a result 30 percent of pregnancies are terminated (Jones et al., 1989:6, 69). At the time of first intercourse, only 20 percent of U.S. women use the birth control pill (NCHS, 1997b:1). The pattern is for young couples to become sexually active and then later to begin contraception. In the Netherlands, by contrast, 56 percent of adult women use one of the effective forms of contraception and only 11 percent of pregnancies end in abortion. In addition, most of the cross-societal variation in abortion occurs among young women, aged 15 to 30. This fact suggests both a specific strategy and a target population for reducing the rate of abortion.

I say this because disparities in abortion do not occur by accident; they reflect deliberate policy choices. In *Pregnancy, Contraception, and Family Planning Services in Industrialized Countries,* Elise Jones and her colleagues enumerate some of the strategies used in the Netherlands (1989). To begin with, abortions are free, covered under the national health insurance plan. They are also easy to obtain. Yet the Dutch regard abortion as a necessary backup, not an acceptable method of birth control. Hence, their orientation is to prevent abortions by making contraception widely accessible at no cost. Furthermore, the confidentiality of adolescents is protected by law. In addition, Jones and her colleagues observe that the media treat sexual issues as a topic for public education; they generally do not sensationalize sexuality. As a result, the Dutch population is sophisticated about all forms of birth control. And the Dutch rate of abortion is the lowest in Western Europe.

The Dutch, however, believe that too many abortions occur. As in the United States, poor and young women are most likely to become pregnant accidentally and seek abortions. In response, physicians have proposed making the birth control pill available without prescription. Other strategies involve better outreach attempts to inform people about contraception. Thus, the Dutch accept the fact that women (and couples) want to limit fertility and that the young will become sexually active. Although abortion constitutes one mechanism for preventing births, public policy in the Netherlands is designed to eliminate its need.

The situation in the United States is, of course, quite different (Jones et al., 1989). Abortions are difficult to obtain, especially for the young, the poor, and those living in rural areas. One out of every eight young women (aged 15 to 19) becomes pregnant each year, and nearly all of these are unwanted pregnancies. So unwanted births occur because contraception is not as accessible as in other nations. Those seeking the birth control pill, for example, must pay for a doctor's visit. If they have insurance (and many do not), they may be reimbursed for this cost later. Physicians in the United States typically insist on a pelvic examination as part of the visit, a difficulty for some girls and young women. Moreover, specialists, who are typically more expensive than family doctors, usually provide the prescription. Although the pill is also available from clinics, they are usually oriented to serving the poor, which discourages many high schoolers from going there. Finally, once they have obtained a prescription, recipients must pay for the pills. Moreover, the U.S. media tend to use sex to titillate rather than educate the public. These factors produce a very high abortion rate.

Implications

In John Irving's book *The Cider House Rules,* the main character, Homer Wells, is taught to perform illegal abortions (safely) by a physician who directs an orphanage (1985). An orphan himself, Homer comes to believe that abortions are wrong after doing an autopsy on an embryo. He vows never to do one again. Many parents agree that abortions are wrong, until faced with their daughter's pregnancy. Many women also share this belief, until faced with a mistake that will transform their lives. Ultimately, Homer confronts a situation in which he believes he must perform an abortion. Irving's point seems to be that such acts should be kept rare.

A simple solution exists: contraception. A commitment to birth control would reduce the level of abortions by about half, a result that would make the U.S. rate similar to those of other Western nations (Westoff, 1988). In general, whenever relatively obvious solutions are rejected, you can be sure underlying issues exist. Thus, the debate about abortion is about gender relations, the centrality of motherhood to women's lives, and the nature of family life. This fact can be seen when strategies for dealing with abortion are considered.

One option is to make getting an abortion as difficult as possible while also limiting access to contraception. This paradoxical strategy constitutes public policy in the United States. It appears to accept unwanted births as a penalty for those who are sexually active prior to marriage. It implies that women ought to remain in the home, serving bread to their breadwinners.

Another option is to make abortions available because of the desire to control fertility but to work actively to prevent them by emphasizing contraception. From this angle, abortion is a failure, its high rate a crime against women. This point of view implies that women and men may choose how they organize their lives together, may choose whether and when to bear children.

So that is where we stand. And there is no scientific way of deciding what should be done. It is safe to say that the fight over abortion will continue; the womb will remain the body's Atlas.

Notes

1. This chapter is an updated and abridged version of a similar one in my *What Does Your Wife Do? Gender and the Transformation of Family Life* (Beeghley, 1996b).

2. In the next two paragraphs, I portray the "pro-life" and "pro-choice" positions as logically coherent ideologies. In so presenting them, I have constructed an "ideal type" (to use a phrase of Max Weber's). This strategy provides observers

with a common reference point from which to compare actual positions taken by people and organizations. For an explanation, see Turner, Beeghley, and Powers, *The Emergence of Sociological Theory* (1995).

3. It has been hypothesized that women have used a variety of plants as abortifacients since ancient times (Riddle et al., 1994).

4. It is notable that the American Medical Association argued against abortion in the nineteenth century in terms similar to the "pro-life" position today: Women who get abortions are selfish and self-indulgent, they are denying their "true place" in society, and men will lose their authority over women. See Carole Joffe, *Doctors of Conscience: The Struggle to Provide Abortion Before and After Roe v. Wade* (1995:29).

5. On these issues, see Zuravin (1991), Boyer and Fine (1992), Ahn (1994), Kallmuss and Namerow (1994), USDHHS (1996), and Manlove (1997).

6. On these issues, see Hein et al. (1990) and Hack (1994).

7. In *The Armada,* an analysis of the British defeat of the Spanish armada in 1588, Garrett Mattingly observes: "In the 16th century, as throughout the Middle Ages, privacy had been the unenvied prerogative of hermits. The greater a man was the larger the crowd in the midst of which he was expected to pass most of his waking life. It was probably his increasing passion for privacy rather than his conventional piety which led people to feel, as he grew older, that there was something monkish about [King] Philip [of Spain]" (1959:74).

8. For further explanation, see my *Structure of Social Stratification* (Beeghley, 1996a).

Recommended Reading

Jones, Elise, Jacqueline Darroch Forrest, Stanley K. Henshaw, Jane Silverman, and Aida Torres. *Pregnancy, Contraception, and Family Planning Services in Industrialized Countries* (New Haven, CT: Yale University Press, 1989).

Luker, Kristin. *Abortion and the Politics of Motherhood* (Berkeley: University of California Press, 1984).

Mohr, James C. *Abortion in America: The Origins and Evolution of National Policy* (New York: Oxford University Press, 1978).

Solinger, Ricky. *The Abortionist: One Woman Against the Law* (New York: Free Press, 1994).

3 Gender Inequality

Outline of Chapter 3

When I was born, just after World War II, most people wanted a house in the suburbs. From there, Mom was supposed to watch the kids and Dad leave for work. He was supposed to compete with other men to produce goods and services, make public policy, interpret God's will, and cure the sick. It was a "Father Knows Best" world. Indeed, in the television series of that name, Jim Anderson left each day in the family car to sell insurance, while Margaret remained at home, isolated and dependent. She had no job and probably not even a driver's license. Her tasks were to watch the children, clean house, order deliveries of groceries, prepare dinner, and do anything Jim needed. In fact, his company assumed that she provided support services. On arrival home, the children presented their father with minor problems, which he resolved prior to the end of each show. The point, of course, was that "father knows best"; in retrospect it seems like a (very) bad after-school special. But this show suggests how people thought married life ought to be: One sex was supposed to serve as domestic servants for the other. Or to put it more charitably, married women's family duties were supposed to be the center of their lives. In contrast, men's economic abilities were supposed to be the center of their lives.[1]

Many families, of course, could not live up to this ideal; some women have always worked for pay. Most married women, however, found it hard to obtain "respectable" jobs, since so-called protective laws and discrimination forced them into dead-end positions. Such practices enjoyed overwhelming support. For example, a 1945 Gallup poll asked a nationwide sample of people: "Do you approve or disapprove of a married woman earning money in business or industry if she has a husband capable of supporting her?" Only 20 percent of women and 16 percent of men approved. Thus, the vast majority believed that women should stay at home (Niemi et al., 1989:225). The impact of this norm, of course, was to control women's behavior by keeping them economically dependent.

Earning and spending money, it seems, is not a neutral thing; it has (nonobvious) social meaning. In *The Social Meaning of Money*, Viviana Zelizer shows that as the middle class expanded after 1870, husbands usually controlled the family's money and wives did not know how much their husbands earned (1994). The money needed to run the household was either doled out to wives irregularly or provided via an allowance. Zelizer notes, however, that men often opposed allowances precisely because it increased a wife's independence. Whether they received a dole or an allowance, middle-class women used devious strategies to obtain additional money. For example, they would take change left in their husband's pockets, have shopkeepers add bogus items to bills and keep the difference, retain money from goods and services produced at home (e.g., by renting rooms and sewing), and save money from housekeeping expenses. The situation differed for working-class families, of course, since their incomes were lower and more uncertain. According to Zelizer, husbands usually withheld some amount from their pay envelope for their own pleasure and turned the rest over to their wives (people were paid in cash in those days, not by check). Again, wives often did not know what their husbands earned. Regardless of class, then, women carried on a private battle within the family to obtain a little economic independence. Throughout this period, the law said family income belonged to the husband. He earned it; he could dispose of it as he saw fit. Thus, the Jim Andersons of the world, for all their admirable qualities, kept their wives economically dependent.

But norms about earning money have changed. In 1993 a random sample of people was asked the question about married women working for pay: By then 78 percent of women and 80 percent of men approved of a wife's employment. But do not be misled by these high percentages: A great distance exists between attitudes and action. In fact, the typical point in studies of gender is that if much has changed, much remains the same. Thus, although an income increases independence, women remain dependent. And that is the theme of this chapter.

Dimensions of Gender Inequality

In modern societies, people earn income by producing goods and services. This is why people are known by their occupation; it is why the question "What do you do?" is so important. Thus, women's employment affects their status because, as Zelizer shows, those without an income may share (some of the) resources obtained by their husbands but do not control them; they remain dependent, like children. In contrast, those with an income have some independence (and power), both within the family and in society.

Historical Dimensions

The steadily growing proportion of women in the labor force provides one of the most significant indicators of changing gender inequality over time. During the past century, 1890–1990, a stable 75–80 percent of all men have worked for pay. By contrast, whereas only 17 percent of all women were employed in 1890, 59 percent had jobs in 1996 (Hayghe, 1997). But included in these figures are single women. The degree to which married women with children are in the labor force provides a better sign of women's dependence and hence inequality.

Figure 3.1 displays this information. It reveals that only 5 percent of all married women were in the labor force in 1890. Such women were usually impoverished or African American or immigrants whose families could not meet the ideal. In considering these data, you should note that

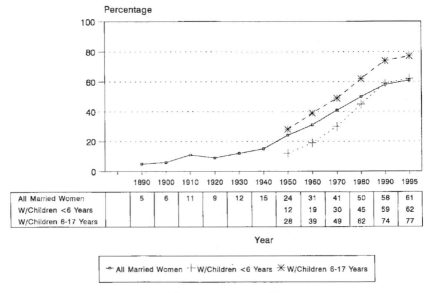

FIGURE 3.1 Labor Force Participation of Married Women, 1890–1996
SOURCES: USBC (1975:133, 1996d:400); Hayghe (1997).

during the nineteenth century women often produced income for the family without being counted as part of the labor force (Bose, 1987). For example, working-class women performed piecework inside the home. Similarly, farm wives produced income. Finally, families (which is to say wives) operated boardinghouses. Thus, wives were often economically productive but either publicly invisible or discounted by Census Bureau enumerators. All the resulting income, of course, belonged to husbands. Figure 3.1 shows that the employment rate of married women rose over time until, by 1996, 61 percent worked outside the home.

The figure also demonstrates that the employment rate of married women with children increased as well, although the data do not go back so far. In 1950 only 12 percent of married women with young children had paying jobs, a percentage that rose to 62 percent in 1996. Similarly, the labor force participation rate among married women with children of school age increased from 28 percent to 77 percent. These data mean that most married women now work for pay.

It is precisely the public recognition of their employment that signifies greater independence for women. But two qualifiers: First, a large minority of women remain out of the labor force. I come back to this issue later in the chapter. Second, my point here, women usually work at different jobs than men. The empirical generalization is: *The level of occu-*

pational segregation by sex was high and stable from about 1900 until 1960, declining slowly since that time (Jacobs, 1990). Job segregation implies not only differences in prestige and income between men and women but also the continuing dependence of women.

This finding can be illustrated by examining the proportion of women in specific job categories, as shown below. In order to see the decline in occupational segregation, scan across the rows. The proportion of women rose in some occupations. Thus, although the data are merely illustrative of a few white-collar jobs, employed women are less segregated from men than they were in the past (Rytina and Bianchi, 1984; USBC, 1996d:406).

Job Category	1970	1995
Engineers	2 percent	8 percent
Architects	4	20
Physicians	10	24
Registered nurses	97	93
Teachers	71	75
Secretaries	98	99

This same conclusion applies to African American women: They are less segregated from both men and whites. As recently as 1940, three-quarters of African American women were employed in only two job categories: as private household and farm workers. Although they remain disproportionately employed in private household work today, their representation has widened over time such that it now looks like that of white women (King, 1992).

In order to see the continuity of occupational segregation, look down the column for the year 1995 in the table just above. These data show that women are underrepresented in high-paying, high-prestige jobs and overrepresented in low-paying, low-prestige jobs. Thus, few women are engineers or physicians, and far more are nurses, teachers, and secretaries.

The continuity of occupational segregation can also be illustrated by other, more subtle indicators (Reskin and Padavic, 1994). (1) Women and men in the same job category often work for different companies, with significant economic consequences. Thus, high-priced restaurants employ waiters (men) whose income is relatively high, whereas low-priced restaurants employ waitresses (women) whose income is relatively low (Hall, 1993). (2) Men and women in the same job category work in different industries, again with significant economic consequences. Thus, women are often employed in the textile industry, where the pay is low, whereas men work in the petroleum industry, where the pay is high. (3) Even when men and women appear to have similar jobs within a com-

TABLE 3.1   Women's Income as a Percentage of Men's (year-round, full-time workers)

Panel A

		Women's Median Income Compared to Men
	1950	54%
	1960	61
	1970	59
	1980	60
	1990	70
	1995	69

Panel B

Group	1995 Median Income	Percentage Compared to White Men
White men	$29,865	—
White women	20,707	69
African American women	17,688	59
Hispanic women	14,634	49

SOURCE: USBC (1996b:38).

pany, the former often have more and the latter less income and authority. Just because a person has the title of manager does not mean she controls resources or makes fundamental decisions. Occupational segregation means inequality and dependence.

This inequality occurs because women earn less than men. In 1890 women employed full time earned only 54 percent as much as men (Goldin, 1990:60). This difference was relatively stable over much of the twentieth century, rising in recent years—as shown in panel A of Table 3.1: Women who work year-round, full time, now earn 69–70 percent as much as men. There are, however, significant differences by race and ethnicity, shown in panel B: Compared to white men, white women earn 69 percent, African American women 59 percent, and Hispanic women 49 percent. It is harder for women of color to be economically independent.

But less inequality exists among new entrants to the labor force. Shown below are the mean incomes of two age ranges of women and men employed full time in 1995 (USBC, 1996b:35).

Age	Women	Men	Women's Percentage
25–34	$25,100	$32,300	78 percent
45–54	$28,800	$49,600	58 percent

These age ranges identify people starting their work lives and in their peak earning years. As you can see, older women do not earn much more than younger women on average; this is because the former have often left the labor force for extended periods of time and suffered more from discrimination (issues to be discussed later). However, younger women's average income is closer to younger men's, which may mean they suffer less discrimination. As before, racial and ethnic variations exist.

But do not be misled by the fact that younger women are better off. The data presented in this section show clearly that most women in the United States still find it difficult to be economically independent. Most, including younger women, still rely on their husbands for economic support. This situation is also true in other societies.

Before turning to that topic, however, a few words of caution about these numbers: Data extending into the nineteenth century are always more subject to error than those gathered by current methods. As mentioned, women's economic contributions were significantly under-counted in those days. Moreover, the occupational structure has changed considerably over time, with some jobs disappearing (e.g., corset maker) and new ones emerging (e.g., computer programmer). Methods of classifying occupations have changed as well. Nonetheless, the general truth of the findings reported here remains even after these issues are taken into account (Jacobs, 1990; Goldin, 1990). Hence, in my judgment, they mirror the pattern of stability and change that has occurred over time.

International Dimensions

Women remain dependent on men in Western industrial nations besides the United States. Shown below are international comparisons of labor force participation in 1994 (USBC, 1996d:842).

Netherlands	57 percent
France	60
Germany	62
United States	64
United Kingdom	65
Canada	68
Sweden	74

The data reveal that the U.S. rate is about in the middle among these nations. But this fact hides much variation (Blossfeld and Rohwer, 1997). Sweden, for example, displays a higher level of employment among women and (not shown) less income inequality between the sexes. Germany displays about the same level of employment as the United States, but German women are more likely to work part time. Despite these differences, women are unequal to men in all Western nations.

Taken together, the data shown here reflect the theme mentioned earlier: Women have greater independence today than in the past, but most continue to be dependent on men. Although I later suggest hypotheses that explain these facts, before doing so, I want briefly to examine some of the consequences of gender inequality for women and men.

Consequences of Gender Inequality

The inequality described in the previous section extends to all areas of life, even the mundane. For example, an automobile executive recently claimed that "cars today are genderless" (NYT, 1994:12). If this is true, how come automobiles do not have a convenient place for women to put their purses? Who designs cars? For whose benefit? Perhaps the lack of a built-in spot for purses suggests that women should be like Margaret Anderson: left at home? The example may seem trivial, but it symbolizes the way men exercise authority (the design and production of cars) and make women victims (in this case by inconvenience). Of course, male authority and female victimization have far more serious consequences for gender inequality.

Male Authority

A person with authority asserts a right to make decisions influencing others, who believe they must obey (Weber, 1920). This shared notion of right and duty limits the use of force as people with authority mobilize others, obtain the money to get a job done, and hire and fire. Authority occurs in marriage as well, symbolized by a wife's pledge to love, honor, and obey her husband. Although my impression is that this vow occurs less often today, men still have authority in most areas—including marriage.

Men make most economic decisions. Only 2 percent of vice presidents, presidents, and chief executive officers of Fortune 500 corporations are women (Catalyst, 1996). Of all corporate officers, only 10 percent are women. Thus, men choose what products to produce, how much they will cost, and the conditions of work. When they design assembly lines, men determine the height of the conveyor belt or machine. Unlike the purse example, this is not just inconvenient; the organization of factories influences women's ability to work in high-paying blue-collar jobs. Finally, since men occupy the top positions, they determine how occupations are evaluated and paid; they have decided, for example, that engineering is more important and requires more skill than, say, teaching.

A similar pattern exists in government. Men, not women, enact and enforce legislation. Only 8 percent of U.S. senators and 11 percent of representatives are women. This is one reason the distribution of birth control information and abortions remained illegal for most of the twentieth century. It is why women were denied civil rights until recently, including the ability to control income they earned, own property, obtain credit, and sue in court. And this legislative gender bias remains in place today, when Congress considers issues important to women.

Religion is much the same. God nearly always talks through men. Only 11 percent of the clergy are women (USBC, 1996d:405). One leader of a conservative faith group tried to justify this situation (Shimron, 1997:1): "We believe in the full equality of men and women. But we don't believe God calls women to be senior pastors of a church. It grows out of our commitment to Scripture. The husband is in the position of leadership, and the wife is the helper and complement to that. God designed a woman to be a nurturer and a mother. God created men to protect and provide." It should be no surprise, then, that God, however known, is usually defined as masculine. Is it any wonder that he decided to defend developing embryos rather than the women who carry them? Is it any wonder that he has always justified men's hitting women and children (Greven, 1991)?

The courtroom is no different. Male judges exercise authority there, deciding how laws are to be understood and enforced. It should not be surprising that child support payments are set very low in the United States and child support laws often go unenforced (Glendon, 1987).

So it is with medical treatment. Physicians are nearly always men who decide who enters the field, its priorities, and how much treatment will cost. Remember, men drove women out of medicine at the end of the nineteenth century as more women began seeking abortions (see Chapter 2).

Finally, higher education displays the same pattern. Administrators and faculty are nearly all male and the secretaries nearly all female. Sociology departments are no exception (Beeghley and Van Ausdale, 1990). Thus, men's history and exploits have always been emphasized, since men assumed (wrongly) that analyzing women's experiences would yield little new insight.

These examples suggest that it remains odd for women to have authority. Think about women in decisionmaking roles: as the chief executive officer of Chrysler, as the Speaker of the House of Representatives, as a priest in your local parish. Or consider how women in some occupations are referred to: "lady policemen" and "lady doctors." Such dismissive wording immediately points out that the individuals are odd and perhaps ought not to be there. Similar language is typical at colleges, where the term "lady" usually refers to women's athletic programs—as in "Lady Wildcats" and "Lady Anteaters" (honest, at UC Irvine). It is not accidental that men's and women's sports are always unequal. In effect, the use of "lady" as a prefix implies that women ought to remain at home, where they can be protected by men. Yet such protection occurs neither in the house nor on the job.

Female Victimization

Inequality leads to female victimization, such as sexual harassment, rape, wife abuse, and child sexual abuse. All involve men's asserting power over women. And when force is implied or used, women become victims and men's authority is buttressed.

Sexual harassment takes two forms: (1) The attempt at extorting sex via implicitly or explicitly threatening one's job, grade, or letter of recommendation. (2) Repeated verbal, physical, or symbolic actions that create a hostile work (or educational) environment. In nearly all cases, males harass females (Schneider, 1991). Although harassment often happens when women occupy subordinate positions, it comes from colleagues as well as supervisors (AMA, 1996). About half of all women are harassed sexually at some point in their academic or working lives (Fitzgerald, 1993:1071). The behavior takes a number of forms: pressure for sexual cooperation, repeated phone calls or letters, repeated pressure for dates, repeated physical touching, and repeated sexual remarks. Other mechanisms for creating a hostile working environment include plastic displays of sexual body parts or nude pinups used as dartboards. Men's imagination is the only limit to ways of showing women that they are unwanted on the job. Thus, millions of women endure insults and assaults simply because they choose to earn a living.

Many women find that sexual harassment is a crime without a remedy. Shakespeare points out why in *Measure for Measure,* written around 1603 (1991). In act 2, scene 4, Isabella says to Angelo:

> *With an outstretched throat I'll tell the world*
> *aloud*
> *What man thou art.*

Angelo replies:

Who will believe thee, Isabel?
My unsoil'd name, th' austereness of my life
My vouch against you, and my place i' th' state
Will so your accusation overweigh
That you shall stifle in your own report,
And smell of calumny.

In short, people do not believe the accuser, who will herself be accused of trying to harm another's reputation. After making their own accusations, the perpetrators of sexual harassment go on to become chairs of academic departments, supervisors in government agencies, and judges (Engelberg and Sontag, 1994).

Sexual harassment has negative consequences for victims (Wagner, 1992). Some are fired from their jobs after they complain of harassment or quit because of the stress (Coles, 1986). In addition, the trauma takes an internal toll, causing such physical ailments as headaches and ulcers. The psychological impact ranges from loss of self-esteem and increasing anxiety to *clinical depression*—essentially, psychological incapacitation: Victims lose interest in daily activities for an extended period; they have little energy, feel worthless, and find it difficult to concentrate (APA, 1994). Depressed persons often consider suicide and are prone to drug use and abuse. Although this is speculative, it appears that when women enter traditionally male occupations, their male colleagues want to remind women of their "true place" (at home) by using sexuality as a demonstration of power. The resulting trauma limits women's ability to be economically independent.

Rape has a similar impact. According to self-report data, about 700,000 adult women are raped each year (NVC, 1992). This estimate probably covers less than half the total rapes, however, since about 60 percent of all victims are under 18. Even those who have not been raped may alter their behavior for fear of being attacked; women learn not to make themselves vulnerable by going out after dark or working in the evening (Koss, 1993). Yet long hours are necessary in many occupations. Thus, women who are prudent are victimized without being raped. It turns out, however, that 75 percent of rape victims know the perpetrator; most are family members, friends, or acquaintances. Rape leads to many difficulties (NVC, 1992). Clinical depression eventually affects about 30 percent of rape victims. About 31 percent eventually display *post-traumatic stress disorder,* which refers to reaction to trauma: intense anxiety, inability to concentrate, becoming easily startled, nightmares, flashbacks, and insomnia (APA, 1994). Victims also exhibit physical symptoms such as stomachaches, ulcers, and headaches. Moreover, drug abuse is higher among rape victims than other women. Finally, about 33 percent of victims consider suicide, and about 13 percent attempt it. So rape has a long-term disabling effect. Like sexual harassment, rape uses sex to assert power; it is a way to control women, to let them know where their "true place" is (Searles and Berger, 1995).

Yet, again, staying home (and being dependent) does not guarantee protection. Think about "wife abuse": threatening or actually injuring one's wife or companion. I use this term rather than the more common "spouse abuse" because men initiate the violence in most families (Herman, 1992). Although women harm men as well, their actions are nearly always reactive. About 14 percent of women say their husbands or boyfriends have threatened or struck them, with about 2 million episodes occurring each year (FVPF, 1993). About half of all murders of women are committed by their male partners (Browne and Williams, 1989). In addition, of course, wife abuse has psychological consequences, such as post-traumatic stress syndrome, clinical depression, and suicide (Herman, 1989). As in other forms of sexual intimidation, wife abuse is about power: Men use violence to keep women dependent. It makes them constantly fearful and thereby prevents them from leaving. In the jargon, the victims suffer from *learned helplessness* (DeMaris and Swinford, 1996). Such results rarely lead to economic independence.

Neither does "child sexual abuse," which refers to adults sexually molesting or penetrating children. It appears that about 20 percent of girls and 9 percent of boys endure sexual abuse, nearly always perpetrated by males, with over 400,000 episodes taking place each year (NRCCSA, 1992). Like the other acts outlined here, child sexual abuse involves the use of sex to express power. In effect, adult males act sexually with the defenseless young as a way of feeling powerful. The victim responds, of course, by feeling powerless (Jacobs, 1994). Male victims often display contradictory responses, sometimes showing aggression (especially toward women) and sometimes clinical depression. Female victims often become clinically depressed and see themselves as dependent on men. As a result they often become sexually active at younger ages and endure early pregnancy (and abortion or birth), early marriage, and early divorce (Boyer and Fine, 1992; Stock et al, 1997). Victims of both sexes frequently use and abuse drugs and think about suicide. These outcomes limit their employment and income as adults.

Such behaviors suggest that instead of needing protection by men, women need protection from men. When some men use sex as an assertion of power, the benefits redound to all men because women are encouraged to remain at home: dependent. Thus, although it may never occur to men like Jim Anderson to threaten women like Margaret, their family life is buttressed by the victimization of women by men. Gender inequality results.

Individuals and Gender Inequality

Consider the case of Susan Jones, who enrolls at Slippery Rock State with excellent test scores and good grades. She can select almost any major. She thinks about engineering and does well in the first course. Eventually, however, she decides on teaching.

After graduation, she becomes, at age 23, an elementary school teacher. She marries Isaac Godbolt and supports him for two years until he gets an engineering degree. Then they leave the hills of Pennsylvania and settle in (of all places) Mayberry. For the next five years, she teaches and takes charge of the house. Then Isaac is offered a job that would mean relocating to (let us say) Metropolis. A debate ensues—a major fight actually—during which Isaac throws the phone at Susan, giving her a black eye. So they move and decide to start a family (a common pattern). After giving birth, Susan, now 30, drops out of the labor force and spends three years raising her child and taking care of Isaac and the house. She then returns to teaching, again starting near the bottom of the salary scale because her previous tenure only partially transfers. Hence, Susan not only earns far less than her husband, she also earns less than those who graduated from Slippery Rock at the same time but worked steadily. Also, though Isaac helps (a little), Susan remains in charge of child care and housekeeping.

Two years later, Isaac gets another job and the couple move again, over Susan's objection, to (where else?) Gotham City. They decide to have a second child, and Susan stays out of the labor force for two years this time, returning to teaching again at age 35. Still, she remains near the bottom of the salary scale. Five years pass. Isaac, now earning big bucks, begins hating the rat race he is in. He has an affair, divorces Susan, and marries his secretary. He takes his engineering degree (which Susan helped him get), his pension (which Susan helped him get as well), and the new wife to Kansas in search of a better life at the end of the rainbow. Susan receives no income support, of course, since she has an occupation. She gets custody of the children and child support, but after a short time the payments stop arriving. Today she cares for her children on her teacher's salary of $30,000 per year.

Although this vignette is oversimplified, it nonetheless reflects many women's lives. Susan chose to teach rather than, say, design highways; women more often want jobs that involve helping others (Bridges, 1989). She married rather young; such women tend to lower their career aspirations (Murrell et al., 1991). She gave up income, job security, and an advanced degree of her own by supporting Isaac while he completed his degree, taking charge of child care and housework, leaving paid work twice to care for infants, and following her husband's moves (Presser,

1994). In general, about 82 percent of corporate moves involve men's needs to relocate (ERC, 1992). Like many women, Susan went through a divorce, and child support proved unreliable. Only about half of those awarded support receive the full amount; about one-fourth collect half, and one-fourth get nothing (USBC, 1995a:7). With the exception of the divorce and its aftermath, all these decisions were Susan's. Many women make choices like these, and it is important to know their implications for dependence and independence.

Women's Choices

Economists posit that the job market is "efficient" such that sex-related differences in income occur because women are less productive than men. Productivity is measured by workers' *human capital*, as indicated by their skills (education; work experience; tenure in their current jobs) and employment priorities (staying in the labor force continuously; choosing part-time employment; absenteeism due to children's illness; leaving a job due to a spouse's mobility). The human capital hypothesis can be formally stated: *The fewer skills people acquire and the lower the priority they place on employment versus other activities, the lower their income.*

As the vignette about Susan suggests, the hypothesis is plausible because it focuses on the choices people make. Their decisions about education and work experience lead to the development of certain job skills. Along with these skills, people's employment priorities indicate their productivity and thus their income. So Susan's selection of education over engineering produced skills (presumably) worth less than Isaac's. Similarly, her decision to leave the labor force was a free choice, but it made her "less productive." Other women make different but similarly self-limiting decisions that reflect the importance of their jobs compared to other values, such as raising a family. From this point of view, then, women deserve lower incomes because they are less skilled and less devoted to (paid) work. Their priorities are housework, child care, and following their husbands. An earnings gap results.

Yet two incongruities call this hypothesis into question. First, although its logic implies that women who stress family obligations would pick jobs that fit with the duties of wives and mothers, many of the occupations in which women cluster do not mesh with caring for children and husbands. For example, they usually do not provide more flexible hours. Secretaries and private household help must typically keep rather rigid schedules. Nurses must often work nights and weekends. In fact, it appears that men's jobs often carry more flexible hours, more unsupervised leave time, and more sick leave and vacation, which means that their jobs are more compatible with family responsibilities. Second, although the hypothesis suggests that single women (who have fewer family burdens) would avoid low-paying, female-dominated occupations and instead seek higher-paying, male-dominated ones, such women are as likely as married women to be employed in female-dominated jobs (Reskin and Hartman, 1986). Such incongruities indicate that job markets are not "efficient"; more is going on than a simple distribution of skill and employment priorities.

How much more is revealed by tests of the hypothesis. Only about 40 percent of the income difference between men and women results from factors like dropping out of the labor force (England, 1992:27). These findings mean that although the human capital hypothesis provides part of the explanation for why individual women earn less than men, something else must be operating.

Discrimination

That "something else" is discrimination, people's unequal treatment because of their personal characteristics, in this case gender. And, I would like to suggest, discrimination against women starts at home. First, girls and boys learn they are unequal via the socialization process, which teaches them to accept traditional gender relations (Kelly, 1997). Thus, girls like Susan Jones are taught that raising children is their primary responsibility and as adults they neglect to establish their economic independence. Similarly, boys like Isaac Godbolt are taught to assume that their wives should take care of their children and their house. Put bluntly, when children are socialized in such ways, discrimination is occurring. Second, the process of victimizing women described earlier is discrimination. After all, when he thought he might not get to move to Metropolis, Isaac had a temper tantrum and hit Susan with the telephone. So, like all women, Susan knew that force was always possible, directed either at her or the children. More generally, the possibility of sexual harassment, spouse abuse, rape, and child sexual abuse makes all women cautious and fearful, whether they actually are subjected to these acts or not. Third, when couples obtain a divorce, women are treated unequally when the tangible and (more important) the intangible assets are divided (Beeghley, 1996a). Even though Susan saw herself in partnership with Isaac and chose to help him obtain an advanced degree rather than get her own, took care of the house and children for twelve years, and followed his occupational moves, she received no income support when the marriage broke up. "After all," she had her own career and source of income. Similarly, Isaac took his pension benefits with him. "After all," despite his wife's sacrifices, he earned them.

Discrimination starts at home and continues at work, although it is illegal. The Equal Pay Act of 1963 and the Civil Rights Act of 1964 prohibit the unequal treatment of women in earnings and occupation. Nonetheless, discrimination occurs covertly.

When a company has job openings, it must use some mechanism for filling them (Beeghley, 1996a). The most common strategy is word of mouth. A notice is posted or employees are told of job openings, and, quickly and efficiently, applicants appear. The advantage of this process is that employees, aware of their employer's biases, refer potential applicants to what the company considers gender-appropriate jobs. A second strategy is to hire an employment agency. Since such headhunters are paid only for locating acceptable candidates, the reward for acceding to the employer's bias is great. A third strategy is advertising in newspapers or other outlets. Employers who use this tactic sometimes discriminate overtly. For example, a "gender-inappropriate" caller (say, a man inquiring about a salesclerk job or a women looking into a shift supervisory job) will be told that the personnel manager is out, whereas a "gender-appropriate" applicant claiming similar credentials will be asked to come for an interview. A fourth strategy involves tailoring the job description for a prearranged "inside" applicant. My guess is that this tactic occurs more often with academic and government jobs, since the law generally requires that vacancies be advertised.

Once job candidates are identified, they must be screened. One screening device is an interviewer's conclusions about an applicant's "demeanor," "self-esteem," and "psychological stability." These judgments are legal as long as their connection to the job can be shown. So gender stereotypes easily enter the process. How, after all, does a male candidate with "high self-esteem" differ from a female who is "too pushy"? Another screening device is to manipulate the selection criteria. The lack of perfect candidates, especially for white-collar jobs, makes this tactic easy. Let us say that a job is advertised requiring a master's degree and five years of experience and that the two best candidates are a woman with a bachelor's degree and ten years' experience and a man with a master's degree and one year's experience. Note that the woman has less education but more experience. In this situation, it is reasonable to decide that his higher level of education makes the man more qualified. Now assume the same outfit has another opening a few months later. This time, however, the two best applicants are a woman with a master's degree and one year's experience and a man with a bachelor's degree and ten years' experience. Note that I have now reversed the combination of education and experience such that the woman applicant has more education and less experience. This time the employer decides that his wealth of practical experience makes the man the better-qualified candidate. In both cases the "better" candidate was chosen in a situation where a trade-off occurs between education and experience. When a company's labor force remains occupationally segregated over time, it is reasonable to hypothesize that discrimination is at work.

To complicate matters, think about the way minority women fit into this process. Imagine comparing Hispanic or African American women and men to white men, taking into account each individual's mix of education and experience. Once again, discrimination often results (Beeghley, 1996b).

The combination of the choices women make and discrimination helps to explain why many individual women earn relatively low incomes. But this analysis remains incomplete. Women, like men, choose among the opportunities available. Women, like men, value good pay and prestige. Thus, as shown earlier, when the chance to find work in architecture, engineering, and other fields improved in recent years women flocked into them. In order to grasp the range of choices women have and how these choices changed over time, a structural analysis is necessary.

Social Structure and Gender Inequality

In the 1870s, the neurologist W. Weir Mitchell, a specialist in "women's nervous disorders," developed a "rest cure." The patient was placed in isolation (e.g., a bedroom) and forbidden any activity. The goal was for the patient to want "to do the things she once felt she could not do," that is, return with unquestioning acceptance to housekeeping, mothering, and caring for her husband. Shortly after her marriage in 1884, Charlotte Perkins Gilman was given the "rest cure" by her husband. In 1892, after her divorce, she wrote *The Yellow Wallpaper*, which describes how the "cure" almost drove her insane. Gilman finally figured out that only her work (writing) would free her. Mitchell's method was widely used; one can only shudder at the many undocumented cases of torture. *The Yellow Wallpaper* is not only Gilman's critique of psychiatry as a tool for oppression, it also shows what happens when the range of choices for women is so narrow that they are forced to be economically dependent on men. Although the range of choice has widened over time and a job increases the possibility for independence, continuing inequality keeps women dependent. The source of this paradox must be structural: Identifiable factors both maintain and reduce gender inequality.[2]

The Preservation of Gender Inequality

In a context where pregnancy could not be controlled and wives managed productive enterprises around the home, it made sense to divide labor in traditional ways. Today, however, it is not wise for a wife like Susan Jones to give up income and seniority for her husband's job advancement. Yet many do precisely that. And most men, it seems, expect such sacrifice from their wives and have temper tantrums if they do not. The source of such expectations must be structural. My hypothesis is *the preservation of gender inequality reflects (1) the salience of traditional gender norms and (2) institutionalized discrimination.*

The Salience of Traditional Gender Norms. Traditional gender norms dictate that men and women should have different spheres. Although women might be bright or artistic, they ought to bear children, raise them, and care for husbands. In performing these tasks, they should be in touch with their own and others' emotions, sensitive to the needs of others, and nurturant of their children and husbands. In contrast, men's nonreproductive abilities should constitute the center of their lives. Hence, men ought to compete with one another, earn a living, and support their families. In performing these tasks, they should not be overly emotional, sensitive, or nurturant, and they should not be economically dependent. After conception of children, men's roles within the family are more limited than women's because of the need to work outside the home and the psychological characteristics that outside jobs impose. I have constructed this portrait of traditional gender norms as a "pure type" (after Max Weber). Real people adhere to them in varying ways:

(1) A large percentage of women remain unemployed by choice. As Figure 3.1 shows, 61 percent of all married women are in the labor force, meaning 39 percent do not earn a living. They are housewives, reliant on their husbands for status and livelihood.

(2) About 30 percent of employed women work part time, compared to 14 percent of men (USDL, 1996:6). A similar discrepancy exists among those without jobs but looking for them. Women prefer part-time jobs in order to reduce the conflict between outside work and household duties.

(3) Husbands do not like cleaning toilets; wives, of course, don't either, but they are usually the ones who do it. I use this image to symbolize the fact that husbands tend to expect their wives to do most of the work around the house, regardless of the wives' employment status. Husbands spend fourteen hours each week on housework compared to thirty-three for wives (Blair and Lichter, 1991). Specifically, husbands spend two hours each week fixing meals compared to nine for wives; husbands spend about two hours cleaning house compared to more than eight for wives. Outdoor chores and auto maintenance constitute the only areas in which wives work less. More generally, "sharing" household tasks usually means that wives arrange and control them; in effect, husbands occasionally "help" wives do "their" work. Thus, employed wives perform two jobs—at home and at work—suffering from work overload and depression as a result (Perry-Jenkins and Folk, 1994).

Egalitarian marriages are rare, whether wives have full-time jobs or not, and even when they earn more than their husbands (Brines, 1994). This fact lends credence to the comic's line that "a man around the house is an inanimate object."

(4) Workplaces continue to be gendered; that is, they are organized so as to benefit men (Reskin and Padavic, 1994:128). When men like Jim Anderson left for work in the 1940s, their employers assumed they could stay long hours because they had a support staff at home to take care of their children and personal needs. Employers still make such assumptions. For example, few provide child care on site or make provisions for the care of sick children; the best employees are men whose wives take care of such things. Similarly, employers often create an environment that fosters sexual harassment by ignoring the creation of a sexually charged atmosphere, discriminating against women at promotion time, and fostering the notion that the workplace is a masculine locale.

That many women remain at home or do part-time paid work suggests the continuing significance of traditional gender norms. Men's opposition to housework indicates this salience more directly. And the organization of the workplace not only reinforces traditional gender relations, it leads to the systematic unequal treatment of women.

Institutionalized Discrimination.   Inequality is also preserved by *institutionalized discrimination*, the unequal treatment of people with different characteristics that is embedded in the social structure.

The gender ratio in work groups provides one example of the way in which unequal treatment is structurally induced. Recall that few women are employed in many white-collar jobs, for example, as architects. The skewed gender ratio (a high percentage of men and a low percentage of women) in such work settings means that women are "tokens," treated as representatives of all women, as symbols rather than individuals (Kanter, 1978). Discrimination occurs for three reasons. First, token women are watched closely by supervisors and colleagues, which generates performance pressures. Second, the work group becomes polarized, with tokens excluded, making it difficult for them to obtain information and learn the informal norms that can provide keys to success. Third, token women are assimilated into the work group on men's terms, which may preclude rising to the top because of the job roles forced on women. Such roles may include nurturing male colleagues, being treated as a seductress (regardless of the woman's actions), or being regarded as the group's pet. A woman who tries to remain independent risks ostracism.

Such risks limit women's choices. One option is to overachieve, but not everyone can do this. Another option is to strive for success more covertly. Rosabeth Kanter believes that women's so-called fear of success may actually be an attempt at keeping a low profile in a threatening context, thus preventing retaliation (1978). This strategy is hard to maintain, however, because achievement in competitive jobs often requires sponsors or mentors. Yet polarization of the work group makes it difficult to develop ties with more experienced persons. Further, success in such jobs often depends upon inclusion in informal gatherings, where information is exchanged, contacts made, and bureaucratic lessons learned; yet women are often excluded from such events. In addition, of course, polarization allows plenty of opportunity for discrimination, which men do by sexually harassing women. Some women cope by trying to prove group loyalty in order to become insiders, leading to the "queen bee syndrome": women discriminating against other women.

Occupational segregation provides a second example of unequal treatment built into the social structure. I noted earlier that men determine how occupations are evaluated and paid and that women and men still work at different jobs. As new occupations were created over time, (male) employers "gendered" them; that is, they set pay and organized the work process with one or the other sex in mind. This remains true; the introduction of new technology in an industry always leads to the reorganization and continuation of a gendered division of labor (Acker, 1990). As a result, women are concentrated in jobs that involve helping and nurturing others, whereas men are more likely to be in jobs that involve exercising authority. And occupations with authority are more highly valued and better paid than those involving nurturance. Thus, men decided that the skills needed to build highways and bridges are more complex and have greater long-term implications than those needed to build children. I use the phrase "building children" to emphasize that like the highways and bridges engineers design, children are constructed; they are turned into functioning adults. Melvin Konner ends his book *Childhood* by observing that "children are living messages we send into the future, a future we will not see. . . . In effect we are building the house of tomorrow day by day, not out of bricks or steel, but out of the stuff of children's bodies, hearts, and minds" (1991:428). Child care workers and teachers are paid very low wages compared to engineers, a matter of political rather than economic judgment. It is more accurate to see men and women as having different skills (England, 1992:18). Thus, institutionalized discrimination is a two-part process. Employers first segregate men and women, then pay the latter lower wages even if their jobs are of comparable worth. Once this phenomenon is recognized, the data presented earlier make sense.

Taken together, traditional gender norms and institutionalized discrimination constitute inertial forces, preserving inequality between men and women. Yet these processes are social products; they illustrate how human beings can control and change their range of choices (see Chapter 1). In the next section, we look at some factors that transform gender relations and increase choices.

The Decline of Gender Inequality

Societies are not monoliths: massive, uniform, and unchanging. Discrepant tendencies coexist. At the same time, then, gender inequality is both preserved and reduced. Regarding the latter, my hypothesis is that *the decline of gender inequality reflects (1) industrialization, (2) female labor force participation, (3) advances in medical technology, (4) legal changes, and (5) the rise of feminism.*

Industrialization. As observed in Chapter 2, for most of human history whole families have scratched the soil, dividing work in light of the practical problems they faced. In such environments, women and men were much alike: Both labored at backbreaking tasks. The work women performed—such as baking, making soap, brewing beer, harvesting garden crops, and managing barn animals—was extremely hard. On top of this, women became pregnant often and had six to eight children. Of course, childbirth was a productive act. For most families, survival in such contexts was precarious.

The situation in urban areas at the dawn of capitalism was similar. For example, in his *Autobiography*, which appeared in 1795, Benjamin Franklin recounted how his wife, Deborah, helped "cheerfully in my [printing] business, folding and stitching pamphlets, tending shop, purchasing old linen rags for the papermakers, etc." (1961:92). Franklin, of course, defined the print shop as "my business." Men were in charge of the nascent cash economy, and women's work was not paid. As already noted, early census takers rarely counted the work of women like Deborah. In any case, industrialization transformed this lifestyle as new forms of energy replaced muscle power and productivity increased dramatically. Driving machines with fossil, steam, and other types of energy demands a more complex division of labor than that found at home. It also requires that people work at one location in order to reduce the cost of energy, raw materials, transportation, and distribution. So the production of goods moved out of the home and family members could no longer labor collectively. Since pregnancy and birth continued to be problematic, most wives stayed home. Most husbands left; they had jobs and earned incomes to support their families.

But the new emphasis on administration, coordination, and record keeping meant that reliance on thinking replaced reliance on lifting. Women could, in theory, compete equally with men in all sorts of jobs.

In this new context, an increasing proportion of women began working for pay.

Female Labor Force Participation. One of these many unknown women, Dorothy Richardson, wrote an autobiography around 1905 describing what it was like for a woman to be employed at the end of the nineteenth century (O'Neill, 1972). After leaving home at age 18 and moving to New York City, she worked in entry-level positions at several companies. Richardson titled her book *The Long Day*, emphasizing not only the length of her workday but also the hard labor and the difficulties she had making ends meet on low wages. In her time, the average employed person worked ten hours per day, six days per week. Despite this schedule, however, Richardson enrolled in night school and acquired education and commercial skills. She eventually found work as a stenographer and became "prosperous," by which she meant independent and self-supporting. The story of the past century is one in which more and more individuals like Richardson have earned incomes.

The rise in women's labor force participation reduces their economic dependence on men, thus altering their choices and transforming the family. Some women, such as Dorothy Richardson, became like men in this new industrialized context: They supported themselves. It was often the case that such women, especially those with college degrees, never married precisely because they earned a living (Rothman, 1984; Goldin, 1990). Of course, most people find celibacy difficult to maintain. Early in the century, women usually quit their jobs to marry—a "choice" fostered by societal norms and reinforced by law. Over time, however, increasing numbers of married women overcame these restrictions and stayed in the labor force. An important implication is that the divorce rate rose when more women had incomes. A woman with an income need not remain in a marriage that has broken down. Thus, female labor force participation has an insidious result: It overthrows traditional gender relations because economic independence leads inexorably to a desire for equality. This is why all employed women are feminists.

When the opportunities presented by industrialization were combined with increasing labor force participation and the income that resulted, the differences between men and women narrowed. The impact of these two factors, however, was limited by the degree to which reproduction could be controlled, which in turn depended on advances in medical technology.

Advances in Medical Technology. The application of science to solving practical problems creates choices, allowing behavior that was impossible or immoral in the past. For example, as described in Chapter 2, the condom, the intrauterine device, and the birth control pill led to an increase in the rate of premarital sexual intercourse. In the same way, the ability to perform safe abortions allowed greater sexual freedom as well. As indicated previously, gender relations underlie these issues. After all, if pregnancy and birth cannot be controlled, women must be dependent on men for economic security.

A mental experiment suggests why. Imagine that in an industrialized society women do not have access to either birth control or abortions. If a talented woman wants to become an architect, should a school of architecture admit her? School officials could argue that she will be like most women and marry and become pregnant many times. In this context, they could say, it would be a waste of time to train a woman to be an architect. Furthermore, even assuming she receives a degree, should a company employ her? After it devoted time and money to her training, she would eventually leave, either because of pregnancy or to follow her husband's occupational moves. Birth control changed this situation.

Yet legal restrictions on women's activities made it difficult for them to take advantage of the new choices resulting from advances in medical technology. Put simply, women possessed neither civil rights nor reproductive rights.

Legal Changes.   Laws regulate action and serve as formally stated norms. They constitute a collective decision about what actions are good and bad. It follows that citizens with different characteristics are often treated differently under the law. Children, for example, enjoy both special rights and special restrictions. Treating them differently is seen as appropriate because children are relatively powerless compared to adults. Until recently, treating women differently has been seen as appropriate as well. (Here the focus is on civil rights, since changes in reproductive rights were described in Chapter 2.)

Women were denied civil rights because, it was said, they need to be protected. One type of "protective legislation," as it was called, restricted the number of hours women could work—for pay outside the home, not for free inside it. Thus, although prior to the 1880s no state limited women's hours of employment, by 1919 forty states had passed such laws (Goldin, 1990:190). Another category of legislation allowed unequal treatment in hiring and retaining women on the job. For example, married women could not be hired as teachers in 61 percent of all school districts in 1928; after marriage they could not be retained in 52 percent of all school districts (Goldin, 1990:161). Such statutes were one reason so many women "chose" to quit their jobs at marriage: They were forced to. A third category of laws legalized occupational segregation. This meant that women were typically hired for jobs that did not allow for promotion. Thus, a 1940 study of 260 companies showed that 74 percent limited women to specific jobs and 70 percent limited men to specific (and different) jobs (Goldin, 1990:112). Such policies were both legal and cause for company pride; they were advertised to the public. Limits on hours of work, hiring and retention, and job type constituted only a few of the constraints on women that, taken together, meant that they were not fully endowed citizens.

There are two opposing explanations of protective legislation (Goldin, 1990:192). One interpretation is that young, single, employed women could be easily exploited and, like children, needed protection. In addition, it has been argued, protection had a paradoxical and positive impact in that it led to improved working conditions for both men and women. The average number of hours of work declined from about sixty per week during the late 1800s to about forty by the 1930s. Another interpretation is that such laws restricted women's choices in order to keep them at home and dependent. According to this argument, it is not surprising that these statutes were passed between 1880 and 1930, the same period that rates of premarital sex, abortion, and divorce rose; the same period when industrialization flowered and female labor force participation grew. These laws constituted responses by men and their elected representatives (male legislators) to rising competition; men wished to retain power and privilege—both at home and in society at large. Of course, the justification for such laws was found in traditional gender norms.

The drive to "protect" women generated much conflict as feminists pushed for equality. For example, led by Alice Paul, the National Woman's Party was organized in 1921 and submitted an equal rights amendment to Congress. But despite the morally powerful arguments for equality, movement toward this goal remained ineffectual for a long time. Between 1890 and 1960, laws continued to focus on "protecting" women, expressing the fundamental belief that men and women are not and should not be equal. Women ought to be like children: dependent on others.

Like so much else, however, this collective judgment changed during the 1960s, when women gained full civil rights. Yet it is worth noting that in at least one case this situation arose by accident. The Civil Rights Act of 1964 did not include women until just prior to passage. When a southern member of Congress introduced an amendment to include sex along with race, the media reported that there was laughter in the Congress; it was seen as a joke, part of a strategy by southern lawmakers to propose "silly" amendments aimed at defeating the bill (Bird, 1968). But they misjudged the situation, and this amendment became part of the civil rights law passed that year. One result is that employment discrimination against women became illegal. Combined with the Equal Pay Act of 1963, title 9 of the Educational Amendments Act of 1972, and other legislation, much of the legal buttress for gender discrimination disappeared. Thus, the law has been fundamentally changed so as to require equal treatment of men and women. The logic is that human beings have dignity and worth, that they should not be treated unequally based on personal characteristics. Behind these legal changes was the reemergence of feminism.

The Rise of Feminism. When oppressed people strive for equality, they usually rely on ideology and an organized social movement. As emphasized previously, feminism provides both. It has been linked to women's ability to engage in sexual activity with whom they wish, to regulate their fertility, and to end marriages of sorrow. But exercising these abilities requires economic independence. Without that, all else is a sham. Because such independence is limited by women's continued victimization, feminists have increasingly focused on this issue.

In *Trauma and Recovery,* Judith Lewis Herman emphasizes the many negative consequences for victims of sexual harassment, rape, wife abuse, and child sexual abuse (1992). It turns out, however, that the most common location of such trauma is not in the midst of war or even in violent neighborhoods but within the family and workplace. Such venues continue to be regulated by traditional gender relations. Because these norms dictate that men ought to dominate women, they deny the existence of sexual trauma and thereby perpetuate economic inequality. In fact, Herman argues, what haunts women even more than the crimes themselves is the silence surrounding them: bystanders' denials that crimes have been committed. She says that the study of trauma endured by women depends on a political movement for equality: feminism. Without a movement, the process of bearing witness becomes meaningless because traumatic acts are not acknowledged; they are forgotten. Placed in the context of a movement for equality, these same acts are understood as examples of oppression, of tyranny. They allow victims to find a transcendent meaning in their experiences. They galvanize others and translate a personal tragedy into a social problem. Herman argues that women's activities as adults cannot be like those of men until women are no longer victimized. This change requires economic independence.

Implications

When problems persist over time, it is useful to ask a simple question: Who benefits? Do women benefit from being unable to regulate pregnancy? Or do men? Do women benefit from job segregation? Or do men? In an industrial society, it takes strong norms, upheld by religious sanctions, to persuade people that women benefit from being kept dependent and unequal. And this is precisely what traditional gender norms do. As a result, it can be argued that men are no different than other dominant groups in history: They exploit women to gain money, power, and prestige. Men resist equality, then, because they do not want to give up their dominant position. Although there is truth to this explanation, it is crude, bereft of subtlety. Men and women live together and love one another, or try to, so there has to be more going on than simple exploitation. Here are some ideas (Goode, 1982).

Let us begin from the fact that as things now stand, men run the nation, regulate the economy, interpret God's will, make the law, provide for higher education, and determine medical treatment. This is what men have always done. They dominate and expect to dominate. In this context, men have been socialized that it is their obligation to support and protect women, who function in turn as domestic servants.[3] Men have also learned that women are sexual objects whose primary task is to satisfy men and reproduce. As a result, many men do not regard women's desires as important. It is a sociological principle that dominants always know less about subordinates than subordinates know about dominants. So women's desire for equality simply mystifies many men. From this angle, traditional gender relations feel right, and men wonder why "radicals" want to change them. Moreover, because the men alive today did not create the system that provides them with advantages, they reject charges that they have conspired to dominate women. They believe that the different activities of women and men and the consequences that follow exist as part of the natural (God-given) order; they constitute social facts, as Durkheim would say. They are not men's fault and men do not want to be blamed. Nor do they readily notice the talents or achievements of women, which means that women of accomplishment still seem odd. Men take their advantages for granted, remaining unaware or denying that the social structure provides them with an edge. But despite their denial, men define even a small loss of opportunity or deference as threatening and exaggerate the potential problems that might result. This is because they feel as if women are invading high-prestige and powerful positions.

Although these remarks are admittedly speculative, I mean to suggest how difficult it is for many men to recognize their benefits and give them up. They are being asked, as adults, to change ingrained psychological responses (such as defining women as sexual objects rather than colleagues while at work). This kind of transformation is difficult. So the abandonment of traditional gender relations does not come easily.

Some women resist equality, too, though their motives for resistance probably differ. I mentioned earlier that employed women are feminists in fact, if not in ideology, because they have the potential to be independent. Yet many women reject the label "feminist." For example, I have had female students say, "I am not a feminist, but I believe in equal pay" (or "equal rights" or "the right to an abortion"). They are ambivalent. Maybe, in an inarticulate way, they feel as if they are being offered a variant of "Sophie's choice." In the novel of that title by William Styron, the Nazis force Sophie to choose which of her children will die (1979). By analogy, women may sense that feminism forces a choice between two parts of one's self: dependence or independence, heart or mind, the inner world of family or the outer world of work. Maybe it creates a conflict between basic emotional needs learned as children and the demand for fair treatment in society. Perhaps many women fear they cannot have both and that feminism means picking the latter. Again, this analysis is speculative, but it provides a way of explaining the strange phenomenon of middle-class women's demanding equality while supporting political candidates who oppose the means to achieve it.

Although such dissonance probably exists for many working-class women as well, their material situation differs. Their jobs are often less interesting and less well paid, and they usually have less education. Working-class women, in short, have fewer resources than their middle-class counterparts. This difference means that it is more difficult for them to win economic independence. It means further that for them divorce sometimes leads to poverty, so holding on to a man who is a good provider becomes more essential. Thus, when their economic circumstances are bolstered by religious teachings that specify time-honored (and different) tasks for each gender, these women support traditional gender relations. In effect, working-class women may believe that egalitarianism promises fewer benefits than traditional relationships.

Although history is not predetermined, it is useful to recognize its direction. One way to do this is with a mental experiment. Can you imagine going back to a preindustrial existence, forcing women out of the labor force, or denying them civil rights? Can you imagine denying them the benefits of medical technology? My guess is that unless these sorts of structural changes occur, the impact of traditional gender relations will decline over time, and so will discrimination. Equality is a powerful idea.

Notes

1. This chapter is an updated and abridged version of a similar one in my *What Does Your Wife Do? Gender and the Transformation of Family Life* (Beeghley, 1996b).

2. On Mitchell, see Ann Lane's *Charlotte Perkins Gilman Reader*, which includes *The Yellow Wallpaper* (1980).

3. The negative consequences of this arrangement for men is illustrated in Charlotte Perkins Gilman's story "Mr. Peeble's Heart" (Lane, 1980). All his life, Mr. Peeble runs a store he hates in order to support women (his mother, sisters, and wife). He is trapped: bored, angry, resentful, and not even aware of why. His sister-in-law, a physician and "new woman," persuades him to sell the store and travel by himself. He returns "enlarged, refreshed, and stimulated." His wife, forced to take care of herself, develops "feet of her own to stand on." Like most of Gilman's stories, this one ends happily, as their relationship is transformed.

Recommended Reading

Beeghley, Leonard. *What Does Your Wife Do? Gender and the Transformation of Family Life* (Boulder, CO: Westview, 1996).

Herman, Judith Lewis. *Trauma and Recovery* (New York: Basic Books, 1992).

Lane, Ann J. (ed.). *The Charlotte Perkins Gilman Reader* (New York: Pantheon Books, 1980).

Zelizer, Viviana A. *The Social Meaning of Money* (New York: Basic Books, 1994).

4 Racial and Ethnic Inequality

Outline of Chapter 4

American history, we are told, is the story of how rugged individuals left the tyranny of the Old World to conquer the wilderness and build a better life in the New. Over time they created the first new nation, one that, in Thomas Jefferson's words, holds "these truths as self-evident, that all men are created equal. They are endowed by their creator with certain unalienable rights, such as life, liberty, and the pursuit of happiness."

And indeed, the story goes, today's freedom and prosperity result from the efforts of those intrepid pioneers.[1]

Like most myths, this one has elements of truth. The United States was indeed new, for the moral standard that all human beings are created equal and ought to be free had not existed before. And it can be argued that the story of the past two centuries has been the gradual realization of this new value, not only here but around the world. Moreover, the society that arose over time was new as well—industrialized and capitalist—characterized by a dynamism perfectly fitted to the new value. Much progress has occurred.

But like most myths, this one also misleads. Reality is more complex; progress and exploitation are intertwined. Jefferson failed to live up to his own moral standard (Ellis, 1997). He was a slave owner, and like most of the new Americans, he believed in the inferiority of those in bondage. Thus, whereas some Americans' ancestors came here to escape tyranny, others were brought here to further it. Some made the perilous voyage across the Atlantic to better their lives; others came in chains and remained that way. Slaves built Jefferson's home, Monticello. Slaves made the land prosperous for their southern masters. Slaves made the North rich as raw materials from the South were manufactured and traded. Capitalism and industrialization arose based on slavery.

And on conquest. If some Americans came here to escape tyranny, those already here were either killed off or made subject to it. The Native American population fell from about 2.5 million in 1600 to about 200,000 in 1850, primarily through disease brought by the Europeans, starvation due to displacement from the land, and murder (Spinden, 1928; Snipp, 1989). The remainder were placed on reservations, where many still live. Although the population has rebounded recently, a 92 percent decline is a good definition of genocide.

The United States still lives with the twin legacies of progress and conquest. At this point two definitions are necessary: *Race* refers to groups identifiable by their physical traits, such as skin color. Thus, African Americans, whites, and Asians are usually defined as races. *Ethnic group* refers to aggregates with distinct social attributes, as shown by their customs, language, religious heritage, and other elements of their background. Thus, the Irish and Italians are typically defined as ethnic groups. So are persons who came from or whose ancestors came from various Hispanic and Asian nations. The current U.S. population is about 260 million people, of whom about 74 percent are white, 12 percent African American, 10 percent Hispanic, 3 percent Asian, and 1 percent Native American (USBC, 1996d:22). Yet these categories, though useful, are also completely arbitrary. They serve as metaphors for the long-term racial and ethnic divisions afflicting the United States.[2]

These divisions were established early. In 1790, just after the Constitution was adopted, 60–80 percent of the white population was of English origin (USBC, 1975:1168). All other groups had to adjust to English norms and values and endure their prejudice and discrimination. Once again, definitions are necessary. *Prejudice* refers to people's hostile attitudes toward others in a different group or toward other groups as a whole (Allport, 1954). *Discrimination,* as mentioned in Chapter 3, refers to the unequal treatment of individuals and groups due to their personal characteristics, such as race or ethnicity.

Most people now embrace the value of equality, especially when phrased as equality of opportunity. Prejudice and discrimination have declined, especially since the late 1960s. Despite these changes, however, many Americans oppose policies designed to provide equal opportunity. For example, although nearly all whites say that African American and white children should be able to attend the same schools, 62 percent oppose busing children to achieve integration, even though busing was used to maintain segregation for many years (GSS, 1996). Similar differences exist when whites are questioned about access to housing and jobs. Even if they accept equality, then, whites remain willing to tolerate inequality.

Dimensions of Racial and Ethnic Inequality

This continued willingness to tolerate (high levels of) inequality sometimes makes it seem as if the United States is not one society but a giant centrifuge in which people, especially people of color, are flung about. At other (more optimistic) times, however, it seems the country is (slowly) becoming like a merry-go-round that Americans ride together. This paradox is not unique to the United States; it exists in most nations with heterogeneous populations.

Historical Dimensions

Civil Rights.   By the term "civil rights," I mean citizens' legal guarantee of equal participation in society without discrimination. Those with civil rights can vote. They can buy food at grocery stores or eat in whatever restaurants they like. They can purchase houses wherever they choose. They can obtain jobs. They can worship God, however known. And they can marry whom they wish. Civil rights guarantee individual freedom. Without them, the law itself can be used to exploit and oppress (Aguirre and Turner, 1993).

In 1790 only property owners who paid taxes could vote. In effect, this limitation meant that only men of English origin had civil rights. Over time, despite and because of much protest and violence, those who did not own land and various white ethnic groups (German, Scandinavian, Irish, Italian, etc.) obtained their civil rights.

Native Americans were less successful. Although whites repeatedly promised, by treaty, to deal with the original inhabitants of this land fairly, as sovereign nations, Western concepts of property (e.g., land titles and transfers) were unknown in Native American cultures, and the law was used to take their land (Churchill and Morris, 1992). In so doing, the United States removed the basis for political sovereignty of Native American nations, substituting the regulation of their civil rights by the Bureau of Indian Affairs, run by white administrators in Washington (Deloria, 1992).

Those of Asian ancestry were also less successful in obtaining civil rights. The few Chinese and Japanese who came to the United States in the second half of the nineteenth century faced high levels of prejudice and discrimination (Takaki, 1989). For example, Japanese Americans were jailed and their property stolen during World War II (CWRIC, 1982). More generally, restrictive immigration laws were used to keep down the numbers of people of Asian heritage.

Hispanics fared no better. By origin, the Hispanic population is about 60 percent Mexican American, 12 percent Puerto Rican American, and 5 percent Cuban American, with the remainder coming from various Central and South American nations. The early settlers from Mexico displaced the Native Americans and regarded the Southwest as their homeland, until the Anglos invaded and made it part of the United States. Mexican Americans were subsequently treated as second-class citizens, segregated and deprived of civil rights. Similarly, in the North the small communities of Puerto Rican Americans were kept segregated and denied their rights, partly by custom and partly by law. More recent immigrants from Cuba and other nations have endured less discrimination, benefiting from legal changes that have occurred since the 1960s.

Finally, the Civil War's promise of freedom was empty, as African Americans went from slavery to serfdom in the form of sharecropping. At the end of the war, the South began an immediate campaign of terror against the former slaves that not only denied them civil rights but kept them in a system of segregation and debt peonage that lasted for another century (Kennedy, 1995; Oshinsky, 1996). The South lost militarily but won substantively, and the North acquiesced. It has been said that 200 years of slavery and its 100-year aftermath were America's original sin.

The denial of civil rights did not end until the 1950s and 1960s, with court decisions and new laws. For example, the Supreme Court ruled in 1954 in *Brown vs. Board of Education* that segregated schools were unequal and therefore unconstitutional. This was but one decision in a series by which the Court destroyed the legal basis for unequal treatment. In addition, beginning with the Montgomery, Alabama, bus boycott in 1959, minority groups moved their struggle for civil rights into the streets. At first the conflict was nonviolent, but it became violent over time. During this period, Congress passed a series of civil rights laws that among other changes made it illegal to deny people the right to vote, access to public accommodations, and access to housing. Civil rights, however, are only one dimension of inequality. Moreover, although the law is less often a vehicle for discrimination, enforcing civil rights is another matter—and so is equality of opportunity.

Infant Mortality. Equality of opportunity does not exist when the *infant mortality rate* varies by group. The term refers to the number of live babies who die within the first year of life. Infant mortality is an especially useful measure of equal opportunity not only because people who die cannot succeed but also because it reflects families' levels of nutrition, sanitation, housing, and medical treatment. Here is the infant mortality rate in 1900 for several groups (Lieberson, 1980:46):

Deaths per 1,000	
Native-born whites	142
English immigrants	149
German immigrants	159
Italian immigrants	189
African Americans	297

At this time, because they had the lowest infant mortality rate, native-born whites showed the highest standard of living, with various white immigrant groups arrayed below them. The infant mortality rate among African Americans was much greater than that of immigrants and twice that of native-born whites. This difference reveals just how bad life was in the years after the Civil War.

The relative position of African Americans and whites has not changed over the years, even though everyone is healthier now. Thus, in 1915 the African American infant death rate of 181 per 1,000 was about double the ninety-nine for all whites (USBC, 1975:57). Infant mortality rates declined steadily during the twentieth century, such that by 1996 about fifteen per 1,000 African American infants died compared to six whites (NCHS, 1996b:26). To put this difference into perspective: The infant mortality rate of African Americans today is identical to that in Bulgaria and close to that in Bangladesh (USBC, 1996d:839; McCord and Freeman, 1994).

The only U.S. minority group with a comparable level of infant mortality is Native Americans, with thirteen deaths per 1,000 in 1985–1987 (Singh, 1995). Other groups are better off: Asian Americans displayed an infant mortality rate of eight in 1985–1987. The Hispanic American rate was six in 1995, although with considerable variation among ethnic groups (NCHS, 1997c:68): The rate among Puerto Rican Americans (more of whom are black) was nine, whereas that among Cuban Americans (more of whom are white) was five. Whites rarely notice these differences in equality of opportunity because they tend to live in other neighborhoods.

Housing Segregation.   When minority groups are isolated from whites because they reside in different areas, they have less equality of opportunity. Housing segregation increases the price of minorities' housing (because it allows them fewer choices). It decreases the quality of education available and restricts employment opportunities. It raises the odds of being the victim of a crime. It limits access to community services, such as libraries and parks. It exposes children to neighborhood disorganization (e.g., drugs; see Chapter 6) and thereby makes growing up harder. It influences, in short, every aspect of life (Massey and Denton, 1993).

Before World War I, African Americans were not as isolated from whites as they are now (Harrison and Weinberg, 1992). In the North, the average African American lived in an area in which only 7–10 percent of the residents were African American; nearly all the rest were white. This situation was possible because the African American population in the North was small. In effect, whites reacted to African Americans' migration to the North from 1920 to 1970 by increasing their isolation, by segregating them. Passage of the Fair Housing Act in 1968 was supposed to prevent such unequal treatment. But it was a mere symbol, a law without teeth. African Americans remain highly segregated. In 1990 the average African American lived in a neighborhood in which 63 percent of the residents were African American. This result is not accidental.

The level of residential isolation is less for other groups (Harrison and Weinberg, 1992).[3] The average Hispanic lives in a neighborhood in which 52 percent of the residents are Hispanic. Remember that many Hispanics, such as those of Cuban ancestry, look white, so they endure less segregation (Massey and Denton, 1993). Among Asian Americans, the average person lives in an area in which 28 percent of the residents are of Asian heritage. This lower level of housing segregation suggests that these groups are seen as less threatening by whites, partly because they remain small populations. As a result, their relative social position is better, as their occupations and incomes show.

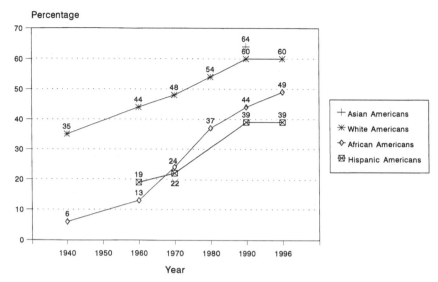

FIGURE 4.1   Percentage of Racial and Ethnic Groups in White-Collar Jobs, 1940–1996
NOTE: The system of occupational classification changed between 1970 and 1980.
SOURCE: USBC (1975:381, 1996d); USBLS (1997:170).

Occupation and Income.   This nation has always displayed a high degree of occupational segregation, with whites having higher-prestige jobs and higher incomes than Hispanics, African Americans, Asians, and Native Americans. Minority groups have been improving their situations over the past few years, however, as illustrated in Figure 4.1. Thus, in 1940 only 6 percent of African Americans had white-collar jobs, compared to 49 percent in 1996. The pattern is similar for Hispanics: a change from 19 percent in 1940 to 39 percent in 1996. Although the percentage of Hispanics doing white-collar work remained the same between 1990 and 1996, the data represent a significant temporal improvement relative to whites. Finally, as of 1990, 64 percent of Asian Americans were employed in white-collar jobs. The population of Native Americans remains small, and comparable data are not available. But members of this group tend to be less well educated (only 66 percent have high school degrees) and hence are less likely to have white-collar jobs. In general, then, the changes shown in Figure 4.1 reveal less inequality than in the past.

The pattern of declining yet continuing inequality can be seen in the table below, which focuses on a few specific occupations (USBC, 1974:352; 1996d:405). In order to see the decline in racial inequality, scan across the rows for African Americans in 1970 and 1995: In each case, their percentages have increased, which suggests declining inequality. Temporal data for other groups are not available over this same time.

Job Category	African Americans 1970	1995	Hispanic Americans 1995
Architects	2 percent	8 percent	6 percent
Engineers	1	5	3
Physicians	2	4	3
Lawyers	1	4	3
Insurance agents	3	6	5
Electricians	3	9	7
Firefighters	2	15	5
Police	6	17	7

Despite these changes, job segregation persists. Although African Americans are 12 percent of the population, in 1995 they made up only 8 percent of architects and 4 percent of lawyers. Similarly, although they are about 10 percent of the population, Hispanics make up only 6 percent of architects and 3 percent of engineers. These data show continuing inequality.[4]

Data on income reflect this continuity. As shown below, the income of families varies by racial and ethnic group, and the rank order follows the pattern shown in Figure 4.1 (USBC, 1995d:49; 1996b:13).

		Median Family Income
Asian American	1993	$44,500
White American	1995	42,600
African American	1995	26,000
Hispanic American	1995	24,500
Native American	1990	21,800

Thus, Asian and white Americans have the highest family incomes, with African and Hispanic Americans significantly lower. Native American families are much worse off than any other group.

As I noted earlier, the United States is a heterogeneous society, comprising a variety of racial and ethnic groups who are unequal to one another. The existence of differences in access to valued resources (life, housing, jobs, and income) is not unique to this country; other nations show a similar pattern.

International Dimensions

Although the European nations I use for comparison in this book are relatively homogeneous by race and ethnicity, the colonial legacy of the

TABLE 4.1   Unemployment by Racial and Ethnic Group, United Kingdom and United States, 1991

	Unemployment Rate (%)
United States	
White	6
Hispanic	10
African American	12
United Kingdom	
White	9
Indian	13
Black	21
Pakistani	29
Bangladeshi	32

SOURCES: USBC (1992:39); Rees et al. (1995:580).

United Kingdom makes it an exception. So I compare it to the United States by focusing on a crucial issue: unemployment. After all, those with jobs usually enjoy a higher standard of living than those without jobs.

The UK population of about 56 million persons comprises 1.5 percent who are black from various Caribbean and African areas, 1.5 percent of Indian origin, and smaller proportions from Pakistan, Bangladesh, China, and other Asian nations. Racial and ethnic minorities total almost 6 percent of the population (ONS, 1997:31).

Table 4.1 displays unemployment rates in the United States and the United Kingdom by race and ethnicity for 1991. It reveals that whites in both nations are significantly less likely to be out of work than members of racial and ethnic minorities. Other indicators of inequality, such as those used earlier in this section, show that racial and ethnic minorities in the UK suffer discrimination similar to that in the United States (Joshi, 1989).

The data presented in this section lead to three conclusions. First, racial and ethnic inequality in the United States has declined in certain areas, such as civil rights, infant mortality, and occupational prestige. Things are better now than in the past, which means that members of minority groups have more opportunities to succeed. Second, much inequality still exists, as shown by enduring contrasts in infant mortality, residential segregation, occupational prestige, and income. Third, inequality among racial and ethnic groups in the United States resembles that in the UK. These conclusions suggest that even though inequality has declined, the divisions established when the new nation was formed continue today.

Consequences of Racial and Ethnic Inequality

One result of continuing inequality based on discrimination has been the creation of an *underclass:* people who are persistently poor, residentially homogeneous, and relatively isolated from the rest of the population. More graphically, the term connotes people confined to a ghetto (an area inhabited by one group). The obvious candidates in this country are whites living in certain areas of Appalachia, Native Americans living on reservations, and African Americans. I focus on the last, who compose about 60 percent of the underclass (Ruggles, 1990:112).

As mentioned earlier, beginning around 1920 large numbers of African Americans migrated out of the rural South to northern cities. They sought freedom from serfdom; they found a trap in the form of housing segregation. In addition to the generally high level of housing segregation that all African Americans endure, sixteen large U.S. cities display hypersegregation: Only a few African Americans live in integrated areas; most reside in neighborhoods that are virtually all black. They are more isolated than any other minority group. The increasing rate of poverty that occurred during the 1980s (described in Chapter 5) has made this problem worse.[5]

Today large areas of the nation's central cities are composed of the poorest segments of the African American population. Since the early 1970s, manufacturing jobs have moved to the suburbs, which are inaccessible to central city residents. So unemployment is rampant. Many have learned to live without work for long periods. Looking around, all they see is others like them.

An anomic setting has been created; *anomie* refers to a lack of connection between valued goals and the means to achieve them (Merton, 1968a). Thus, people are still taught—at home, at school, and in the media—that hard work will lead to success. They are, however, unable to achieve success in normal ways: by employment. In this context, young persons grow up without positive role models. They do not observe stable families with adults going to work each day and children doing well in school. Social life has been stood on its head. People living in such environments react in predictable ways. All too often, they lose hope. They become alienated. *Alienation* refers to people's belief that they have little control over their lives, that trying to improve their situation is futile; they develop oppositional strategies as a way of coping with persistent assaults on self-esteem. The result is high rates of crime, drug use, and sexual acting out.

Some alienated people become angry. And angry people become violent. Crime becomes normal, an illegitimate means to "success." For example, 75 percent of the inmates in New York state prisons come from only seven neighborhoods in New York City, all of them African American and Hispanic (Clines, 1992). The carnage is self-destructive. Murder has become the leading cause of death among African American men aged 15–24 (NCHS, 1996a:31). It does not take much psychoanalytic insight to suspect that when young African American men kill young African American men, they are shooting into a mirror. The consequences are debilitating. A significant proportion of the young African American male population resides in jail. Those not in jail, male and female, do not feel safe. Children are traumatized.

Some alienated individuals turn their anger inward. Their self-loathing often leads to drug dealing and drug abuse. Drugs reduce the pain, so it should not be surprising that such persons consume substances with the most immediately destructive impact: alcohol, crack cocaine, and heroin. In *Streetwise: Race, Class, and Change in an Urban Community,* Elijah Anderson shows how "the roles of drug pusher, pimp, and (illegal) hustler have become more and more attractive" (1990:76). Street-smart young persons working in the underground economy appear successful and become role models for others. This process leads, of course, to an increase in crime and violence and the further decline of the area. So large areas of central cities resemble war zones, filled with people preying on one another, many disoriented, others traumatized.

Finally, some alienated people act out their anger sexually (Anderson, 1990). Men and boys make women and girls pregnant. Women and girls desire to become pregnant and give birth. After all, in an anomic setting, making babies is one of the few tasks at which people can succeed. It becomes a mark of their humanity in a dehumanized environment. Below is a simple indicator of how extreme segregation, race, and the creation of an underclass lead to behavioral outcomes: the percentage of babies born to unmarried women by race and ethnicity in 1995 (NCHS, 1997d:38).

African American	70 percent
Puerto Rican American	60
Mexican American	38
Cuban American	24
White American	21

African Americans display the highest rate of unmarried births. Among Hispanics, the rate of unmarried births corresponds to the degree of housing segregation and the proportion whose members look white (Massey and Denton, 1993).

These responses to anomie are not confined to one race (Ogbu, 1978). Whenever a group lives in an upside-down world, some of its members react in ways such as those described here (Innis and Feagin, 1992). Liverpool, England, for example, is like many U.S. cities except that its population is nearly all white. As in U.S. cities, manufacturing jobs have left Liverpool, and the unemployment rate is about 25 percent. It is now normal for young adults there to learn to live with long-term unemployment. Poverty is widespread, and poor people are concentrated together and isolated from the rest of the nation. They compose an underclass. And the same problems appear: high rates of crime, drug use, and sexual acting out. Unfortunately, these consequences are not amenable to quick fixes. Individuals without hope for the future do not easily alter their view of the world or their behavior. This situation constitutes a legacy of three centuries of oppression.

The extent of racial and ethnic inequality and its consequences lead to two questions. At the individual level, in what contexts does discrimination occur, and what is its impact? At the structural level, why have members of some racial and ethnic groups succeeded at greater rates than others?

Individuals and Racial and Ethnic Inequality

The connection may seem far-fetched, but the contexts in which discrimination against individuals occurs can be illustrated by a nursery rhyme: "Humpty Dumpty sat on a wall. Humpty Dumpty had a great fall" (Wright, 1916:40). Although it is an unsolved mystery in the context of the rhyme, I have always wondered why he fell. Let us consider an explanation. Since we are dealing with a sentient egg, it makes sense to think he took precautions against falling. If so, he probably did not fall accidentally. I conclude that someone pushed Humpty Dumpty. The reason: He was a brown egg. But why? Perhaps the white eggs were not used to seeing someone like him on top of the wall and assumed eggs like him ought to remain at the bottom. Perhaps they resented eggs like him appearing so high and mighty. "All the king's horses and all the king's men could not put Humpty together again." Again, why? Since the number of spaces on the wall is scarce, perhaps they did not try hard. After all, if he is gone, a white egg can replace him. Although this analysis may be flawed (!), it makes sense of the rhyme. And it demonstrates my point: People of color have always been pushed off the wall by prejudice and discrimination.

Moreover, the analysis suggests some of the contexts under which prejudice and discrimination occur. One hypothesis, for example, emphasizes the importance of contact and familiarity: *The less experience people from different groups have with one another, the more likely are members of the dominant group to display prejudice.* When whites interact only with other whites, they tend to see the world from a narrow perspective and, in the absence of personal experience, develop negative stereotypes about those who are different (Case et al., 1989; Fuchs and Case, 1994). This tendency is why in interpreting the nursery rhyme I suggested the importance of being used to seeing someone who is different in an equal or superior position. The prejudice that results when this does not happen could have been why Humpty Dumpty was pushed. Two venues in which people become familiar with others from different groups are schools and neighborhoods. But data show they remain segregated.

Another context in which prejudice and discrimination occur is when people from different groups seek the same jobs, land, or other valued resources (a place on the wall), as in the following hypothesis: *The more people from different groups compete for scarce resources and the more members of the dominant group perceive a threat, the more likely they are to display prejudice and to discriminate.* Members of the dominant group act to protect their interests and, in so doing, develop rationalizations (prejudices) about those at the bottom that justify keeping them there (Aguirre and Turner, 1993). Such reasoning vindicates practices that would otherwise be seen as unjust. This logic, I thought, might explain why "all the king's horses" stood aside while Humpty Dumpty lay broken. Not hiring others of a different race or ethnic group (or gender) functions in the same way.

Such problems were supposed to have ended with the civil rights movement of the 1960s. Yet the data presented earlier on infant mortality, housing segregation, and occupational and income difference show that inequality of opportunity remains. But the slights and slaps of daily life cannot be shown with numbers; they do not reveal how individuals try to climb walls only to be shoved off when they succeed. Two contexts that illustrate the hypotheses above are discrimination in public places and by organizations. Although I focus here on African Americans, the ideas apply to all minorities.

Public Place Discrimination

Whites rarely consider how their skin color might affect their treatment. In contrast, as African Americans go out and about they confront the impact of their color each day.

Discrimination can take several forms (Allport, 1954). Avoidance is one. Simply getting a cab in a large city is often hard for minority individuals. Many drivers avoid picking up nonwhites; it is a chance to act on one's prejudice without being caught. Other forms of avoidance are more subtle: Whites may cross the street to avoid African Americans. I have seen whites take their children away from play sites (e.g., a jungle gym) when joined by dark-skinned children. So whites must be put at ease. Some African American males apparently whistle classical music while walking down the street as a sign they are not dangerous (Bradley, 1997). The need for such behaviors adds stress to daily life.

Rejection is a second form of discrimination (Graham, 1995). One way is to provide poor quality of service. Middle-class African Americans often wait a long time to be seated in restaurants. While waiting, they are sometimes handed coats to be checked. When their meals finally arrive, they are cold. Another form of rejection is subtle harassment on the way to the office: African Americans might be frisked on suburban commuter trains or mistaken for delivery people when they enter the buildings where they work. Finally, rejection occurs in the office. Clients seem to wonder, "Why did I get the black lawyer?" (or accountant, etc.); this concern is manifested in questions about qualifications ("Where did you get your degree?") that clients would not usually ask. Such experiences mean that ordinary interaction is often tinged with anger.

Harassment, verbal and nonverbal, is a third form of discrimination. Whites shout racial epithets—when it is safe: from a car, for example. The "hate stare" seeks to intimidate without overt violence. These attacks are mostly suffered without response, since replying can be either futile or risky. Anger and stress mount.

Violence is the final form of discrimination. Whites hurl cans or bottles from moving cars. Sometimes, if they are in the "wrong" (i.e., segregated white) neighborhoods, African Americans are taken from their cars or stopped on the street. They may "only" be threatened. Police usually provide little help; in fact, they are often the perpetrators. One study of police violence against citizens shows that in nearly all cases, 93 percent, white officers attacked African Americans (Lersch, 1993). Such episodes and the daily recognition of their potential make life harder.

These kinds of experiences wear people down. They make occupational success more difficult. One person describes the long-term impact (Feagin, 1991:115–19):

> If you think of the mind as having 100 ergs of energy, and the average man uses 50% of his energy dealing with the everyday problems of the world . . . then he has 50% more to do creative things that he wants to do. Now that's a white person. Now a black person also has 100 ergs; he uses 50% the same way a white man does . . . , so he has 50% left. But he uses 25% fighting being black and what that means. Which means he really only has 25% to do what the white man has 50% to do, and he's expected to do just as much as the

white man with that 25%. . . . You just don't have as much energy left to do as much as you know you really could if you were free, [if] your mind were free.

White students in my courses sometimes say that minority persons are too touchy, they should simply ignore small slights. They do—every day. But think about the impact of always being shoved off the wall and shattered (psychologically, if not physically). The long-term effect leads to fury that can be hard to contain.

Discrimination by Organizations

One location for discrimination by organizations is in housing. In the past, the white public, real estate agents, and government acted overtly: As African Americans migrated to the North after World War I, they were trapped in ghettos far more systematically than previous waves of European immigrants or Asian or Hispanic Americans (Massey and Denton, 1993). The strategies used to create and maintain black ghettos were straightforward: (1) Violence in the form of riots, bombings, physical harassment, and threatening letters intimidated any African American family attempting to buy a house in white areas. (2) Neighborhood "improvement" associations formed and inserted restrictive covenants in deeds so that it became illegal to sell to African Americans. (3) Real estate agents made huge profits by restricting African Americans to ghetto areas to increase demand and thus prices. They regulated the expansion of the ghetto by blockbusting. This process began when real estate agents would sell an African American family a house in an area next to a ghetto; real estate agents then bought the remaining houses at low prices as whites fled; finally, they sold those homes at high prices to African Americans. (4) After World War II, housing guidelines established by the Federal Housing Administration and Veterans Administration directed inexpensive mortgages to suburbs where whites lived, stimulating the greatest increase in home buying in American history— by whites. African Americans were excluded.

This brutal system was supported by most whites. In 1942, 84 percent of a random sample of whites agreed that "there should be separate sections in towns and cities for Negroes to live in" (Massey and Denton, 1993:49). Similarly, in 1962, 61 percent of whites agreed that "white people have a right to keep blacks out of their neighborhoods if they want to and blacks should respect that." This question has been repeated over the years, and the percentage of respondents who agree has declined steadily: 28 percent in 1984 and 12 percent in 1996 (GSS, 1996). Nonetheless, most cities remain segregated. Although whites appear to accept open housing, in practice they remain prejudiced against African American neighbors, especially if there is more than one family.

Banks and real estate companies know these feelings and continue to discriminate covertly. A scene from an Eddie Murphy skit (I think it was on "Saturday Night Live") illustrates how: Murphy, dressed impeccably, applies for a mortgage loan. Bankers greet him warmly, give him forms to fill out, and assure him with smiles that his application will be given careful attention. As the door closes behind Murphy, the bankers wink, laugh, and toss the application into the wastebasket. A white person then enters the bank and begins filling out an application. But the bankers explain this step is not necessary; they take him to the vault and throw the door open to him. The scene is chillingly accurate. At every income level, African Americans are much more likely than whites to be turned down for loans (Massey and Denton, 1993:108).

Real estate dealers smile as well but deceive African Americans and Hispanics in order to make it harder to rent or buy homes in white neighborhoods, as housing audits show. In these audits, African Americans, Hispanics, and whites posing as clients present matching qualifications to agents. As displayed below, nationwide data indicate that minorities seeking housing, either to rent or buy, are often treated unequally: They are shown fewer units in white areas or steered to minority neighborhoods and get less information about houses they do see (Fix and Struyk, 1993:20).

	Denied Opportunity to See Houses	*Denied Information About Houses*
Black renter	46 percent	15 percent
Black buyer	50	8
Hispanic renter	43	12
Hispanic buyer	46	8

In general, when neighborhoods remain segregated over time, you can be sure that discrimination is occurring. Remember: the issue here is not the wonderfulness of white areas; rather, the issue is the resources accompanying housing that lead to equal opportunity.

Another location for organizational discrimination is in the hiring of employees. Recall from Chapter 3 that perfect job candidates rarely appear, and so companies must weigh qualifications. Imagine, for example, that the Widget Corporation advertises a job requiring a master's degree and five years' experience. Imagine further that the two best applicants are a Hispanic male with a bachelor's degree and ten years' experience and a white male with a master's degree and one year's experience. The Widget Corporation hires the white male because of his educational qualifications. Now imagine that Widget has another opening a few months later and the two best applicants have reverse qualifications (the Hispanic with more education and less experience). This time Widget hires the white male because of his greater experience. After this process occurs many times, a workforce will remain white and male—but no discrimination will be apparent. This is because the "best" applicant was always selected.

Hiring audits done in three large cities show that when a young Hispanic with an accent applies for a job advertised in the newspaper, about 31 percent of the time he or she will be denied an application, refused an interview, or not hired (Fix and Struyk, 1993:22). A similar result occurs about 20 percent of the time when the applicant is a young African American. In general, when an organization's workforce remains segregated over time, it is plausible to hypothesize that discrimination is taking place. This is another way of describing unequal opportunity, of course. Nonetheless, despite the controversy over affirmative action in recent years, discrimination persists, and its effect on individuals remains significant. Yet as I have argued previously, a focus on individual experiences leaves the analysis incomplete.

Social Structure and Racial and Ethnic Inequality

Today some whites claim they simply want a "level playing field" in which everyone has an equal opportunity to climb the wall of success. My impression, however, is that such persons usually have few friends who are members of racial or ethnic minorities, send their children to segregated schools, and live in segregated (often gated) neighborhoods. These people not only ignore the history of discrimination, they ignore the fact that the field is not level, that the social structure has always restricted the opportunities available to minority groups. In this section, I try to explain how these restrictions have affected people over time.

The issue is important because whites often wonder why members of minority groups, especially African Americans, have not succeeded at a greater rate. As Figure 4.1 shows, only 6 percent of all African Americans were white-collar workers as recently as 1940. Although the proportion has risen over time, both African Americans and Hispanics are still less likely than whites to have white-collar jobs. This seemingly odd situation sometimes leads to insensitive conclusions, in part because many whites have learned how their ancestors arrived as immigrants and struggled to succeed. They farmed or built a trade or business. Whole groups—Germans, Irish, Italians, Russians, Swedes—succeeded in this way. Figure 4.1 shows that Asian minorities have also advanced in recent years. Their experiences suggest that the United States remains a land of opportunity. But African Americans lag behind. At the risk of unduly simplifying a complex historical process, I offer the following hypothesis: *African Americans' relative lack of economic success in comparison to other immigrant groups reflects historical differences in (1) conditions of settlement, (2) prejudice and discrimination, and (3) affirmative action.*

Conditions of Settlement

By *conditions of settlement,* I mean the situation in a group's homeland and the United States when the immigrants appeared on American shores (Smith, 1987). The first condition was the situation under which immigration occurred. Some groups arrived voluntarily; others were brought involuntarily and remained slaves. Immigrants who came voluntarily were reacting to economic changes in their country of origin. Irish and German immigrants who settled in the Midwest between 1820 and 1840, for example, had been expropriated from their lands. Members of other groups possessed useful skills and were recruited by American companies. Thus, the reason for immigrating was the hope for a better life. And over time, usually two or three generations, members of these groups succeeded. In contrast, African persons were brought to the North American continent as forced (often skilled) labor. Slavery produced profit—for others. As I indicated in the introduction to this chapter, as plantation owners gained directly, northern shipowners, bankers, and others also benefited from slavery. The often unrecognized reality is that the American economy was built on forced labor. Generation after generation of enslaved people lived and died, unable to the pursue the opportunities available to others.[6]

The second condition of settlement was the size of North America. The European immigrants defined it as an open continent free for the taking. Despite repeated promises, the history of U.S. relations with Native American nations indicates that they were always seen as problems to be put aside, by law if possible, by force if necessary. As the frontier moved west, it seemed the land could accommodate an infinite number of white immigrants. Slaves could not take advantage of this situation.

The third condition of settlement was the opportunity presented by industrialization. As new forms of energy were substituted for muscle power over the course of the nineteenth century, the kinds of skills needed changed. In the early years, stonemasons, bricklayers, loggers, carpenters, and the like fueled economic development. Later the ability to use (or learn to use) power-driven machines became important. In addition, openings for merchants and traders grew steadily. Thus, the expanding economy provided opportunity for new arrivals, but not slaves.

After the Civil War, new immigrant groups arrived from Scandinavia, Italy, Russia, and other places. Many settled on the prairie. Others found economic niches that fit their skills in northern cities. After two or three generations, they became prosperous. In the South, however, President Andrew Johnson pardoned former Confederate soldiers, thus allowing them to reclaim their land. As a result, most former slaves became sharecroppers, trapped by a system of debt peonage (Smith, 1987). Later, Jim Crow laws institutionalized discrimination (Woodward, 1966). This process effectively prevented freedom for another century.

This rather sketchy description is designed to indicate that white ethnic groups faced conditions of settlement that facilitated long-term success. Over time, they assimilated and flourished. In contrast, African Americans faced many disadvantages.

Prejudice and Discrimination

As my (perhaps too facile) interpretation of "Humpty Dumpty" suggests, people in every society tend to deny equal opportunity to those who are different. Prejudice, of course, often underlies such treatment. And the basis for such feelings can vary; religious beliefs are one. For example, the United States in the nineteenth century was viciously anti-Catholic, which meant that immigrants from Ireland and southern Europe faced huge obstacles to success. Nonetheless, a continuum of desirability existed (Lieberson, 1980). The majority of native whites came from northern Europe and ranked immigrants from these nations as the most desirable. Those from central and southern Europe followed, even though they were Catholic. The third rank comprised Japanese and Chinese immigrants. Even small numbers of Asian immigrants seemed to spark a high level of prejudice. Thus, in 1924, after legal constraints ended immigration, fewer than 150,000 people of Japanese origin resided in this country, and the number of Asian persons in the United States remains low. The fourth rank consisted of African Americans, who endured greater prejudice and discrimination than any other group (except Native Americans). The data on infant mortality and housing segregation presented previously only suggest the difficulties faced by former slaves and their descendants.

Despite religious differences, immigrants from southern and central Europe shared a common cultural heritage with other whites. In addition, because Catholic immigrants were not physically identifiable, they blended into the new society by changing their names, dress, and accents. Moreover, when the harshness of their lives here proved too much, some went back to their homelands. These nations sometimes pressured the United States not to discriminate and assisted migrants after their arrival. These factors reduced prejudice and discrimination directed at southern and central European immigrants.

In contrast, nearly all African Americans lived in the South, usually in rural areas, and their "freedom" was a sham. Their skin color made them easily identifiable, and their cultures were devalued. Home governments did not exist to provide protection. So discrimination was institutionalized, limiting opportunities. Although blacks' "freedom" seemed to hold the promise of economic opportunity in the North, they were never allowed to realize this potential (NACCD, 1968:143–44).

> Had it not been for racial discrimination, the North might well have recruited southern Negroes after the Civil War to provide labor for building the burgeoning urban-industrial economy. Instead, northern employers looked to Europe for their sources of unskilled labor. . . . European immigrants, too, suffered from discrimination, but never was it so pervasive. The prejudice against color in America has formed a bar to advancement unlike any other.

In comparing European immigrants and African Americans in this way, I am not suggesting that assimilation was effortless for the former; it cannot be easy to begin again in a new land. But I am suggesting that southern and central European immigrants had an easier time assimilating because there were fewer structural barriers to equality. In contrast, African Americans have had to endure widespread discrimination, and such treatment was often legal. Freedom is impossible when people are denied civil rights. Although systematic unequal treatment is usually concealed today, it still exists and it still prevents equal opportunity.

Affirmative Action

By *affirmative action* I mean public policies designed to give advantages to members of one group over others. Affirmative action has become contentious recently because many whites think it is unfair. After all, policies that give (a little) extra opportunity to African Americans, other minorities, and women—in job hiring, for example—seem discriminatory. They are. All whites (say they) want is a level playing field, a color-blind society. But that is not the real issue; the real issue is power. As Stanley Lieberson points out, racial and ethnic relations always involve obtaining a piece of the pie (1980). Lieberson's metaphor suggests that valued resources in society—jobs, land (or housing), and education—are like a pie. People fight and use the law in order to obtain (or retain) their "fair" share. "Fair," of course, means a bigger piece. Most groups do not want to diet. So the question becomes how the pie is going to be divided up. Historically, affirmative action in the United States has meant giving advantages to whites.

Land is one piece of the pie. I noted previously that German immigrants located in the Midwest. They did not randomly choose this site.

The Land Act of 1820 provided them slices of the pie, since immigrants obtained 80 acres of land on credit, with payment at $1.25 to $2 per acre. Such prices meant that the land was basically free. In the years following the Civil War, the prairie west of the Mississippi River was settled by Scandinavian immigrants. Again, this location was not accidental. The federal government subsidized railroad expansion and enacted the Homestead Act of 1862. The latter said that settlers who farmed 160 acres for five years could purchase the entire parcel of land for $10. Once again, such prices meant giving the land away. When land was combined with access to eastern markets via the railroads, the settlers had a rather large piece of government-provided pie.

In contrast, during these same years the former slaves were promised 40 acres and a mule as their share of the pie. And in fact, General William Tecumseh Sherman signed an executive order dividing almost half a million acres into 40-acre parcels that (along with work animals) were given to the newly freed people. If this promise of land and the means to farm it had been kept, J. Owens Smith suggests in *The Politics of Racial Inequality,* millions of African Americans would have been truly free and, by the second or third generation, would have been prosperous (1987). They would have been like the Germans and Scandinavians. But when President Johnson revoked Sherman's order and pardoned former Confederate officers, they reclaimed their lands and kept "freed" slaves on as sharecroppers. Whites combined systematic terror and the law to deny people not only land but basic civil rights.

Access to education is a second piece of the pie. In 1862 Congress enacted the Morrill Act, which funded land grant colleges in every state. According to Smith, the federal government spent more than $250 million (in the nineteenth century!) under the principle that "every citizen is entitled to receive educational aid from the government" (1987:115). Yet this incredible expenditure of money did not benefit "every citizen." The University of Florida, where I teach, did not admit an African American student until 1969. An alternative system of African American colleges was established, mainly by white private philanthropists. The strings attached to the little money available meant accepting a philosophy of "racial adjustment" (i.e., that African Americans should know their place). A second Morrill Act in 1890 created separate (and unequal) land grant colleges in the South, such as Florida A&M. The point of this law was to keep places like the University of Florida eligible for federal support while providing an unequal education to small numbers of African Americans.

This last statement summarizes the educational opportunities available to African Americans in the South from the time of the Civil War until recently. Lieberson hypothesizes that *the greater the proportion of African American citizens in an area, the less the educational opportunity available to them,* and he is probably right (1980:149). By "less educational opportunity," he means inequality in virtually every aspect of the public school system: funding, teacher training, supplies, length of the school year, and so on. For example, African Americans could attend only a few schools: There were a total of sixty-four high schools open to African American students in the eighteen southern states in 1911, none in Atlanta and other major cities. The situation was only a little better in the North. Lieberson shows that in every context where African Americans have had a chance at education they began catching up to whites. Yet their piece of the educational pie was tiny, and progress was very slow.

Access to a job is a third piece of the pie. Even though they were denied land and education, African Americans might have become more upwardly mobile as industrialization developed had they not faced job discrimination as well. But job opportunities did not occur. I mentioned earlier that because of racial prejudice European immigrants were recruited into northern factories in the years after the Civil War. Northern employers, however, soon discovered a use for African Americans: as strikebreakers (Grossman, 1989). Although nonunion European immigrants were also exploited in this way, they were eventually incorporated into the union movement. African Americans were not. As a result, when Congress was considering the National Labor Relations Act (NLRA) in 1935, pleas by African American leaders to include an antidiscrimination clause fell on deaf ears. The NLRA put wages, hiring policies, and layoffs under the rule of law and helped many (white) people to a higher standard of living. In addition, organized workers obtained good credit rating, group insurance, group discounts, easier qualification for home loans, and other perquisites that further improved their living standard.

But the NLRA left unions free to discriminate, which they did. Over time, Smith argues, whites parceled out jobs to kin and friends (1987). For example, the National Apprenticeship Act of 1937 established government training programs under union control for skilled workers. This program covered not only blue-collar jobs but also training as occupational and physical therapists, librarians, medical technicians, and many others. In 1964, the same year the Civil Rights Act was passed, the federal government paid $4 million in subsidies to the apprenticeship program. Over the life of the program, virtually all the participants were white. Although this was a relatively minor initiative, it illustrates a more general point: Little of the job pie has historically gone to African Americans.

In considering affirmative action, I have adopted Stanley Lieberson's metaphor that valued resources can be like a piece of the pie, in which power determines who gets a bigger share. Whites have always used public policy to provide opportunities for whites. Beginning, however, with the administration of President Lyndon Johnson in the early 1960s, the federal government instituted a variety of programs designed to provide opportunity for minority groups to increase their share of the pie, especially in terms of access to jobs and education. The data presented earlier show that such programs have been effective (again, very imperfectly), as more African and Hispanic Americans have moved into white-collar jobs. But in recent years whites have protested that such policies are unfair.

Implications

The United States continues to live with the progress and exploitation established when the nation was founded. On the one hand, the data show that racial and ethnic inequality along with prejudice and discrimination have declined. On the other hand, the data also show that racial and ethnic inequality remains substantial and that it is buttressed by prejudice and discrimination.

This complexity means that commentaries often resemble Emile Zola's "J'accuse" (1996): No matter which side observers take, the issues are so serious that the analysis is often suffused with a moralism that inevitably becomes tiring. For example, those who argue against affirmative action are implicitly asserting that racial and ethnic inequality has declined so much that people ought to compete with one another without help or hindrance. In contrast, those who argue in favor of affirmative action are implicitly asserting that racial and ethnic inequality remains so pervasive that public policy ought to give minority groups a small advantage. The possibilities for name-calling in this context are great. And science cannot resolve this issue. We can, however, describe (albeit imperfectly) some of the implications of the current situation.

The study of occupational mobility reveals a stable finding of great relevance: *The class structure reproduces itself over time.*[7] This empirical generalization means that although a great deal of mobility occurs, most people usually end up in the same job category as their parents. Parents in blue-collar jobs tend to have children who work in blue-collar jobs, and parents in white-collar jobs tend to have children who work in white-collar jobs. This continuity exists mainly because children's educational attainment, the key to success, reflects their parents' education and occupation.

This finding means that people's location in the class structure decisively affects their opportunities in life. Think about the data presented earlier. Different levels of infant mortality mean not only that fewer minority children survive but those that do have fewer opportunities.

Housing segregation means not only that minority children are isolated from whites but that they have fewer opportunities. Occupational and income differences have a similar impact. Precisely because they have less opportunity to succeed, the odds of occupational mobility are stacked against many minority children—simply because of their class of origin.

Here is an example. Most people learn about jobs from their relatives and friends (Grieco, 1987; Morris, 1992). This pattern has enormous implications because whites, African Americans, Hispanics, Asians, and Native Americans usually participate in different social networks. As shown previously, whites work at different jobs than do Latinos and African Americans. They live in different neighborhoods. Their children go to different schools (Orfield, 1997). They also attend different churches (Beeghley et al., 1996). These differences suggest how the social structure affects interaction patterns: contact, friendship formation, and the like. The members of each group lead separate lives. As a result, individual whites, African Americans, Latinos, and Asians tell their relatives and friends about different job opportunities. Even in the absence of prejudice, then, this process produces a high level of occupational segregation and inequality. And this pattern will continue into the future.

One way to break this cycle is via racial preferences in college admissions—affirmative action in other words. Since the 1960s, many selective colleges and universities have granted extra "points" to minority students applying for admission. The result has been an increase in the number of minorities attending and graduating from college, law school, medical school, and the like. Recall the data presented earlier: Between 1970 and 1995, the number of African Americans in the law, medicine, and other professions grew significantly. This change was deliberate; it shows that affirmative action works.

It has, however, become controversial. In California and Texas, for example, using race as one criterion in admission is now prohibited (Applebome, 1997). As a result, the number of African American and Hispanic college students is declining precipitously in these states. Some now favor using class (instead of race) in combination with test scores, grades, and letters as admission criteria. But this change will not work if the goal is a racially and ethnically diverse student body (Kane, 1997). The reason is that minority groups are also a minority within each class. If more working-class applicants are admitted to selective colleges, most of them will be white.

In this context, the benefits and liabilities of affirmative action ought to be considered. Here I focus on higher education. First, the benefits: (1) An increasing minority presence on campus produces a more diverse student body, members of which learn about each other and become used to one another. (2) When minorities graduate, they change the occupational structure, demand better housing, and integrate society at all levels. (3) Minority graduates also tend to provide better services to minority people and neighborhoods. (4) In moral terms, this strategy helps to remedy the historical legacy of prejudice and discrimination. As for the liabilities of affirmative action: (1) Over time, preferences can become an entitlement, enforced by power, and merit-based college admissions are deemphasized. (2) Whites with higher test scores or grades are admitted in lower numbers; they are discriminated against. (3) In moral terms, treating people unequally in today's society just does not seem right.

Ultimately, there is no right answer. The issue is what kind of society do we want to have, now and in the future?

Notes

1. This chapter is an updated and abridged version of a similar one in my *Structure of Social Stratification in the United States* (Beeghley, 1996a).

2. These categories are really bizarre. First, race is meaningless at the genetic level; skin pigmentation merely reflects long-term adaptation to climate (Cavilli-Sforza et al., 1995). So race has been made socially significant. The "one drop rule" historically defined a person who had a single drop of "black blood" as "black" in order to enlarge the slave population with the children of slaveholders (Wright, 1997). Second, categories change over time; those used today were developed in the 1970s and differ substantially from those of the past (Lott, 1997). Third, many people grouped together do not see themselves as sharing a common culture; rather, they identify themselves by nationality—for example, as Italian Americans, Chinese Americans, Mexican Americans, Jamaican Americans, or Navaho—because each displays a distinct language, culture, and organizational pattern. Yet these categories remain important, not only as a way of presenting data but also as mechanisms for monitoring and enforcing civil rights laws and as markers for distributing certain government benefits.

3. Native Americans are an exception, since a high proportion still live on reservations.

4. Although the data presented here show that Asian Americans are relatively well-off today, they are also discriminated against (USCCR, 1992). For example, well-trained professionals of Asian heritage often face a glass ceiling preventing advancement in management.

5. In this section, I am simplifying a very complex situation that has developed over the past century. For more detail, see Douglas S. Massey and Nancy A. Denton, *American Apartheid: Segregation and the Making of the Underclass* (1993). This is sociology at its best.

6. Many African slaves were like European immigrants in one sense: They had useful skills. Some were bilingual; others had agricultural expertise. For exam-

ple, in *African Americans at Mars Bluff, South Carolina,* Amelia Wallace Vernon shows that Africans with knowledge of rice growing were imported precisely because the English-born planters were ignorant of this kind of farming (1993). This book is also useful because Vernon reveals how despite centuries of subjugation some cultural characteristics of African people survive in South Carolina to the present day.

7. For a summary of this literature, see Beeghley (1996a:47–79).

Recommended Reading

Anderson, Elijah. *Streetwise: Race, Class, and Change in an Urban Community* (Chicago: University of Chicago Press, 1990).

Aguirre, Adalberto, and Jonathan H. Turner. *American Ethnicity: The Dynamics and Consequences of Discrimination* (New York: McGraw-Hill, 1993).

Lieberson, Stanley. *A Piece of the Pie: Blacks and White Immigrants Since 1880* (Berkeley: University of California Press, 1980).

Massey, Douglas S., and Nancy A. Denton. *American Apartheid: Segregation and the Making of the Underclass* (Cambridge: Harvard University Press, 1993).

Smith, J. Owens. *The Politics of Racial Inequality* (New York: Greenwood Press, 1987).

Vernon, Amelia Wallace. *African Americans at Mars Bluff, South Carolina* (Baton Rouge: Louisiana State University Press, 1993).

5 | *Poverty*

Outline of Chapter 5

I. Dimensions of Poverty
  A. Historical Dimensions
  B. International Dimensions

II. Consequences of Poverty

III. Individuals and Poverty
  A. Low-Wage Job Skills
  B. Unemployment
  C. Family Instability
  D. Age of Household Head

IV. Social Structure and Poverty
  A. The Long-Term Fall in the Poverty Rate
    1. Industrialization
    2. Class Differences in Fertility Rates
    3. Declining Discrimination
  B. The High U.S. Poverty Rate
    1. The Reproduction of the Class Structure
    2. The Vicious Circle of Poverty
    3. Macroeconomic Policy
    4. The Structure of Elections
    5. The Structure of the Economy
    6. Institutionalized Discrimination

V. Implications

James Hilliard works at a fish-processing plant in Cedar Key, Florida, a small town on the Gulf Coast. His wife, Mary, works at a convenience store. Late one afternoon, he stepped onto the porch to greet his children and collapsed with a seizure. Mary took him to the nearest hospital (90 miles away), where he remained for three days. He then spent several weeks recovering at home.

This example illustrates some of the dilemmas the poor face. The Hilliards did not have insurance, a common situation. In the aftermath of James's illness, they faced debts of more than $10,000, which they had no means of paying. He lost his job. They were evicted from their small house. After the Hilliards had lived in their car for a few days, their friends found out and arranged to keep the children and for James and Mary to sleep in the storeroom of their church. Finally, they found a one-bedroom mobile home in which to live.

The example also indicates some of the dilemmas faced by those who would help the poor. James and Mary have no immediate family, but they do have a network of friends, all of whom live near the edge of poverty. This similarity means their ability to help is limited. When physicians saw James, they not only diagnosed an illness, they confronted poverty: The Hilliards often had to choose between buying medicine and paying rent. When teachers sent work home, they confronted not only education but poverty: The children had no space in which to do their homework, since they were living in a car and then with friends; later, they had only the cramped room of the mobile home. When James began drinking too much in the aftermath of his illness, a counselor would have confronted not only self-destructive behavior but poverty. Since no treatment was available in this isolated environment, James and Mary simply dealt with the problem as best they could.

Poverty affects every dimension of life. The term refers to an income level below which persons or families have difficulty subsisting. The word "subsist" is key: Poor people find it hard to obtain food, shelter, and medical treatment. Although the Hilliards are a fictional family, they represent this predicament. In effect, we demand heroic behavior on the part of people like them, people who have few choices, and then condemn those who fall by the wayside. We make such demands mainly because of our lack of familiarity with what it means to be poor in an affluent society.[1]

Dimensions of Poverty

One way of becoming familiar with poverty is to count the poor. But this task is more difficult than it seems, especially if one wants to obtain a historical and international view of the problem.

Historical Dimensions

Historical data are hard to come by because standards of living have changed over the years. In 1900 only 1 percent of all families possessed a car, which meant that social life did not require high-speed transportation (USBC, 1975:717). Today, however, people who want to get to work, buy groceries, or go to the doctor usually need an automobile. In 1900 only 12 percent of families had running water in their homes. Nearly everyone used outhouses, which exposed them to disease. Today, however, outhouses are illegal in every city, and poor persons must have the money to pay for utilities (not only water but heat, electricity, and a telephone as well). The cost of utilities illustrates how the ability to fully participate in a modern society now depends on financial resources: a cash income.

These changes in standards of living make it difficult to assess trends in poverty over time. A tentative albeit imperfect strategy is to focus on changes in the proportion of the population that finds it hard to subsist. Figure 5.1 presents these estimates. The figure suggests that about 45 percent of the population was poor in the years 1870–1880. But there is a certain arbitrariness to this number. In *America's Struggle Against Poverty, 1900–1985*, James T. Patterson shows that estimates for this period are in the 40–60 percent range (1986). I selected a percentage at the low end of this continuum to avoid overstating the level of impoverishment. What you should remember, then, is that the proportion of the population having trouble subsisting was very high during these years. But it began dropping around the turn of the century. In assessing the long-term trend, ignore the sharp declines caused by World Wars I and II and the great increase during the Depression. After World War II, the poverty rate probably stood around 30 percent (with a narrower range around the estimate). It declined to about 22 percent in 1960 and to 11–12 percent during the 1970s—the lowest level ever attained in the United States. The poverty rate rose, however, during the 1980s to about 14–15 percent and remains at that level. Notice that since 1960, the data reflect the government's official poverty line. They are the most accurate—assuming you agree that the poverty line is a practical measure (more on this later).

The poverty line for a family of four in 1996 was $16,036 (USBC, 1997b:A–3). This figure is the most familiar cutoff, since it refers to a stereotypical family of four—such as the Hilliards. The threshold differs, however, by family size; it is less for a family of two and more for one of six or seven. It is also lower if the head of the household is aged. The poverty line does not change by region or location (rural or urban) be-

Percentage

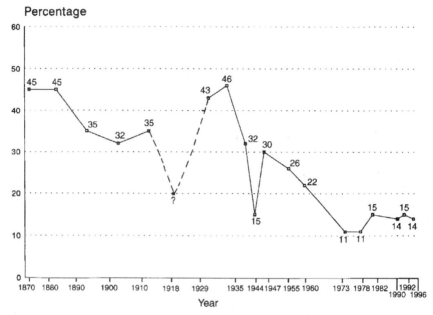

FIGURE 5.1   Poverty Estimates in the United States, Selected Years, 1870–1996
NOTES: There are no data for the World War I period. I have used dotted lines to suggest that the poverty rate probably fell during this period.
SOURCES: For 1870–1910, Hartley, (1969: 19); for 1929–1944, Ornati (1966:158); for 1947–1955, CEA (1969:154); for 1960–1996, USBC (1997b:v).

cause such distinctions have proven too difficult to make. In sum, these criteria mean that in 1996 about 14 percent of the population, 36 million people, lived in poverty (USBC, 1997b:vii). About 14 million of them were children, which means that more than one in five young persons live in poverty today.

Before continuing, I should make clear that contrary to popular stereotypes, the poor population is a rather unstable aggregate in that the same people are usually not impoverished from one year to the next. Most individuals become poor for a short period, typically two years or less, and then improve their economic situations (Ruggles, 1990). They are replaced by others whose situations have worsened. This turnover means that a relatively high proportion of the total population experiences poverty over, say, a decade.

Figure 5.1 shows that poverty declined over time in the United States before rising since the late 1970s. In order to understand this pattern and to place it into perspective, such data should be supplemented with information from other nations.

International Dimensions

International data are difficult to obtain because there is no agreed-upon way of measuring poverty. Of the Western nations usually referred to in this book, only the United States and United Kingdom have "official" measures. The best that can be done is to assess the proportion of the population that earns less than 40 percent of the median income. This indicator provides data that nearly match (within 1 percent) the ratio of the U.S. poverty line to the U.S. median income. These data are below (Smeeding, 1997).

	Population with Income Less Than 40 Percent of Median
United States	13 percent
United Kingdom	7
Canada	7
Germany	5
France	4
Netherlands	4
Sweden	4

When these data are considered together with Figure 5.1, it becomes apparent that although the proportion of people who found it hard to subsist declined in the United States (until recently), the level of poverty in comparable Western European nations fell much further. Even so, the data probably exaggerate the level of impoverishment in these nations because they provide more in-kind (noncash) benefits for all citizens, regardless of ability to pay. Thus, not only are there fewer poor, but being poor is not nearly so onerous in other Western societies as in the United States.

These differences carry an important implication: The level of poverty in a modern society reflects political choices. Public policies can be devised that put people to work, which prevent situations like that of the Hilliards. The United States, however, chooses to maintain a rather large impoverished population and to live with the consequences.

Consequences of Poverty

Another way of becoming more familiar with the poor is to outline a budget on which they must live. This exercise also introduces some of the consequences of poverty. Recall that because of his extended illness, James Hilliard lost his job at the fish-processing plant. Unemployment in Cedar Key is high, and others are eager to take his place. He now remains at home, caring for the children and maintaining the house. Mary continues working full time, forty hours a week, fifty-two weeks per year, at the convenience store. She does not get paid holidays or vacation time. She has worked at the store for many years and is now the manager, earning $7.50 per hour, or $15,600 annually. This places the family just below the poverty threshold of $16,036. Although her income is high for the kind of work she does, setting it lower would leave the family too far below the poverty line for my purposes.

In order to calculate a family budget, it is first necessary to subtract Social Security taxes (at 7.5 percent): $15,600 − 1,170 = 14,430. Mary chooses not to have federal income taxes withheld, since her income is so low she will have no tax liability. If the Hilliards use one-third of their income for food, as posited by the poverty line (see note 1), their monthly budget looks like this: $397 for food, $806 for nonfood. Thus, the food allotment provides for $3.31 per person each day, assuming a thirty-day month. The amount will be slightly more in February, and the Hilliards will fast one day in each month that has thirty-one days. This last is sarcasm, of course, but with a serious message: The Hilliards cannot obtain a nutritionally adequate diet on $3.31 per person per day. (Actually, you cannot even go to Burger King and get a Whopper meal for that amount.) Moreover, poor persons nearly always pay more for food because nearby markets are either mom-and-pop operations or franchised small stores. So it is hard for the Hilliards to remain within their food budget. They are, however, eligible for food stamps. At their income level, they receive about $150 per month in coupons, $1.25 per person each day. (They can now afford a Whopper meal.) But even with this supplement the Hilliards are like most poor families: They spend more than one-third of their income on food, which means they must use part of their nonfood budget in order to eat.

But the nonfood budget is not adequate either. It allows $806 per month for rent, utilities, automobile maintenance and transportation, medical and dental bills, clothing, school expenses, entertainment, and all else necessary for living in the United States. A few assumptions show how hard it is for the Hilliards to subsist on their nonfood budget (even if food costs do not encroach on it): Let us assume rent is $350, utilities $160, and transportation $100, leaving $196 for everything else.

These assumptions are difficult to sustain in practice but necessary at this income level. The figure for rent, $350, is often low. Among the poor, about 81 percent of renters and 69 percent of owners spend more than half their income on housing (Lazare and Leonard, 1992). Actual prices for gas, electricity, and a telephone add up to more than the assumed utilities cost, $160. For example, many poor families pay far higher heating bills than do the nonpoor (meaning middle-class people, for the most part) because their homes are so badly insulated. Finally, the

transportation cost of $100 is not enough for gasoline and auto mainte-
nance, although it might work if the Hilliards lived in a large city and
used public transportation exclusively. It is not clear, at least to me, how
the remaining $196 can cover medical bills (for the adults; the children
are covered by Medicaid), clothing, purchases necessary for school-age
children, and entertainment, just to name the most obvious expenses.
Forget about going to the dentist. Even the cost of birth control pills is
high, given this budget. And if Mary becomes pregnant, the family's fi-
nances fall apart completely. Hence, the Hilliards find it nearly impossible to subsist on the nonfood budget. Yet as noted above, this family
cannot stay within its food budget either.

As an aside, recall that the Hilliards were homeless for a few weeks after James got out of the hospital and lost his job. They filed federal income tax forms, however, and received an earned income tax credit of,
let us say, $3,500. They used the money to pay for first and last months'
rent on the mobile home, utility deposits, and a few (not all) of the debts
that had accumulated as a result of James's illness. The lesson is that
even when poor families live on their budgets, one emergency leads to
disaster. And most families at all income levels have emergencies. The
difference between the Hilliards and, say, a middle-class family is that
the latter has the resources to deal effectively with crises.

These considerations show that even though the method for measuring poverty has been criticized (Citro and Michael, 1995), it does one
thing very well: It shows that the 36 million people living poorly in America are truly poor (Beeghley, 1983). Poverty means that families like the
Hilliards must often choose between paying for utilities and food, or
housing and food, or medical treatment and food (Frank et al., 1992). It
should not be surprising, then, that *the greater the poverty, the more
likely are homelessness and hunger to occur* as a consequence.

Homelessness means lacking access to a conventional dwelling: a
house, apartment, mobile home, or rented room (Rossi, 1989). Homeless people sleep in places not intended for such use: cars, scrap metal
shacks, and public areas (such as bus stations or fire grates outside
buildings). Some also sleep in shelters. The usual guess is that on any
given night 300,000–500,000 people, 20 percent of whom are children,
are homeless and that about 1 million people will be homeless in any
given year. Again, the usual guess is that about one-third of them need
mental health treatment, one-third need drug rehabilitation, and one-
third just need housing. The word "guess" here should be taken seriously, as precise counts are hard to obtain. Regardless of the exact number or proportion, the homeless are very poor.

They live in grief and on grates. The impact is most obvious in children. About 40 percent of homeless pregnant women receive no prena-

tal care (Bassuk, 1991). So the odds of bearing low-birth-weight babies, with all the human tragedy and costs they entail (see Chapter 9), become much higher. Children in shelters or on the streets are more likely to be abused or neglected. They display chronic medical and psychological problems. They do not attend school or do so irregularly, which means they fail to develop the skills necessary for success. Like hunger, the impact of homelessness redounds to affect the entire society.

Although the United States does not display starvation like that in some Third World nations, many people go hungry. *Hunger* means the chronic underconsumption of nutrients. The usual guess (with the usual qualification) is that 20–30 million people suffer from hunger in the United States, which makes sense in light of the family budget described earlier (Brown, 1992). The presence of food distribution centers in every city suggests that the nutritional needs of many people go unmet. Such centers fed 26 million people in 1993 (SHNFBN, 1994).

The long-term impact of hunger is devastating, especially for children. Physicians in low-income areas commonly see 6-year-old kids who look 3 (Brown and Pizer, 1985). They display slow growth and mental deficiencies as a result of hunger. Put simply, children become stupid because they have not had enough to eat during the first years of life. They never recover. Malnourishment makes people more susceptible to disease and less capable of recovering. This is important because many common illnesses have a long-term impact. For example, if strep throat, a typical childhood disease, is not treated with antibiotics, it can lead to heart and kidney damage. The result is a sickly adult who is less productive. A nutritious diet can help prevent strep. Again, the long-term impact of hunger redounds to affect the entire society.

In addition to homelessness and hunger, a glance at the topics covered in this book indicates some of the consequences of poverty. All of these findings are empirical generalizations: *Compared to the nonpoor, (1) poor women are more likely to lack access to birth control, become pregnant, and give birth or obtain abortions; (2) poor people are more likely to use drugs and less able to obtain treatment; (3) poor people are more likely to commit and be victims of homicide (and other crimes); and (4) poor people have less access to medical treatment, worse health, and shorter life spans.* These considerations, which do not exhaust the impact of poverty, suggest the importance of social class in modern societies: *The lower the social class, the fewer the choices people have and the less effective they are in solving personal problems* (Beeghley, 1996a).

How do individuals like the Hilliards end up in a situation of limited choices? The angle of vision implied by this question applies a basic sociological orientation to understanding impoverishment: Individuals act on and react to the situations in which they find themselves. It lowers the possibility for self-deception and provides a clear, if cynical, view of U.S. society. It makes the unfamiliar familiar.

Individuals and Poverty

Most people in this country work hard and strive to succeed. And in most cases they survive. Poverty, when it occurs, is short-term. Even so, getting out of poverty rarely brings economic security, since any unexpected drop in income leads back into it. The specter of hunger or homelessness is never far away. Most people simply hope for the best, in spite of characteristics that make them prone to poverty.

Low-Wage Job Skills

The fewer the job skills people possess, the greater the likelihood of poverty. This finding means that a lot of employed people are poor. Mary Hilliard, for example, earns almost $7.50 per hour and works full time all year long, yet her family remains below the poverty line. Although the Hilliards are a hypothetical example, they represent millions of people. Among poor persons over age 16, 41 percent work at least part of the year and 10 percent work full time year-round (USBC, 1997b:viii).

One reason employed persons are poor is that they have low-wage skills. One indicator of skill is education. The poverty rate among individuals aged 25 years and older with less than a high school diploma is 25 percent, compared to only 3 percent for those with a college degree (USBC, 1997a). In the case of the Hilliards, for example, although Mary has a high school degree; James does not. It is not clear how someone like James, who has worked (very hard for many years) in a fish factory, can develop marketable skills in a new industry, no matter how great his motivation. Many people find themselves in his situation.

Unemployment

But regardless of motivation, jobs do not always exist. Plants close, leaving entire communities out of work. In a modern economy, those without paid work often become poor. *The longer the unemployment, the greater the likelihood of poverty.* For example, among persons age 16 and over, only 3 percent of those working all year long are poor, compared to 14 percent of those unemployed for part of the year and 23 percent for those unemployed all year (USBC, 1997b:17). James Hilliard had a stable albeit low income job for many years. But he had no job security and no disability insurance. After his illness, he was unable to find a new job. And one parent's unemployment hurts the entire family.

Family Instability

Two-parent families are less likely to become poor than families headed by women. Thus, only 6 percent of two-parent families are poor, compared to 36 percent of female-headed families (USBC, 1997b:2). Before James Hilliard lost his job, the family had a low but steady income, around $25,000 per year. They managed the stresses inherent to their economic situation. Since losing his job, however, James has felt helpless because he cannot provide for his family. Fights between James and Mary have increased, partly because he feels so bad (and has been drinking too much) and partly because money has become so tight. It will take courage for them to remain together. Millions of couples find themselves in situations like this. Some break apart. This is why more than half of all poor families are headed by women (USBC, 1997b:viii).

Such personal experiences are connected with individual characteristics: age, race and ethnicity, and gender. I am not going discuss gender or race here, however, since they were considered in previous chapters.

Age of Household Head

Families headed by young adults and aged persons (over 65) are more likely to be poor than those with household heads of other ages. Thus, only 8 percent of those in which the household head is 25–34 years of age are poor, compared to 14 percent when the head is less than 25 (USBC, 1997a). Families headed by young adults have a greater rate of poverty because the young have not yet acquired education or job skills. For them, the decision to establish an independent household is often unwise. One factor leading to this decision is pregnancy. Yet public policy makes it hard for young persons, especially the poor, to obtain contraception (recall Chapter 2). Sadly, sometimes girls who live in abusive or otherwise deprived situations become sexually active; they confuse sexual intercourse with love and conceive a child as evidence of their humanity, their adulthood (Sgroi, 1984). Boys from poor backgrounds often react similarly: They make girls pregnant to prove their manhood (Marsiglio, 1993). Hence, young persons decide to form families in contexts of limited choices in which they believe (sometimes falsely) they will be better off.

How does one become better off? That is the question. The common-sense approach to understanding poverty blames individual deficiencies: The poor should be like the rest of us, it is said; they should work. Some observers translate common sense into academic jargon by seeing poverty as the result of low human capital. As indicated in Chapter 3, *human capital* refers to job skills or education, which can be converted into skills that produce income (Becker, 1975). This angle of vision suggests that poor persons should simply make their services more valuable and then they would find jobs, and even those with low human capital should at least look for work. Yet even if someone like James Hilliard does get a job, this strategy will solve only his individual problem. It will not reduce the high rate of poverty. The reason is simple: There are not enough jobs. A large proportion of those out of work have become so discouraged they have quit looking for jobs. (This is why official unemployment figures understate the "true" level of unemployment.) If discouraged persons were suddenly to seek jobs, they would overwhelm the vacancies at the lower skill levels (Kasarda, 1990). And most would still be poor. Hence, promoting self-help strategies as the solution to poverty—whether as common sense or dressed up as academic jargon—is impractical. Such proposals affirm dominant values without increasing familiarity with poverty. The latter occurs only when structural questions are asked.

Social Structure and Poverty

The historical data shown in Figure 5.1 reveal a fundamental transformation: For the first time in history, poverty fell. And this process has occurred in every Western nation. The international data, however, show that the rate in the United States is higher than in nations similar to it. This section attempts to explain both phenomena.

The Long-Term Fall in the Poverty Rate

The commonsense argument, noted above, is that hard work keeps people out of poverty. Students tend to find this point of view appealing because they have learned the association between hard work and good grades. After all, people simply need to take advantage of their opportunities. But this orientation (like the easy quips of radio talk show hosts) misses the underlying issue: Not everyone has opportunity. The structural question is, What factors produced a context in which hard work could pay off? My hypothesis is that *the long-term fall in the poverty rate reflects (1) industrialization, (2) class differences in fertility rates, and (3) declining discrimination.*[2]

Industrialization. *Industrialization,* you should recall, refers to the transformation of the economy as new forms of energy are substituted for muscle power, leading to advances in productivity. As described in Chapter 2, industrialization is linked to other historical changes that have occurred in concert with it: the rise of capitalism, the development of work-centered values, the use of science to solve problems, the emphasis on personal freedom, and an increase in life expectancy. But the change in economic organization is most important here. With industrialization, the proportion of high-paying, white-collar jobs rose steadily over time, whereas the proportion of farming and unskilled, blue-collar jobs fell. Thus, in 1870 only 19 percent of the workforce held white-collar jobs, compared to 58 percent today (USBC, 1996d:405). In 1870, 53 percent of the workforce (more if women's work was counted) held farming jobs, compared to less than 3 percent today.

These data mean that the opportunity structure changed. The new job slots at the top were like a vacuum that needed filling; it pulled people upward, out of poverty. This process occurred because industrialization requires coordination and management. In addition, it requires expertise; entirely new white-collar occupations emerged based on technical knowledge. Who needs a computer programmer when most people are plowing fields—by hand?

Class Differences in Fertility Rates. Except for the baby boom generation, the fertility rate has declined steadily for nearly 200 years. As described in Chapter 2, however, birthrates have varied by social class, with blue-collar and farming families bearing more children. With industrialization and the decline in the number of farming jobs, these "surplus" children were "pushed" up in the job queue by the pressure of numbers. The combined impact of industrialization and class differences in fertility created a context in which people who worked hard could be upwardly mobile. Poverty declined as a result.

Declining Discrimination. But for a long time only persons with certain characteristics benefited from this new historical context. Others were usually excluded. Racial and ethnic minorities were treated unequally, often by law. Deprived of civil rights, they faced further obstacles to opportunity: unequal medical treatment, housing segregation, school segregation, and occupational discrimination. Thus, industrialization provided whites with more opportunities in which hard work could lead to economic success. Although discrimination continues, Chapter 4 showed that there has been improvement. African Americans, Hispanics, and Asian Americans (not necessarily Native Americans) are treated less unequally today than in the past. The result is less poverty.

Discrimination against women was once legal as well. Traditional norms dictating that women and men should have separate spheres provided justification for depriving women the ability to compete fairly and earn a living. In this context, men had more opportunities in which hard work could lead to economic success. Although unequal treatment continues, Chapter 3 showed that women are treated more fairly today.

Now it remains true that regardless of industrialization and class dif-ferences in fertility, people (usually white males) succeeded only by hard work. But these efforts took place in a historical context in which they could pay off. In order to see how this was so, imagine that industrializa-tion had not happened. Instead, for the past 150 years your great-grand-parents, grandparents, and parents have labored on farms: pulling plows, canning produce, doing—by hand—everything they needed to survive. This lifestyle is, of course, your fate and that of everyone you know. In such a context, I submit, little economic surplus would exist and the poverty rate today would be very high, about 40–60 percent of the population (Patterson, 1986). In the real world, however, people's choices changed. Although no one was forced to be upwardly mobile, both the jobs and the people to fill them existed. These new opportuni-ties had nothing to do with each individual's motives or abilities. In Emile Durkheim's phrase, they reflected a change "in the nature of soci-ety itself" (1895:128).

The High U.S. Poverty Rate

Despite the progress in alleviating poverty throughout this century, the United States chooses to maintain a higher rate than other Western soci-eties. My hypothesis is: *The rate of poverty in the United States reflects (1) the reproduction of the class structure, (2) the vicious circle of poverty, (3) macroeconomic policy, (4) the structure of elections, (5) the structure of the economy, and (6) institutionalized discrimination.* These factors exist externally to individuals, determining the range and effectiveness of their choices.

The Reproduction of the Class Structure.   Despite the high level of mo-bility in the twentieth century in the United States and all Western na-tions, the class structure has remained stable over time. Studies of occu-pational mobility reveal that most people end up in the same job category as their parents (Blau and Duncan, 1967; Featherman and Hauser, 1978; Hout, 1988). This finding means that the class structure is continually reproduced.

Because this result is counterintuitive, I digress for a few moments with a vignette about the game of Monopoly. The purpose of this little fantasy is to provide you with a subjective sense of why the class struc-ture is stable.[3]

The game of Monopoly embodies key American values, especially be-liefs about equality of opportunity and the importance of hard work. In the actual game, each player begins with $1,500. By combining luck (represented by the dice) and hard work (represented by purchase and auction decisions), players try to win. Note that when the game begins each participant has an equal chance of winning. The real world, however, differs in that some people begin life with more opportunities than others and the result of their hard work varies accordingly. In order to illustrate this fact, I have constructed a fantasy Monopoly game. Let us start by imagining that four groups of people take part and that they compete both as individuals against each other and, on occasion, cooperatively as members of their particular group.

The first group is small, its members statistically insignificant. But they begin the game with some advantages: They own some property and have $5,000 each. Moreover, people in this group operate the bank, and as a result of this duty and their overall political influence, they get two rolls of the dice each turn. Thus, although these people are statistically insignificant, they are substantively important. The second group is large, but its members have fewer advantages at the start: They do not own property and have $2,000 each. Nonetheless, they maintain that anyone playing the game can move into the first group if they work hard enough. The third group is also large, but its members have still fewer advantages at the start: They do not own property and have about $1,000 each. The fourth group is smaller but significant in size. Its members, however, have the fewest advantages: They do not own property, have only $500 each, and do not know all the rules. Partly as a result, they sometimes lose a turn and are sometimes charged more than list price for properties, rents, and fines. One last point: This is not an evening's entertainment; no one can quit the game. Participants who run out of money or go to jail must beg for cash, serve their time, and continue playing—indefinitely.

Now the contest starts. Monopoly, of course, is played by individuals, and it is easy to look at the decisions each player made and figure out where she or he ended up. Although such an analysis would be useful, it would be misleading to try to understand the game as a whole based on studying the hard work of each individual. This is because the players were divided into groups with unequal advantages when the game began.

In contrast, from a structural angle of vision, it is easy to see how the game will turn out. Members of the first group, whom I will call the rich, will usually stay rich, barring bad luck or lack of wisdom (actually, they will have to be really dumb not to succeed). This outcome occurs precisely because they started the game with built-in advantages and share some of them; for example, they pool their "get out of jail free" cards. Moreover, even though some of them illegally "borrow" money from the bank, the few who get caught pay back only a small part of what they stole.

Similarly, most of those in the second group, whom I will call middle class, will maintain their positions. Although a little mobility will occur, most movement will be short distance and within group. They overlook the reality that they will never be rich and simply enjoy being better off than those who are less advantaged. They assume their lifestyle reflects hard work and ability rather than the advantages with which they began.

The members of the third and fourth groups, the working class and poor, have the most difficulty surviving. Although some upward mobility will occur, most movement will be short distance within or between the lower-level groups. Economic security is always doubtful for these players; they had so few resources at the start that it is hard for them, on their own, to move ahead. Nonetheless, nearly all of them work hard and accept their position in the game.

It should be pointed out, however, that some members of the third and fourth groups become alienated; they believe they are powerless to influence their own lives and find that dominant norms and values are hopelessly remote, even meaningless. Thus, some readjust their goals and only go through the motions of the game. Others, however, just sit at the game board passively while their tokens are moved for them. Still others (surprisingly few) pull out guns and use them to alter their economic situation. But given spatial arrangements separating the various groups, their victims are usually other members of the third and fourth groups. When caught, these people are sent to jail for long periods.

The vignette highlights the fact that the rewards of hard work tend to go to people who are born with some advantages. It also suggests how the social structure sets the range of opportunities for individuals: As social class declines, so do the number of choices people have and their effectiveness. Hence, no amount of effort will change the fact that most individuals will not cross class boundaries. This reality exists independently of them, limiting their choices. In practice, then, most people who work hard will never be poor. Others, including many who work just as hard and have just as much ability, will become impoverished at some point in their lives. In turn, a small proportion of the poor become trapped.

But before pursuing that topic, I wish to pause for a moment. The tendency for the class structure to reproduce itself occurs in all societies, regardless of economic development. In industrial societies, however, this tendency can be regulated by public policies. The following variables suggest how the policy choices made in this country affect the poverty rate.

The Vicious Circle of Poverty. Most poverty, as noted previously, does not last long. But temporary impoverishment occasionally combines with other difficulties, in a vicious circle, to snare people into long-term poverty.

One way people become trapped is that their efforts at escape are thwarted and they become so discouraged they give up. Consider the Hilliards, and remember they represent lots of families. For many years Cedar Key has been a rural backwater. A nice place to live. Not much crime (okay, a few locals run drugs up and down the coast). But few (legal) jobs. In recent years, however, it has become a bit of an artist colony and tourist haven. So James decided to set up a kiosk next to the town dock and sell locally made "art" (junk, but the tourists don't know that). The result was transformative. He started shaving and stopped drinking. He was bringing in an income. But the number of street vendors is limited by law, and after the chamber of commerce protested to the police, James was forced to close his kiosk. So James cleaned up his car and started using it as a jitney, taking tourists from condominiums to the dock area at $1 per person. But after protests by the local cab company, he was again forced to stop. James knows the "American rule": You are supposed to keep trying, find work, and succeed over time. But this effort becomes harder after you are repeatedly thwarted.

These examples are not far-fetched. Although some poor persons are so lacking in job skills that employment would require extensive (meaning years of) training, many can operate small businesses. Lots of jobs— as cab drivers, jitney operators, cosmetologists, and street vendors, to name a few—require little capital or education. They require instead entrepreneurship. But local laws often restrict such activities in four ways (Mellor, 1996). First, arbitrary ceilings are placed on the number of jobs in any one area. In New York City, for example, only 12,187 taxis, 4,000 food vendors, and 1,700, merchandise peddlers may operate. Second, for certain jobs extensive training is required that has little relevance to public safety. In New York, one needs 900 hours of training to become a licensed cosmetologist, compared to 116 hours to become an emergency medical technician and 47 hours to become a security guard (with a gun). Third, interest groups are protected by outlawing certain jobs. Although jitney vans are in high demand in New York, the Transit Workers Union successfully lobbied the state assembly and city council to make such services illegal. Finally, getting a business license takes bureaucratic sophistication along with endless paperwork. In New York, the city's official directory contains seventy-three pages of instructions about places to go and forms to fill out in order to get a license to repair videocassette recorders or open a parking lot. Thus, in New York as in other cities, thousands of bootstrap entrepreneurs operate illegally, on the economic margin, unable to expand their businesses. The long-term impact is to dull ambition, leaving people trapped.

The limits on entrepreneurship mean that some illegal capitalists also rely on public aid. They are, of course, guilty of welfare fraud if caught.

Moreover, the penalties for obtaining legal jobs are severe. Let us suppose that one of James's friends works at a company where a janitorial position opens up, and he gets the job. He now earns $5.50 per hour, or $11,440 per year. (This assumes he works forty hours per week for fifty-two weeks, including Christmas, and is never sick.) But the new job presents a major problem: The children have become ineligible for Medicaid because James and Mary's combined income of $27,400 is so high (!). The Hilliards must choose between work and health insurance for their children. This is a catch-22. In the novel of that title, the character Yossarian could get out of the military if he were crazy (Heller, 1961). But since he sees that the war itself is crazy, he is clearly sane and so cannot get discharged. In the real world, people like James Hilliard sometimes choose not to accept employment. Are they lazy?

Assume for a moment that James turns down the job in order to maintain Medicaid coverage for the children. Their problems are not over. Young Samuel develops an earache. The nearest Medicaid provider is 90 miles away in Gainesville. Out-of-pocket expenses for gas and lunch while the family is at the emergency room of the hospital will be at least $20. So the Hilliards decide to wait and see if their son recovers. And he does. Although this is a reasonable strategy, since some medical problems improve over time without treatment, it has unfortunate results. Sam had otitis media, a common childhood ailment, easily diagnosed and treated. Left untreated, however, it results in hearing loss, even deafness. Thus, Sam now has a long-term disability, one that increases the odds of his doing poorly in school and ending up trapped in poverty himself as an adult. This is the social context in which the Hilliards and millions of real people must act.

The Hilliard vignettes suggest how factors associated with poverty can form a vicious circle that traps people. Remember: Laws regulating small businesses and determining eligibility for welfare reflect policy choices made by the nonpoor. So do macroeconomic decisions.

Macroeconomic Policy. *Macroeconomic policy* refers to the way government regulates the economy, especially inflation and unemployment. Even when both are low, one is usually kept higher than the other (Heilbroner and Thurow, 1982). In the 1990s inflation was 2–3 percent and unemployment 5–6 percent. Underlying this policy choice is the fact that all economic problems are political problems. The decision to stress either low inflation or unemployment harms some people and benefits others. Generally, the poor are hurt more by an emphasis on unemployment: A 1 percent increase in the unemployment rate increases the poverty rate by an almost identical 0.97 percent. In contrast, a 1 percent increase in inflation increases the poverty rate by only 0.12

percent (Blank and Blinder, 1986:187). Thus, unless the situation is atypical, the poor benefit from macroeconomic policies that keep unemployment low.

Since World War II, however, U.S. policy has focused (not always successfully) on keeping inflation in check (Hibbs, 1977). In contrast, most Western European governments have focused (again, not always successfully) on keeping unemployment down; they have sought, in other words, 5–6 percent inflation in exchange for 2–3 percent unemployment. These alternative policies affect the poverty rate, as the data presented earlier imply.

The U.S. focus on low inflation is consonant with the political interests of the middle class and rich, who wish to protect their pensions and other investments from the impact of rising prices. Their representatives try to prevent inflation.

The Structure of Elections. I mean the phrase "their representatives" to be provocative. The middle class and rich vote at a much higher rate than the working class and poor. It is not surprising, then, that elected officials enact policies that reflect the interests of those who elect them. A number of obstacles keep impoverished and working-class people from voting (Beeghley, 1992). First, elections occur on workdays (rather than weekends or holidays). Those who can get to the polls most easily have jobs that are less physically tiring, can take the time off, have child care available, own a car, and live in safe neighborhoods. Second, voting entails registration, which the middle class and rich are more aware of and better able to deal with.[4] Thus, the structure of elections means that macroeconomic and welfare policies reflect the interests of the nonpoor. In this context, the structure of the economy must also be recognized.

The Structure of the Economy. Hard work often does not prevent poverty, mainly because of the structure of the economy. The pay attached to some jobs is low, as shown by the fact that about 10 percent of the poor work full time all year long (USBC, 1997b:viii). Like Mary Hilliard, these poor persons have both motivation and jobs: They lack wages high enough to live on.

In addition, wages and job security differ from one industry to another (Hodgson and Kaufman, 1982). Given comparable skills, people working in industries where the pay is low are more likely to be poor than those in industries where wages are high. For example, if the General Electric Corporation located a plant in Cedar Key and James Hilliard worked as a janitor there (rather than at a small business, say), not only would his income be above the poverty line but he would also have benefits, such as medical insurance. Thus, depending on the industry in which they work and their area of residence, some people become trapped in low-wage jobs—despite their hard work.

Finally, many people face not simply low-wage jobs but the lack of any jobs at all. The Hilliards, remember, reside in a small town where there are few jobs. This problem is typical in rural areas. But urban residents face the same difficulty: Since about 1970, hundreds of thousands of manufacturing jobs have moved from cities to suburbs (Kasarda, 1990). Getting to them from the cities requires a long and expensive commute, usually by car. This mismatch between workers and workplaces especially affects African Americans, who are less likely to live in suburbia because of housing discrimination. One can only guess why industries left the cities: Cheaper land and easier access to transportation (interstate highways and airports) is probably one. Another may be corporate dislike of African Americans (Williams, 1987). Whatever the reason, massive unemployment in central cities has resulted.

Thus, the structure of the economy means that millions of people will be impoverished despite their willingness to work hard. Institutionalized discrimination makes this problem worse.

Institutionalized Discrimination. Chapters 3 and 4 showed the way in which discrimination against women and ethnic minorities is built into the social structure. In Chapter 3, for example, the hypothesis was that gender inequality is preserved by (1) the salience of traditional gender norms (the large percentage of women who remain unemployed and work part time by choice, the extent to which men avoid housework, and the extent to which the workplace remains gendered) and (2) institutionalized discrimination (illustrated by the impact of skewed gender ratios and occupational segregation). Similarly, in Chapter 4 the hypothesis was that African Americans' relative lack of success compared to that of other immigrant groups reflects historical differences in (1) conditions of settlement, (2) prejudice and discrimination, and (3) affirmative action. The same processes help keep women and racial and ethnic minorities poor.

Despite these hardships, the nonpoor display ambivalent attitudes toward the poor. When asked "why there are poor people in this country," respondents agree that the following factors are "very important" (GSS, 1996):

Failure of society to provide good schools	36 percent
Failure of industry to provide enough jobs	36 percent
Loose morals and drunkenness	39 percent
Lack of effort by the poor themselves	46 percent

In my experience, when presented with ethnographic accounts of poverty or the details of poor people's lives in some other way, the non-poor often react with sympathy. At some level, they understand that those with little income face limited choices and see the importance of good schools and jobs. But when discussing "the poor," without specifics, these same persons often revert to stereotypes about morality and effort. There is no question in their minds that the poor, like everyone else, ought to try to help themselves.

This structural analysis, however, should make you aware that poor individuals acting on their own cannot reduce the level of poverty. No amount of moralizing about the importance of self-reliance and individual initiative will change that fact.

Implications

The experiences of other nations show that plausible ways of reducing the rate of poverty do exist. Impoverished people need benefits, training, and—above all—jobs. By "benefits," I refer to programs that prevent poverty over the long term. Access to birth control, for example, would allow poor women to regulate their fertility (see Chapter 2). Access to medical treatment would prevent illness from becoming chronic, especially if the emphasis is on prevention (see Chapter 9). Access to drug treatment would help those who want to help themselves (see Chapter 6). Access to housing would help prevent trauma to children and family breakups. There are other issues, but these indicate the general direction necessary to reduce poverty.

That the United States does not pursue rather obvious strategies to alleviate poverty suggests that the status quo is useful. Who benefits from having lots of poor people around? The nonpoor gain four advantages from the existence of so much poverty (Gans, 1972). First, as mentioned before, the poor absorb the costs of macroeconomic policies designed to keep inflation down. Whenever unemployment falls, the media report that economists believe prices will rise to "unacceptable" levels and that the Federal Reserve Board is under pressure to raise interest rates. Raising interest rates will restrict economic growth, thereby boosting unemployment (at least that is the idea; it does not always work). Second, the poor constitute a class of low-skill workers who perform vital tasks that others do not wish to do. Such jobs come easily to mind: making cloth and clothes, picking and cooking food, cleaning buildings and streets, and all the other dirty, menial, dangerous, low-paying, and short-term occupations that keep a modern society going. Third, by working for low wages, an indigent class subsidizes consumption by the affluent: Food is less expensive, mortgages are reduced, and taxes are low. Fourth, poverty creates jobs and incomes for persons who would regulate, serve, or exploit the less fortunate. For example, people who cannot obtain work sometimes resort to illegal drugs and street crime to sustain themselves, thereby guaranteeing jobs for police officers, lawyers, judges, probation officers, and everyone else connected with the criminal justice system. This (rather cynical) view of the benefits of poverty suggests that resistance will occur whenever programs to reduce the level of poverty are proposed.

Now I am perfectly aware that reducing the rate of poverty will be difficult. But public resistance to antipoverty programs goes beyond a realistic pessimism about the odds of success. What is going on?

One source of resistance is structural: The federalist system of government divides power between a central authority and the states. This system expresses the fear of a strong central government that characterizes U.S. history. Thus, programs to help the poor imply an expansion of what is sometimes called the "welfare state," and when confronted with this possibility, people tend to throw up their hands in despair. A fear exists that the federal government creates problems rather than solves them. After all, it is said, programs against poverty have been tried and failed. But this attitude is self-deceptive. When weapons systems, trade policies, or environmental policies display flaws, they are fixed. Moreover, middle-class and rich people actively use government: looking for tax breaks, contracts, and services. Finally, the falling rate of poverty after World War II until the 1970s (see Figure 5.1) reflects the impact of both an expanding postwar economy that provided jobs and the War on Poverty launched by President Johnson in 1964. It seems to me that the United States did not lose the War on Poverty; it was called off.

Another source of resistance is ideological: the value placed on individualism. As most people use it, the term "individualism" refers to an amorphous yearning to be free of governmental rules, to be free to pursue one's economic and social goals. Remember, the United States is a society of immigrants who overcame great adversity to achieve success. In a self-deluding way, then, people believe they "made it" without the help of government (without affirmative action programs, for example). Despite this individualism, most nonpoor people take government benefits readily. They simply see them as reinforcing their own efforts and therefore as deserved. Thus, they consider Social Security an insurance fund paid into by employed persons (it is not), and they see tax deductions for home owners as assisting hardworking people. Regarding the poor: If they would just work harder . . . which leads to the judgment that they are lazy.

A third source of resistance lies in the racial composition of the poor. The legacy of slavery still haunts the United States, as the poor are identified (inaccurately, because of prejudice) as predominantly African American. Thus, any form of assistance seems to benefit "them," not "us." I am inclined to think that whenever racial differences in a population exist and these differences are related to income and culture, the development of programs to secure jobs, health, and other rights of citizenship (as occurs in Western Europe) will be difficult.

This, then, is the context in which poverty persists. For the majority, the poor remain unfamiliar and, many believe, undeserving. They seem different. So I am pessimistic about plans to reduce the rate of poverty.

Notes

1. This definition is extrapolated from the government's official poverty line, which is "based on the amount [of money] needed by families of different size and type to purchase a nutritionally adequate diet on the assumption that no more than a third of the family income is used for food" (Orshansky, 1969). I show just below, however, that this assumption is inaccurate.

2. The argument in this section is revised and adapted from my "Individual Versus Structural Explanations of Poverty" (1989a).

3. The name of the game, Monopoly, is the trademark of Parker Brothers for its Real Estate Trading Game (Beverly, MA: Parker Brothers Division of General Mills Fun Group, Inc., 1935, 1946, 1961). An earlier version of this vignette appeared in my *Living Poorly in America* (1983).

4. In addition to voting, people participate by contributing money. The rich, of course, invariably have an advantage here. Low voting rates add to it. High rates would reduce it. This is because politicians would have to appeal to the interests of the entire population in order to be elected.

Recommended Reading

Citro, Constance F., and Robert T. Michael (eds.). *Measuring Poverty: A New Approach* (Washington, DC: National Academy Press, 1995).

Kotlowitz, Alex. *There Are No Children Here* (New York: Doubleday, 1991).

Patterson, James T. *America's Struggle Against Poverty, 1900–1985* (Cambridge: Harvard University Press, 1986).

Rossi, Peter H. *Down and Out in America: The Origin of Homelessness* (Chicago: University of Chicago Press, 1989).

6 Drugs

Outline of Chapter 6

Drugs are used in every society because they make people feel "high," another (albeit artificial) way of feeling good. Drug use is especially "high" in the United States and other Western nations. But some drugs are illegal, which gives their use an aura of excitement and rebellion. And because they are illegal, they generate crime and violence, destroy neighborhoods, have inflated prices that attract people into the drug trade, preoccupy the police, and create clogged courts. These problems lead some observers to favor legalizing drugs because they believe the impact of prohibition is worse than the substances themselves.

Yet drugs are often harmful. They damage the body, sometimes causing death, and can lead to loss of job, home, and marriage. So drugs often injure both users and their families. Eugene O'Neill portrays this process vividly in his play *Long Day's Journey into Night*, which describes the impact of his mother's abuse of heroin on her family (1962). Because of these effects, some see drugs as evil and favor laws prohibiting consumption. Drug use, they say, is like a slippery slope: It leads to drug dependence and abuse and demoralizes society.

These different positions are not easily resolved. A story from Greek mythology illustrates the difficulties. The Sphinx was a monster with the face of a woman, the body of a lion, and the wings of a bird. In Sophocles' play *Oedipus the King*, the Sphinx lived on a rock near the road into Thebes and from there she would pose a question to passersby: "What has one voice yet becomes over time four-footed, two-footed, and three-footed; and the more feet it uses the weaker it is?" (1972). Those not able to solve the riddle were eaten by the Sphinx, who enjoyed many delicious meals.

I will tell you the answer to the Sphinx's riddle later in the chapter. For now, some definitions are important in order to understand the riddle posed by drugs. A *drug* is any chemical substance that, when ingested, changes a person's physiological or psychological functioning. This definition is broader than usual in the drug literature. It points out that everyone uses psychoactive substances; it does not matter whether you shoot them or swallow them, whether you get them from a dealer or a doctor. I focus on five drugs—alcohol, tobacco, marijuana, cocaine, and heroin—mainly because they have been controversial for over a century. *Drug dependence* refers to compulsive craving and use, often in increasing amounts. But in fact not everyone who uses drugs becomes dependent. Users can be divided into three categories: (1) Casual drug users consume drugs occasionally, often in social settings. (2) Controlled drug users consume drugs frequently but in moderate amounts, often at home (for example, a glass or two of wine at night constitutes controlled use). (3) Drug abusers become dependent and consume large quantities of a drug over a long period and as a result experience a variety of life problems, such as sickness, death, divorce, loss of job, and arrest.

It sometimes seems that drugs constitute an unsolvable riddle, like that posed by the Sphinx. To keep use low—by keeping drugs illegal—it appears that the United States must endure crime, violence, and other problems. Yet to avoid these consequences seems to invite abuse. But this dichotomy is too simple. Alternatives exist. In order to see the broader picture, it is necessary to begin with the facts about drugs and their use.

Dimensions of Drug Use

On a bleak corner of any city, littered with broken booze bottles, discarded heroin syringes, and empty crack vials, drugs appear to dominate the environment. They seem like the incoming tide. Although drugs are indeed pervasive, and not just in "bleak" areas, differences in use and abuse over time and across societies suggest that the United States is not helpless, that drugs need not be a scourge, and that much of the harm associated with drugs can be reduced.

Historical Dimensions

Figure 6.1 presents data on use levels of the drugs under consideration here. Below I focus on each substance in turn, noting the current situation as shown in the figure and then describing the historical pattern of consumption.

Alcohol.   Most adults imbibe alcohol at one time or another. Panel A of Figure 6.1 shows that it is the most widely used drug in the United States, with 83 percent of the population consuming it at some point in their lives and 51 percent within the past month. Yet—and this is important— most people drink in a casual or controlled way and do not experience any problems as a result. In contrast, a small proportion of the popula-

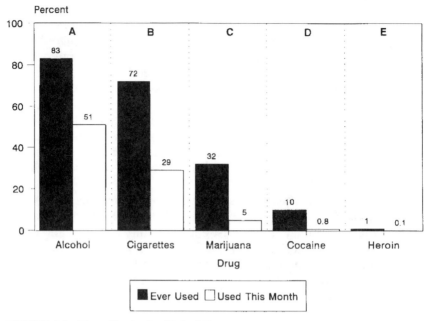

FIGURE 6.1   Drug Use in the United States, 1996
SOURCE: SAMHSA (1997:62).

tion drinks a huge amount: About 10 percent consumes 50 percent of all alcohol and 20 percent consumes 78 percent (RWJF, 1993:24; Skolnick, 1992). Many of these persons are dependent on alcohol; they are drug abusers. Quitting is difficult once one has become dependent; the relapse rate is high (Valliant, 1996).

In *The Alcoholic Republic,* William Rorabaugh estimates that annual per capita consumption of alcohol rose steadily over time from about 7 gallons in 1850 to about 32 in 1910 (1979). He notes, however, that per capita data attribute behavior equally to each adult and, as such, are misleading. Rorabaugh shows that most people consumed little alcohol in the nineteenth century; rather, as today, a small proportion consumed huge amounts. But use dropped abruptly to about 2 gallons per person in 1920, after passage of the Volstead Act (Prohibition), and remained at that level for more than a decade. By 1940, seven years after the end of Prohibition, consumption rose to about 19 gallons and continued rising until peaking at 43 gallons in 1980. Since that time, imbibing has dropped, partly because the minimum drinking age has been raised to 21 in all states and partly because consumers have switched from spirits to wine and beer. Nonetheless, the pervasiveness of alcohol today can be seen by the invitation to "have a drink," since one does not have to qualify it. Plainly, the reference is not to milk.

Tobacco.   Panel B of Figure 6.1 displays tobacco consumption by focusing on cigarettes, omitting other forms of use (pipes, chewing tobacco, etc.). It reveals that most people, about 72 percent, have tried cigarettes in their lifetimes but that far fewer consume them regularly, only 29 percent in the month before the survey was taken. The figure shows that the nicotine in cigarettes is the second most widely ingested drug in the United States.

The long-term trend is curvilinear in the form of an upside-down bowl. Thus, yearly per capita use rose steadily from fifty-four in 1900 (shortly after the cigarette-making machine was invented) to a peak of 4,300 in 1963, when the first surgeon general's report on smoking was published. Since then, use has dropped steadily to about 2,500 in 1993 (USDA, 1994:4). This decline is significant because nicotine is the most addictive of the drugs described in this chapter. People often become dependent after only three to four cigarettes, and casual use is rare. Basically, smokers must ingest nicotine regularly throughout the day in order to keep a specific amount in the body. Some people cannot stop, even when they become deathly ill from long-term use (Brecher, 1972:214). The typical former smoker relapsed three or four times before quitting for good (RWJF, 1993:28). Yet despite the difficulty of quitting, smoking has dropped as people recognize that tobacco contains a dangerous drug.

Marijuana.   Although it is illegal, marijuana is cultivated widely and smuggled into the United States in great quantities (Warner, 1986; Pollan, 1995). Recent data, shown in panel C of Figure 6.1, reveal that about 32 percent of the population has used this drug at some point in their lives, 5 percent in the month previous to the survey.

No plausible data exist on marijuana use before the 1970s. Although its history is a sociological black hole, indirect indicators suggest high consumption (Brecher, 1972). One indicator is that it was a widely cultivated cash crop that was used for rope and cloth in the eighteenth and early nineteenth centuries. It is hard to believe that growers of hemp (one of marijuana's other names) were unaware of its other properties. (It may be untrue, but I cannot help imagining the Founding Fathers and Mothers toking up.) In addition, during the later nineteenth century, marijuana was prescribed for medical purposes, a fluid extract was marketed by drug companies, and hashish was sold as a candy in general stores. These products imply its common use. With passage of the Volstead Act in 1918, marijuana use apparently rose as a substitute for alcohol. Marijuana, in fact, contains the most benign of the drugs considered in this chapter, THC. Casual and controlled use are common. Nonetheless, marijuana became illegal in most states in the 1930s and remains so today, although some have decriminalized possession of small amounts. Survey data on marijuana use from the 1970s to the 1990s reveal a curvilinear pattern. As with all illegal drugs, young adults (18–25) are the biggest users: 48 percent reported they had tried this drug in 1972, a figure that rose to 68 percent in 1979 then dropped to 43 percent in 1994 (NIDA, 1995:23). Thus, marijuana is the most consumed of the illegal drugs considered in this chapter.[1]

Cocaine. Panel D of Figure 6.1 shows that only about 10 percent of the population has ever tried cocaine, less than 1 percent in the month before the survey. As with alcohol, most people are casual or controlled users; only about 7 percent of cocaine users consume 63 percent of supplies, often in the form of crack (Skolnick, 1992). So a few have a serious problem.

Historically, cocaine consumption was nearly zero for most of this century until the 1960s (Ashley, 1975). Kolb and Du Mez, for example estimate that there were about 12,000 regular users around 1920 (1924:1194). As for so many other issues, the 1960s constituted a watershed for cocaine use, with consumption rising. Recent data are illustrative: In 1972 about 9 percent of young adults admitted they had tried cocaine, a rate that rose to 28 percent in 1979–1982 and then fell to about 10 percent in 1994 (NIDA, 1995:29).

In considering the data shown in Figure 6.1 and those for young adults reported above, it is important to remember that cocaine use (in the form of crack) is concentrated among poor people who are less likely to appear in random samples. Although researchers try to obtain samples that represent the population, actual use is probably somewhat higher than reported. Nonetheless, the overall pattern is correct: Cocaine use peaked in the early 1980s and began dropping. This decline is good because, as I describe later, cocaine is dangerous. Remember, the coca plant, which is 1–2 percent cocaine, is not the same as the cocoa bean; the latter is the source of the chocolate milk your parents gave you. In fact, cocaine, especially crack, serves as a metaphor for the 1980s: It gives a brief high, followed by a bad aftertaste and untold bodily damage (Morley, 1989).

Heroin. Panel E of Figure 6.1 reveals that heroin is the least used of the drugs dealt with here: Only 1 percent of the population has ever consumed it, 0.1 percent in the month prior to the survey. Again, those using this drug are mainly poor and less likely to be in random samples. Controlled use is possible, since one does not become dependent on it until a month or so of daily use. The usual guess is that about 500,000 persons abuse heroin (Akers, 1992). Thus, heroin dependence is very low compared to alcohol dependence.

Consumption of heroin was also low in the past. Kolb and Du Mez estimate that regular opium smokers (heroin is produced from opium) rose from about 8,500 in the 1860s to about 59,000 in the 1910s (1924:1192). Courtwright's estimate is higher: About 313,000 opium or heroin abusers prior to the 1914 Harrison Act, which restricted narcotics use (1982:146). He guesses the number of users then fell steadily to about 50,000 in 1940, close to zero in an adult population of 100 million. Heroin use rose in the 1960s so that about 5 percent of young adults said they had tried it in 1972. This number dropped steadily, however, to 0.2 percent in 1994 (NIDA, 1995:102).

Despite a low level of consumption, heroin and other drugs remain controversial, partly because of their harmful impact on individuals and partly because of their (presumed) impact on society at large. Yet the debate over this issue exists in an empirical vacuum because so little is known about international rates of use.

International Dimensions

This empirical vacuum is illustrated by Mathea Falco's *Making of a Drug Free America,* the first sentence of which makes an unsurprising claim: "The United States has the highest rate of drug abuse of any industrialized country in the world" (1994:3). But neither she nor anyone else I know of presents data on this issue. So there is no observational basis for this assertion. Although drugs and drug policy have been incredibly controversial over the past two decades, then, the debates have occurred without any awareness of consumption in nations similar to our own. Hence, this section deals only with alcohol and tobacco.

Alcohol use among selected nations is presented below in terms of liters (not gallons) of pure alcohol consumed per capita from all sources—beer, wine, and spirits—as of 1994 (NTC, 1995:21).

France	11
Germany	10
Netherlands	8
United Kingdom	8
United States	7
Canada	6
Sweden	5

The data show considerable variation. Some nations, like France and Germany, display rather high levels of use. Others, like Sweden and Canada, reveal low levels. The United States falls in the middle.

Although data on cigarettes are not as comparable as I would like, it is possible to get a rough idea of the percentage of smokers in Western industrial societies, as shown below.[2]

France	43 percent
West Germany	43
Sweden	41
Canada	32
United Kingdom	28
United States	23

Thus, the United States and the United Kingdom display the lowest rate of smoking compared to other countries. Programs designed to reduce smoking have only recently started in much of Western Europe.

The historical and (so far as they are available) international data suggest a paradox. On the one hand, despite claims to the contrary (ONDCP, 1994), drug use is not a slippery slope leading to dependence and abuse. This fact is indicated by variation in consumption over time and across societies. It is also manifested by casual and controlled use; with the exception of tobacco, most people can and do ingest drugs (both legal and illegal) in moderate amounts. On the other hand, drugs are so pervasive that, to paraphrase Rorabaugh's title, the United States is a "drug republic."

Consequences of Drug Abuse

Drug abuse is not pretty. Nor are its consequences. Yet, as becomes clear in the remainder of this chapter, some of these consequences reflect not the drugs but their prohibition.

Drug abuse destroys families. O'Neill described it as a long day's journey into night because drugs become central to the abuser's life. The smoker, the alcoholic, the junkie, the crackhead—all wake up in the morning preoccupied with getting the next hit of the drug.[3] One result is financial drain. Do the arithmetic; it is easy to spend well over $1,000 per year on cigarettes and much more on alcohol, and the cost of illegal drugs is fantastically higher. Hence, abusers divert family resources that could be used for food and rent to drug purchases. The conflict (and sometimes abuse) that follows leads to family breakdown. Another result is child neglect and abuse, precisely because the next hit is all-important to the abuser. The rise of crack cocaine in the 1980s lead to a threefold increase in neglect and abuse of children (RWJF, 1993:40). Yet as the data show, few people use cocaine and heroin; alcohol is the greater problem. Between 20 and 25 percent of the population admits that drinking has been a dilemma in their families (RWJF, 1993:40). Regardless of the drug abused, children in such contexts display emotional problems along with a greater likelihood of becoming abusers themselves and acting out in other ways (e.g., sex and crime).

Drug abuse also leads to injury. The consumption of large quantities of drugs over long periods impairs major bodily organs, often sending abusers to emergency rooms and intensive care units of hospitals. Their presence costs a huge amount and strains the nation's medical system. The psychological impact is equally severe. Although the opening lines of this chapter noted that people consume drugs to get high, the word seems rather inadequate at extreme levels of consumption because the consequences are so devastating. Cocaine abusers often become clinically depressed without it or paranoid with it. They also experience formication (note the *m* in the middle of that word). In this hallucination one believes that ants, other insects, or snakes are crawling on or under the skin—which must be a terrifying experience. Such results are not highs. Heroin is different but just as bad. Because frequent users need increasing amounts to obtain the same effect, a casual habit that feels like a caress can become a desperate attempt at avoiding withdrawal. One person dependent on heroin explained the agony of waiting for his dealer: "If sweet oblivion is the initial carrot, savage withdrawal is the enduring stick. In time, the dope fiend is not so much chasing a high as fleeing a debacle" (Shenk, 1995:34).

In addition, drug abuse results in death. Although fatalities from cigarettes have declined significantly over the past three decades, they still account for well over 400,000 each year, due mainly to lung cancer, heart disease, and emphysema (RWJF, 1993). Alcohol leads to about half of all deaths from liver disease and is implicated in nearly half of all auto fatalities. Heroin leads to the transmission of HIV and eventual death because users share infected needles. Death also results from the substances themselves, mainly because of harmful additives and the use of unexpectedly pure or impure drugs. Imagine drinking gin diluted with rubbing alcohol or without knowing its strength: whether it is 5 percent, 55 percent, or 95 percent alcohol. Precisely this situation occurred during Prohibition, and deaths from rotgut booze rose for eleven straight years (Ostrowski, 1989). Today cocaine and its crack derivative induce heart attacks and seizures; heroin overdoses are common. Do not misconstrue this emphasis on the importance of additives and dosage ignorance: Neither cocaine nor heroin is benign. My point is simply that part of their danger stems from their prohibition.

The prohibition of cocaine, heroin, and marijuana also results in other deaths: of innocent bystanders. Some die literally, although the total is impossible to know. What is known is that people who do not use drugs but live in households where they are used are eleven times more likely to be killed as those living in households where these substances are not used (Rivara, 1997). More generally, pervasive violence characterizes the illegal drug market as a new generation of Al Capones competes for turf, protects its profits, and punishes those who fail to pay (Williams, 1990; Sullivan, 1989). Inevitably, onlookers are caught in the middle, sometimes with fatal results. Other bystanders die figuratively, especially children, who experience a sort of death of the soul. Jenner Grade School in Chicago has a shooting drill, and when gunfire in the street becomes heavy (not occurs; becomes heavy!) teachers take students into the hallways until an all-clear bell sounds (Terry, 1992). These children grow up where growing up is an achievement. Yet many develop an overwhelming and pervasive sense of fear and hopelessness, which results in chronic *traumatic stress syndrome* (Kotlowitz, 1991; Garbarino, 1991). They suffer sleep disturbances, eating disorders, and constant physical tension; some cannot get along with others because they are overly aggressive or exhibit quick mood changes, whereas others withdraw into self-imposed isolation or fantasy worlds. As a result, they remain physically alive but become dead inside. How are they to succeed in the classroom or on the job? How are they to nurture their own children? This incalculable tragedy is often portrayed in the media as an unfortunate but inevitable result of drug abuse. In reality, it reflects drug prohibition.

Finally, of course, drugs are associated with crime—in three senses. First, some people are high on drugs when they commit an offense. Alcohol is a major problem, as it induces aggression. At least 18 percent of violent offenders (robbery, assault, rape) had drunk alcohol in 1994 (USDJ, 1995:4).[4] Second, some people commit crimes in order to obtain illegal drugs. The best guess is that abusers steal about $10 billion worth of goods each year (Buckley, 1996). About 25 percent of the street crime in New York City is apparently heroin related (Johnson et al., 1985). Nationwide about one-third of those convicted of burglary committed this offense specifically in order to obtain money for drugs (USDJ, 1995:8). Since these data focus on convictions, my guess is that the percentage is low. In any case, a lot of jewelry and stereos go out people's windows to support drug habits. Third, some people become criminals because they possess or sell illegal drugs. Approximately half of all prisoners in the United States were convicted of possession or low-level dealing to support a habit. Much drug-related crime, then, results from the prohibition of drugs.

The facts and some of the consequences of drugs are now clear. Although uncertainty exists, we know the patterns of drug use and their impact. We also know some of the consequences of drugs and their prohibition. With this knowledge, interesting questions can be asked. Among individuals, what kinds of people use and abuse drugs? Do users and abusers differ? And what are their motives? Structurally, I would like to confront two issues: What factors lead to the high demand for drugs, and why are drugs so plentiful?

Individuals and Drug Use and Abuse

Nearly everyone uses drugs at some point in order to relax and feel good. A few persons, however, abuse drugs. In order to understand such behavior, it is useful to know what personal experiences and characteristics are associated with use and abuse. Unless otherwise indicated, the relationships described here are empirical generalizations. Drawing on the findings, I conclude by exploring the connection among drug abuse, poverty, and alienation. For some people, getting high becomes the focus of their lives; it is important to know why.

Personal Experiences

Unemployment.   When the economy turns bad, people lose their jobs, and some turn to drugs in the aftermath: *Unemployed individuals are more likely to abuse alcohol as well as to use and abuse illegal drugs* (NIDA, 1996). Unemployment is one of the most stressful ordeals people endure (Pearlin et al., 1981). Income declines, daily life becomes unstructured, self-concept falls, and people feel angry. Sometimes drugs make them feel better. Alcohol is the most frequent choice, of course, but unemployed persons are twice as likely to use illegal drugs as those employed.

Family Instability.   Like unemployment, family instability produces stress for members. By *family instability* I refer not only to separation and divorce but also to disorganized families where parental guidance is unclear or nonexistent, abusive families, and families where one or both parents abuse drugs: *The greater the family instability, the more likely are individuals to use and abuse drugs.* In such contexts, members (especially children) feel angry and upset, so they act out: Sex and drugs are the obvious ways of trying to feel better.

School Performance.   School is the primary location for achievement among adolescents, through grades, sports, and other venues. The school—its teachers, counselors, coaches, peers, location—comprises a set of key reference groups. But inevitably some young people are left behind, and they are precisely the individuals most prone to drug use: *The lower the school performance, the more likely an adolescent will use drugs* (Akers, 1992). Low school performance is also related to sexual acting out (Beeghley, 1996a). Seeing a restricted future for themselves, they turn to getting high as a way of hiding from the implications of that reality, a way of feeling better.

Peer Influence. Nearly every teenager has access to drugs, all of which are illegal for them to use. Peers, especially friends, constitute another important reference group for adolescents. This factor is the single best predictor of their drug use: *Adolescents whose friends use drugs are more likely to use drugs themselves* (Akers, 1992). It is rare for young persons to be pressured to use drugs. Rather, they typically choose friendship groups partly in terms of whether the group's members use drugs (Glassner and Loughlin, 1987).

Neighborhood Influence. People living in areas where drug dealing and abuse are pervasive see drugs all around them: *The more widespread and public are drug dealing and abuse in a neighborhood, the more likely are residents to use and abuse drugs.* When drugs are an important part of the environment, as opposed to, say, religious groups or schools or some other socializing influence, those using and dealing drugs become role models. Selling drugs appears to be an avenue to success. It often takes heroic efforts to avoid seeing drugs in positive terms.

Religiosity. The term *religiosity,* remember, refers to a person's identification with and attachment to a faith group. The link between religiosity and alcohol consumption is well known: *Members of faith groups allowing alcohol use are more likely to drink than members of faith groups prohibiting alcohol use* (Beeghley, Bock, and Cochran, 1990). In general, long-term members of faith groups respond positively to the moral messages to which they are exposed. They are, as sociologists like to say, socialized to drink or not to drink.

So far as I know, there are no studies of cigarette use and religiosity. Nor, with the exception of marijuana, is there much research on illegal drugs and religiosity (Goode, 1989:144). Extrapolating from the findings about marijuana, I hypothesize that *the less the religiosity, the more likely is a person to use marijuana, cocaine, or heroin.* All faith groups oppose violating the law, so active participants learn a moral stance opposing the use of illegal drugs. Recall that the proportion of the population consuming these substances is rather low. Both users and abusers tend to be nonreligious.

Personal Characteristics

In addition to their personal experiences, individuals who use drugs tend to have identifiable characteristics.

Age. The relationship of age to drug use is curvilinear in the shape of an upside-down bowl: *As young persons move into adolescence, they be-*

come more likely to use drugs, both legal and illegal. The odds of their using drugs increase during young adulthood (18–25 years), then decline with age (NIDA, 1996). As the importance of family instability and school performance indicates, some drug use among adolescents is a reaction to stress and frustration. Yet almost all teenagers and young adults try drugs, which suggests there is something unique about this period in people's lives. It seems to me that as they wait to grow up, young persons (including college students) do not have much stake in jobs, mortgage payments, and raising kids. So they hang out a lot with their friends, an activity that has always impressed me as being a little like waiting for Godot. In Samuel Beckett's play of that name, remember, Godot never shows up (1954). Boredom results (the play evokes boredom, too, as it is designed to do). In this context, the more adventuresome individuals try drugs. Most do so casually or in a controlled way, although a few become abusers. In effect, drugs constitute a way of making choices by people who can make very few. Once they reach adulthood, where more alternatives become available and the stakes are higher, individuals' drug use declines.

Whether such speculation is correct or not, the relationship between age and drug use carries an important implication. It suggests that the best cure for most drug use is growing older. As people mature, they typically develop ties to the community, as indicated by marriage, full-time jobs (with attendant prestige), home ownership, and participation in churches, clubs, and other organizations. For most individuals, then, the casual and recreational use of drugs—especially when they are illegal—may be part of the process of growing up.

Social Class.   The term *social class*, it will be recalled, refers to people's ranking in the society, as shown by their income, source of income, education, and occupational prestige. The relationship between social class and alcohol consumption is expressed by two contrasting empirical generalizations: *(1) The higher the social class, the more likely is a person to use alcohol. (2) The lower the social class, the more likely is a person to abuse alcohol* (NIDA, 1995). It is probable that these different relationships occur because controlled use of alcohol, as a legal drug, by, say, middle-class persons, is relatively easy. It is also probable that the increased odds of alcohol abuse among the poor reflect their restricted life chances and the alienation that results. I return to this issue just below.

In the past, cigarette use was not related to class; almost everyone smoked. Recent declines in tobacco consumption, however, have occurred mostly in the upper part of the class structure. Thus, the current finding is: *The lower the social class, the more likely is a person to use cigarettes* (NIDA, 1995). The pattern for illegal drugs is similar: *The lower the social class, the more likely is a person to use and abuse marijuana, cocaine, or heroin.* Thus, poor individuals are more likely than any other segment of the population to use and abuse illegal drugs. Why is this so?

Poverty, Alienation, and Drug Abuse

The answer is that poverty leads to alienation, and some alienated people cope by abusing drugs. Such behavior seems irrational from a middle-class standpoint, mainly because individuals who are not poor, such as college students, learn that with initiative they can overcome obstacles. Their behavior is, in the jargon psychologists use, *motivation instigated;* that is, it is a means to an end rather than an end in itself. Such behavior is flexible and adaptive: Actions that help to achieve goals are retained and those that do not are abandoned. These tactics seem rational from the angle of those able to obtain (at least some of) their goals in life—such as admission to a university. This notion of rationality (motivation-instigated behavior) becomes, in fact, a sort of middle-class ideological bludgeon for condemning those who succumb to poverty and drugs: "People should take responsibility for their lives and plan ahead." The reference is to stereotypes, of course, not real persons, who often confront problems without the ability to solve them.[5]

Many impoverished people do not have experiences that lead them to see behavior today as a means toward a future end, even in the short term. For example, poor women have more difficulty preventing pregnancy and obtaining an abortion and therefore must give birth more often than others. In every sphere—looking for housing, seeking a divorce, registering to vote, coping with illness, educating their children—poor people have fewer choices and those choices are less effective. This is why social class is significant for individuals: It dictates their range of choices and their impact (Beeghley, 1996a). I can think of no arena where the poor, faced with a dilemma, have more or more effective (legal) choices than the nonpoor. So poverty means living with pervasive frustration. Thus, poor persons often become alienated; they believe they are powerless to influence their lives. And they are often right.

One response is to persevere, which is what most people do at every class level. But in this country the poor must be especially persevering and heroic in order to survive. Young African American children growing up in housing projects, for example, may not know how to spell "violence," but they know what it means. Going to funerals and counting bullet holes are part of their lives (Kotlowitz, 1991). They do not feel safe. And they are not. Parents, often single mothers, cannot protect their children because anywhere they go can be the wrong place at the wrong time. Teachers cannot either teach or protect their students. Kids die. They witness others die. In such contexts, not everyone can persevere or be heroic. A few, mainly the young, respond by becoming angry; they obtain guns, spray paint, or other implements and subject people and buildings (especially schools) to their displeasure. Although I do not mean to defend either mugging or vandalism, this behavior—which does not appear rational to some—makes sense when seen as a terminal response. It is, to use jargon again, *frustration instigated;* that is, it is not goal oriented or a means to an end but an end in itself. It is neither flexible nor adaptive. Much "senseless" violence simply expresses outrage.

Other poor individuals give up—another form of frustration-instigated behavior—and cope by escaping with drugs. Think about their effects: Drugs bring pleasure; they make people high. Put differently, it can be argued that the consumption of cocaine or heroin or alcohol constitutes a form of self-medication against frustration and helplessness by persons who do not have access to psychotherapy or Prozac. One person described his motivation for abusing crack cocaine in the following way (Skolnick, 1992:155):

> It's not addicting like your body craves it. You're not going to get sick . . . by not smoking. [The] only thing that craves crack is your mind. It's like an illusion. You hit the pipe [and] you are whatever you want to be. . . . Say you're into music and you're basing [using crack], you feel like you *are* James Brown or Stevie Wonder or Michael Jackson.

At least for a short time. In a world where occupational success is a fantasy, one might as well get high and, if possible, stay high. This is, of course, self-destructive behavior. In addition to getting high, the odds of getting arrested are high—and that is not a fantasy. Sellers and users of illegal drugs spend a significant amount of time in jail (Reuter, 1992). Death, whether from violence or from the drugs themselves, is also a possibility as is the loss of jobs and loved ones. Again, this behavior makes sense when it is seen as frustration instigated, even though it does not seem rational from a middle-class angle.

Yet despite middle-class value judgments, surprising parallels exist between use of legally prescribed and prohibited substances. The former are used by those with choices, the latter by those without choices. Consider Prozac. Millions of people use it to deal with their frustration simply by obtaining a prescription from a physician (often without engaging in therapy). Consider Ritalin. Production of this drug rose 500 percent from 1991 to 1996. Although Ritalin was designed to deal with a condition called attention deficit disorder, millions of children and, increasingly, adults use this drug simply because they are frustrated and depressed (Kolata, 1996). Thus, it appears that middle-class people use legal drugs in the same way and for the same reasons as impoverished persons use illegal drugs. Whether from Prozac or crack, Ritalin or marijuana, the feelings that result are similarly artificial. Again, the United States is a "drug republic." Why is this so?

Social Structure and Drug Use

"This is your brain," the television announcer intones while the screen shows a fresh egg. "This is your brain on drugs," he continues over a picture of a frying egg: "Say no to drugs." This commercial was designed to reduce demand for marijuana. It was a minor episode in an eighty-year War on Drugs that began with passage of the Harrison Act in 1914. Although there is no way to evaluate the impact of a specific ten-second spot, it probably had little effect. One problem is that fried eggs taste good; people like them. Another problem was the ad's moralistic approach: It assumed that consuming any drug in any amount is evil and starts people on a slippery slope to abuse. The assumption is simply wrong: People know that use does not necessarily lead to abuse. More important, such appeals get in the way of understanding the riddle drugs pose. In order to explore this dilemma, I deal with the two structural questions posed previously. First, what factors lead to the high demand for drugs? Second, why are these substances so plentiful, despite their prohibition? The answers must go beyond scare tactics epitomized by "just say no" commercials.

The Demand for Drugs

The prohibition of drugs is designed to prevent use and abuse, the goal is a "drug-free society." Yet the data show that millions of people will not "say no," that a high demand for drugs exists. This fact suggests that the desire to get high is built into the social structure. My hypothesis is: *The high demand for drugs in the United States reflects (1) societal affluence, (2) the value placed on pleasure, and (3) the high rate of poverty.* This hypothesis contains a paradox, of course, since it asserts that both affluence and poverty lead to the high demand for drugs. But this seeming contradiction can be resolved.

Societal Affluence. It takes money to buy drugs, which is why most Third World nations usually do not have problems with them. For example, one study of 152 countries showed that those with low rates of drug abuse tended to be poor, developing societies (Smart and Murray, 1982). The more affluent, industrialized nations, such as those considered here, display much higher levels of income and much more drug use and abuse (Smart and Murray, 1983). The reason for this finding must be speculative, but a logical account can be offered: Lots of people have lots of money to spend.

TABLE 6.1   Alcohol Consumption and Gross Domestic Product, per Person, per Year, Selected Countries, 1994

	Liters of Pure Alcohol per Person	Gross Domestic Product per Person
United States	6.6	$24,300
Brazil	3.4	2,500
Peru	1.1	3,000
Thailand	.6	5,500
Morocco	.3	2,500

NOTES: Alcohol data for Morocco refer to beer and wine only. Gross domestic product for Peru, Thailand, and Morocco is for 1993.

SOURCES: NTC Publications (1995:21); USBC (1995e:856); WAB (1995:381).

The association between societal affluence and the rate of drug use is illustrated in Table 6.1, which juxtaposes liters of pure alcohol consumed by each person with the per capita *gross domestic product* (GDP), the total value of all goods and services produced in a nation. The table shows that people in the United States, with one of the highest GDPs in the world, also drink a lot. In poorer nations, by contrast, people drink much less, simply because little money is available to purchase alcohol.

The same point applies to illegal drugs: It takes money to buy them, and unless lots of people have lots of it, not much demand for these products will exist. Thus, unless a Third World nation becomes a center for drug production (as with cocaine in Peru), demand for drugs will be low simply because few people can pay for them. In contrast, demand is high in the United States, where people do have money. A common scene in large cities is for affluent persons to exit the freeway into impoverished areas they would otherwise avoid: centers of the illegal drug trade. They make their purchase and get back on the freeway without leaving their cars. The entire process can take as little as five minutes. Although other ways of acquiring illegal substances exist, this example suggests how easy it is for those with money to buy them.

The Value Placed on Pleasure.   Affluence alone, however, does not produce a high demand for drugs; it merely increases people's choices. Values guide choices. *Work-centered values* dictate that people should work hard, organize their lives methodically, delay immediate gratification, and earn money (Weber, 1905). Success is defined in these terms, and everyone is expected to seek it (Merton, 1968a). It follows that people ought to act responsibly with their money; they should save it, invest it, donate it to worthy causes, repair their houses, and send their children to college, among other conscientious uses. And most people do just these sorts of things; they see themselves and are seen by others as responsible and level-headed. But few people work all the time, and besides, one of the benefits of a modicum of success is to have money to spend on pleasure. *Leisure-centered values* dictate that people should pursue self-expression, enjoy pleasure, and consume goods and services (Campbell, 1987). The contradiction between these values is usually resolved by keeping the settings separate. "It's Miller time," as the old beer commercial said, marking the passage from work to leisure, production to consumption, duty to pleasure. In fact, the mood swings provided by drugs, usually alcohol, both parallel and symbolize the transition (Gusfield, 1987).

For some, this transition occurs on vacation; they might visit Yosemite or another national park. For others, it is a hobby; they learn photography, go to the movies or fishing, listen to compact discs, practice yoga, play softball, and the like. Yet although these activities do bring pleasure, they are safe. A few people want more. They want risk. So instead of admiring El Capitan in Yosemite, a few people climb it. Others go hang gliding and skydiving, activities that provide a thrill absent from daily life (Lyng, 1990). It is normal for even level-headed people to seek adventure, even danger, and purchasing and using illegal drugs constitutes a walk on the wild side. A clandestine buy, whether it means pulling off the freeway or a private meeting in a dormitory room, adds excitement and adventure to life. Can I get away with it? Will I be arrested or mugged? Then comes the pleasure. So the high is twofold: from both acquiring and using illegal drugs.

The demand for this high on the part of casual and controlled users now seems intelligible, for it reflects the combination of affluence and pleasure-centered values characteristic of Western societies. This angle of vision suggests that the demand for drugs constitutes a conventional value: the pursuit of pleasure during leisure time. It is thus intrinsic to modern life. In such a context, it is hard to see how a "war on drugs" can be successful.

The High Rate of Poverty. I showed previously how alienation and poverty can lead to drug use and abuse. When the level of analysis shifts to account for the structural source of the relatively high demand for drugs among poor people, it turns out that they share conventional values.

Poor neighborhoods are often characterized by anomie. As described before, the term refers to a disjunction between conventional values, such as economic success, and the legitimate means to achieve them (Merton, 1968a). The poor, like everyone else, learn work-oriented values, yet they find that good jobs are hard to obtain, since few businesses locate in impoverished areas. This problem is especially acute in some African American neighborhoods (Wilson, 1987). There are sections in every large city where most adults are unemployed. Moreover, these districts are often disorganized in other ways as well: They have inadequate schools, social services, police protection, and infrastructure. Inevitably, some people living in such miasmic environments adapt; they come to terms with the fact that achieving success in the conventional way, through hard work at a job, is unlikely. Although several strategies exist, I mention only two, both of which lead to a relatively high demand for drugs.[6]

First, some people adapt by retreating from the search for occupational success; that is, they abandon work-centered values in favor of leisure-centered values. Drugs provide meaning and purpose to their lives. Despite stereotypes of drug users and abusers, their days are full. Their goals simply deviate from the majority. Thus, heroin abusers have been described as always "taking care of business"; they "are actively engaged in meaningful activities and relationships seven days a week" as they seek to obtain their high (Preble and Casey, 1969:2; Faupel, 1991). For abusers, drugs constitute a different lifestyle; the term, you may recall, refers to people's way of living, as indicated by their consumption habits, use of leisure time, and fundamental choices and values. In a nonanomic setting, people balance work- and leisure-centered values, their daily lives containing a mixture of the two. In an anomic setting, however, such a balance becomes difficult, and some people retreat into drug use and abuse.

A second way of adapting is to seek occupational success in innovative ways, one of which is selling drugs (Sullivan, 1989; Williams, 1990). This strategy turns an anomic setting to one's favor by combining work-oriented values with unconventional means. It is not an easy task, requiring the skills of an adventure capitalist (Weber, 1905). Street dealers must establish a reputation for being reliable and honest, both with their suppliers and customers. Dealers must also develop strategies to avoid arrest and robberies. These chores take administrative skills, since large amounts of money must be kept track of; a staff of runners, lookouts, and others must supervised; and negotiations with suppliers, competitors, and regulatory agencies (corrupt police) must occur. These activities require hard work, methodical lives, and delayed gratification. Thus, dealing mimics ordinary job careers. In an industry with an estimated $49 billion in yearly sales (ONDCP, 1994), beginners start out in entry-level positions, and as in other occupations, most do not make it—in this case, many consume the product. Those who succeed, how-ever, reap rewards; they become the Bill Gates of poor neighborhoods, which is to say they have a steady income in a context where few others do. In one study, for example, street dealers who worked four hours per day earned an average of $2,000 per month (Reuter et al., 1990). In an anomic setting, dealers seek a conventional goal: economic success.

It is important, however, not to romanticize impoverished people who abuse or deal illegal drugs. Their lives are not glamorous but desperate; they confront each day with heartache and trauma. As one person explained (Inciardi, 1986:162):

> You grow up in a place where everything is a real mess. Your father's a thief, your mother's a whore, your kid sister gets herself some new clothes by fucking the landlord's son, your brother's in the joint, your boyfriend gets shot tryin' to pull down a store, and everybody else around you is either smokin' dope, shooting stuff, taking pills, stealing with both hands, or workin' on their backs, or all of the above. All of a sudden you find that you're sweet sixteen and you're doin' the same things.

"Growing up in a place where everything is a real mess" is a good, practical definition of anomie. In such a context, the demand for drugs will be high. And so will their rate of use.

Social structures determine people's range of options. In an affluent society, some of those with money will dabble in illegal drugs. They constitute one among many ways of seeking thrills. A few will abuse them, but most will use them in controlled ways, primarily because they have so many other legitimate choices. At the same time, in an affluent society with a lot of poverty, those with fewer choices are more likely to use, abuse, and deal drugs. So demand will be high. It is hard to see how a "war on drugs" can be won in such a context. In fact, it has not been won.

The Supply of Drugs

It is an economic truism that supply rises to demand. Yet, historically, government policy has been to prohibit drugs in order to curtail demand and reduce consumption. This strategy has not worked. In fact, prohibition has the opposite effect: It spurs both drug trade and drug consumption. Vast manufacturing and smuggling networks exist so that people's desire for drugs can be satisfied (Inciardi, 1986; Warner, 1986). Drugs are easily obtained in this country. The United States, it is said, consumes 60 percent of the world's supply of illegal substances (Goode, 1989). That is a lot of dope. One must simply know where to get it. College students typically find that they can obtain drugs rather easily, through a friend (or a friend of a friend). This experience is confirmed by surveys showing that drugs are readily available in any city (Reuter, 1992). Why is this so? My hypothesis is: *The plentiful supply of illegal drugs in the United States reflects (1) the failure of eradication efforts, (2) economic development in producing nations, (3) open borders, and (4) the limits of law enforcement.*

Failure of Eradication Efforts. Eradication tries to stop drug cultivation in other nations, a strategy that has never worked. For example, marijuana eradication efforts in Colombia in the 1970s led to expanded production in Mexico. Eradication of marijuana production there led to the rise of a U.S. industry operating indoors (Pollan, 1995). Indeed, the domestic marijuana industry is a creation of the War on Drugs. Similarly, at various times Turkey, Mexico, Southeast Asia, and Southwest Asia have supplied the U.S. heroin market. Thus, experience shows that a push-down/pop-up phenomenon occurs: When eradication efforts succeed in one country, others fill the void (Nadelman, 1988). Moreover, profits rise with economic development.

Economic Development in Producing Nations. Most drug-producing nations are in the Third World. The paradox of economic progress in these areas is that it makes drug export easier. My example comes from the construction of the Pan-American highway through the jungles and mountains of Peru in the early 1970s (Inciardi, 1986:73). Financed by a grant from the World Bank, the highway was designed to stimulate economic development by reducing transit costs. It did, and progress resulted. The unintended consequence, however, was that cocaine became more readily available at much cheaper prices. More generally, infrastructure improvements facilitate the transformation of the economy in Third World nations. These changes include communication systems, roads, airports, and seaports. Yet these same changes also facilitate drug smuggling.

Economic development combines with the failure of eradication to ensure that supplies of illegal substances are available to meet U.S. demand. Then the problem becomes smuggling the stuff into this country. This task, it turns out, is easy.

Open Borders. The United States must have open borders in order to stimulate legal trade and allow citizens to travel freely. In fact, open borders have become official government policy since passage of the North American Free Trade Agreement (NAFTA) in 1995. NAFTA is supposed to encourage economic expansion in the countries taking part, an outcome that remains uncertain. What is certain, however, is that it facilitates importation of illegal drugs.

Nonetheless, government agencies try to prevent drugs from entering the country. For example, the United States seized about 752,000 pounds of marijuana, 238,000 pounds of cocaine, and 3,000 pounds of heroin in 1994 (USDJ, 1995:12). The government commonly guesses that it intercepts 10–20 percent of the drugs coming into the United States. Do not, however, believe this figure because no one really knows how much is smuggled in (Warner, 1986). But even if this guess is accepted, increasing drug seizures would have little effect on retail cost. For example, in 1997 it was estimated that a pound of cocaine with a street value of $20,000 or more costs only about $1,200 to produce and smuggle into the United States (Wren, 1997). Hence, increasing drug seizures would not reduce consumption much, if at all. Realistically, however, stopping drugs from coming in by plane, boat, and foot is impossible. Of the 400,000 people who illegally walk across the Mexican–U.S. border each year, the small number carrying cocaine are lost in the mass (Skolnick, 1992). The same principle holds for other modes of transportation. Drug seizures simply indicate that supplies are plentiful.

Drug interdiction, however, carries unintended consequences (Skolnick, 1992). One is to increase drug smuggling. This paradox occurs because interdiction efforts eliminate the less able smugglers and leave the market to the more able. Another unintended result is to change the drugs supplied to consumers. Thus, the emphasis on reducing marijuana imports during the 1980s led smugglers to a more dangerous drug: cocaine. Marijuana was transported in hay-bale-sized bundles that were difficult to hide or dispose of. Cocaine, in contrast, is conveyed in brick-sized (or smaller) quantities. It is not accidental that the amount of cocaine that appeared in the United States rose during this period. A third unintended result is to boost domestic production. In effect, interdiction provided tariff protection for U.S. marijuana growers and distributors (Falco, 1994). Protected from foreign competition, the industry has expanded and kept prices—and profits—high.

The Limits of Law Enforcement.   Arrest and prosecution focus on punishing those who produce, sell, and use drugs. For example, the Drug Enforcement Administration captured and destroyed 393 million marijuana plants and confiscated 134,000 pounds of cocaine and 1,500 pounds of heroin in 1994 (USDJ, 1995:11). Yet like the "body counts" during the war in Vietnam, these figures are meaningless. Once again, seizures merely point up how plentiful are supplies.

In addition, thousands of people are arrested and jailed each year for drug offenses. Nearly two-thirds of federal prisoners were convicted of drug-related crimes (USDJ, 1995:21). State-level data are similar. Thus, like interdiction, law enforcement produces tangible results. This "body count" of prisoners, however, has unintended consequences that reinforce the drug trade. First, locking up dealers produces job openings. It is a little like jailing a corporate executive; the combination of good pay and an appealing job (especially in contexts where there are few other choices) means that someone will move into the office before long (Shenk, 1995:35). Second, putting people in jail provides them with job training. Jails serve a purpose normally associated with academic or business conventions: an opportunity for networking with like-minded people and learning the trade (Skolnick, 1992). Third, the threat of jail produces scientific advances that stimulate the drug trade. In the early 1980s, the government launched a program it called CAMP, the Campaign Against Marijuana Planting, which used aerial surveillance and other methods to capture growers. The result was a horticultural revolution as production moved indoors, where high-potency plants can be produced in a short time under carefully controlled conditions (Pollan, 1995). Law enforcement does not and cannot limit consumption.

The conclusion is clear: Drugs are like other commodities in that supply rises to meet demand. Trying to restrict supplies has the opposite effect. I cannot imagine a scenario in which the War on Drugs can be won. This result seems like an unsolvable riddle. Ah, the riddle. As Sophocles tells the tale, when Oedipus neared Thebes he was stopped by the Sphinx and asked the question. Oedipus replied that the answer is human beings, because they walk on their hands and feet when young, on two feet in midlife, and with a cane or staff in old age. Alas, the correct answer caused the Sphinx to go mad and throw herself off the rock to her death. This extreme response typifies our approach to drugs. Perhaps some moderation of our polices might be more useful (Musto, 1996).

Implications

Drugs scare the public, many of whom fail to recognize alcohol and cigarettes, Ritalin and Prozac, even caffeine (see note 3) as psychoactive substances. In addition, drug use is usually equated with abuse. The public ignores that most people consume drugs in a casual or controlled manner. Drugs are thus linked with stigmatized people engaged in immoral behavior. Deviance, Emile Durkheim taught, produces a sense of solidarity among those who conform, strengthening their sense of morality and probity (1893). The result, in the case of drugs, is to draw an artificial boundary between them and us. Even though most drug users and abusers are white, these considerations have overtones for the racial and ethnic divisions in our society.

Historically, drug policy has served as a cover for prejudice. For example, underlying the Harrison Act of 1914 was anxiety about Chinese

American men using opiates to lure white women into having sexual intercourse and cocaine-crazed African American men assaulting white women (Sandmeyer, 1939; Morgan, 1978; Musto, 1973). There was also a fear of a cocaine-induced "black rebellion" against segregation. Similar phobias underlay the Marijuana Tax Act of 1938: It was said the drug made Mexican Americans violent (Becker, 1963; Dickson, 1968). The bizarre quality of these fears can be seen by the transformation of the "problem" posed by marijuana in the 1960s. Instead of being a "killer weed," it was said to be a "dropout drug," producing a decline in achievement motivation among the young and causing them to be unpatriotic by opposing the Vietnam War (Himmelstein, 1983). I know this last example sounds peculiar, but having matured during this period, I can tell you that drugs were blamed for many of the ills of the decade. And that is the pattern: Drug policy symbolizes other fears people have.

This pattern continues today (Jones, 1995). Under federal sentencing guidelines, persons convicted of possessing crack cocaine without intent to sell are sentenced to mandatory minimum five-year prison terms, often longer. In contrast, persons convicted of possessing powdered cocaine without intent to sell are sentenced to a maximum one-year jail term, often less. It is now well known that nearly all those convicted of crack possession are African American, whereas many of those convicted of powdered cocaine possession are white. More generally, the consequences of drug prohibition described earlier—deaths and injuries from impure drugs, the destruction of neighborhoods and deaths of innocent bystanders, crime—fall disproportionately on minority groups. It thus appears that current laws continue to go after those perceived to be the "dangerous classes." One must ask whether drug laws reflect the prejudice of the majority of the population.

This issue is important because although there are no easy solutions to the drug problem, alternatives exist. In my judgment, we need to begin by recognizing two simple facts: The demand for illegal drugs is high and is likely to remain so, and supplies are going to remain plentiful. Hence, all drug policy choices are really about how these substances will be distributed to the public and who will control and benefit from their disbursement. Although the goal of reducing consumption in a humane way, at a low cost, and with minimum disruption is laudable (I believe in it), it will occur in this context. Given this reality, I would like to suggest four choices as topics for discussion.

One choice is simply to legalize marijuana, cocaine, and heroin. This strategy would eliminate the negative consequences that follow from keeping drugs illegal. Deaths and injuries due to impurities would fall. Profits would stay in the country and be taxed. Urban neighborhoods would become less violent. Other benefits would probably ensue (Ostrowski, 1989). Even if use rates went up, it is possible that people would consume less dangerous drugs rather than alcohol and cigarettes. Moreover, if legalization were coupled with honest educational campaigns and radical increases in the number of treatment facilities for those who wished to stop abusing drugs, overall use rates might not rise. The long-term impact of the campaign against cigarette smoking is a good model of what can happen. Note the words "possible," "might not," and "can happen" in the previous three sentences. The level of use in a context where these drugs are legal cannot be known.

A second choice is to keep marijuana, cocaine, and heroin illegal but arrest fewer people and redirect resources to education and treatment. The education must be honest and emphasize family, school, and community involvement. There is no reason to believe that "just say no" strategies affect drug use decisions. Treatment facilities must be widespread and easily available. Treatment is cost effective. Outpatient programs cost $2,000–$4,000 per person each year, compared to $35,000 for keeping someone in jail (Falco, 1994:138). But expectations about treatment must be realistic. It is not like taking out an appendix: here today and gone tomorrow. It is more like treating someone with high blood pressure: a continuing process that takes time (Falco, 1994:108). Moreover, "successful" treatment does not always mean abstinence. Just as people with high blood pressure may eat foods they should not, those in treatment sometimes use drugs—but less often and in smaller amounts than before. They also commit fewer crimes.

A third option would be to decriminalize drug use, retain all the laws against smuggling and distributing drugs, and emphasize education and treatment. With regard to marijuana, for example, it could be legal to grow your own supply but illegal to sell it. Given the hardiness of this plant, the illegal drug industry would decline greatly with this simple step. Again, I am simply proposing an alternative that is worth discussing.

A final option is more indirect: Reduce the level of poverty in the United States by increasing employment opportunities. This strategy would be designed to get at the underlying causal factors producing a high level of drug use and abuse. Those who are most successful at getting off drugs have jobs and other external supports (Falco, 1994). The more people have hope, stability, something to do, and meaning in their lives, the less likely they are to retreat or seek alternative means to success. It should be recognized, however, that achieving this goal would not be easy.

Such alternatives are rarely discussed. It has been said that you can outlaw political corruption but you cannot make it unpopular. Drugs, I fear, are similar. The riddle lives.

Notes

1. The reason is not hard to fathom. Most users report feelings of mild euphoria and relaxation. They also describe a keener sense of sound. (I guess that is why users often play music.) Finally, they experience a dry mouth and increased appetite. (Perhaps that is why ice cream stores flourish near college campuses, even in the north, even in winter.)

2. The data for the United Kingdom and the United States come from nationwide random samples (CSO, 1995:127; NIDA, 1995:29). Those from other nations refer to male adults, aged 35–64, living in various urban areas during the mid-1980s (WHO, 1996:185).

3. So, of course, do ordinary people who do not think of themselves as drug dependent. When I wake up in the morning, I want a cup of tea with its hit of caffeine. And the later it gets before obtaining my drug, the more withdrawal symptoms set in: a headache and nervous anxiety. The millions of people taking Ritalin and Prozac each morning are also dependent on drugs.

4. I say "at least" because whether the offender consumed alcohol is only known about half the time.

5. This section reflects the influence of Norman Maier's classic work, *Frustration: The Study of Behavior Without a Goal* (1949). I elaborated on the issues raised here in my *Living Poorly in America* (Beeghley, 1983:117–31).

6. The following paragraphs use (some would say abuse) Robert K. Merton's essay "Social Structure and Anomie" (1968a).

Recommended Reading

Akers, Ronald I.. *Drugs, Alcohol, and Society* (Belmont, CA: Wadsworth, 1992).

Falco, Mathea. *The Making of a Drug Free America* (New York: Times Books, 1994).

Rorabaugh, William J. *The Alcoholic Republic* (New York: Oxford University Press, 1979).

Skolnick, Jerome. "Rethinking the Drug Problem," *Daedalus* 121(Summer, 1992):133–60.

Williams, Terry M. *The Cocaine Kids: The Inside Story of a Teenage Drug Ring* (Reading, MA: Addison-Wesley, 1990).

7 *Homicide*

Outline of Chapter 7

This chapter was coauthored by Terry Danner, Saint Leo College.

When people from the United States visit Europe, they are often surprised at how safe they feel as they wander about. Basketball player Charles Barkley may have felt this way during the 1992 Olympics when he observed: "I miss crime, murder. I haven't heard about any good shootings or stabbings. I miss Philadelphia" (Messner and Rosenfeld, 1997:17). Behind his sarcasm, of course, lay fear. Unlike the Europeans, Americans have an inordinate fear of crime; it is a national obsession. About 42 percent of the public say they are afraid to walk alone near their home at night (GSS, 1996). Minority persons are especially afraid. About three-fourths of African Americans are "very concerned" about being a victim of a crime (BJS, 1996:127).

For some, this fear is realistic. The United States is a violent society, with a homicide rate much higher than that of other Western nations. There were 432 murders in Philadelphia in 1995, but only 113 in all of Sweden in 1993 (FBI, 1996:124; WHO, 1996:525). And Sweden has one of the highest homicide rates in Western Europe. For others, especially middle-class whites, this fear is not realistic. Most crime, particularly the street crime that frightens people, is concentrated spatially and economically: The poor tend to prey upon the poor—with devastating consequences. Because of their high level of poverty and the legacy of discrimination against African Americans, the impact is even greater on them.

Alex Kotlowitz portrays the lives of two African American children living in a public housing project in Chicago (1991:9).

> The boy and the girl were on their way to a nearby shopping strip, where Lafeyette planned to buy radio headphones with $8.00 he had received as a birthday gift.
> Suddenly, gunfire erupted. The frightened children fell to the ground. "Hold your head down!" Lafeyette snapped, as he covered Dede's head with her pink nylon jacket. If he hadn't physically restrained her, she might have sprinted for home, a dangerous action when the gangs started warring. "Stay down," he ordered the trembling girl.
> [After] the shooting subsided, Lafeyette held Dede's hand as they cautiously crawled through the dirt toward home. When they finally made it inside, all but fifty cents of Lafeyette's birthday money had trickled from his pockets.

As Kotlowitz describes it, the children's summer opened and closed in the same way, with gunfire—and murder. This ordeal is common in many neighborhoods, especially where drugs are sold.

Homicide refers to human death purposely and illegally inflicted by another. Although it is an extreme act, its violence typifies other offenses (such as assault, rape, and robbery) and, to a lesser degree, predatory property crimes (such as burglary and arson). So even though less common than these other offenses, murder serves as a metaphor for crime in the United States.

Dimensions of Homicide

And what a metaphor! In 1996 about 22,900 people were murdered in this country, about eight for every 100,000 persons (NCHS, 1997a:14). Most victims were young males; about half were African American. In addition, surveys show that about 540,000 people were robbed and 1 million assaulted (BJS, 1997b).[1] No wonder most people fear crime. It is useful, however, to put this fear into historical and international perspective.

Historical Dimensions

In the Middle Ages, murder and mayhem were frequent. The annual homicide rate in England has been estimated at twenty per 100,000 persons (Spierenburg, 1994). This figure is conservative; other reasonable guesses are much higher (Gurr, 1989:32). Such data along with descriptions of daily life at that time suggest a society in which men (rarely women) were easily and often provoked and unrestrained in the brutality with which they attacked one another. Over time, however, a steady decline in the murder rate occurred: By the fifteenth century the English homicide rate dropped to fifteen per 100,000; by the sixteenth to seven; by the seventeenth to four; by the eighteenth to two; and by the nineteenth to one—about where it stands today. Other Western European nations displayed a similar pattern. The reason, according to Ted Robert Gurr, is that modernization has sensitized people to violence and led them to exclude it as much as possible from daily life.[2]

But the United States is different. Figure 7.1 displays data for this country since 1900. Interpreting these data, however, requires great caution. There is a scene in an old Marx brothers movie where Groucho is trying to con someone: "Who are you going to believe," he asks, "me, or your own eyes?" In Figure 7.1, your eyes may be deceived, especially for the years 1900–1933, and we want you to believe us. This is not a con: The increase shown for these years is much overstated.

Three factors contribute to the overestimate (Gurr, 1989; Lane, 1989). First, coroners and the police became more adept at distinguishing between fatalities due to natural and unnatural causes. They thus identified murders that had previously gone unidentified. Second, police

Rate per 100,000 Persons

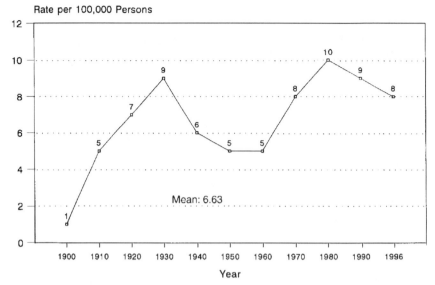

FIGURE 7.1   U.S. Homicide Rate, 1900–1996
NOTE: Because I present the data by decade, I omit some short-term fluctuations.
The rise from 1900 to 1930 is overstated; see explanation in the text.
SOURCE: NCHS (1996d:4).

forces increased in size and efficiency, especially divisions devoted to violent crime. Hence, murders that would have been unknown or ignored previously were now counted. Third, in the years just after the automobile came into use, deaths in accidents were often defined as murder, thereby raising the count. Today they are called involuntary manslaughter. So the rising homicide between 1900–1933 is overstated. But some increase occurred; the United States is, indeed, different. After all, guns were handy and smaller (thus more easily concealed), and the population was dominated by immigrants, many of them young males who found it hard to obtain jobs. Overall, then, as Gurr concludes, "homicide and most other violent crimes declined in the 1880s and 1890s, then increased somewhat (how much remains uncertain) during the first thirty years of the twentieth century" (1989:41).

Figure 7.1 provides a more accurate statistical portrait for the years after 1930. The homicide rate was stable, between five and six per 100,000, from 1940 to 1960 or so. It rose spectacularly after that, however: It was ten in 1980, fell to nine in 1990, and rose again to ten in 1992 (not shown in the figure). It has declined since that time, however, to about eight in 1996. Even given the recent dip, the U.S. level of homicide is very high, as can be seen when the United States is compared to other nations.

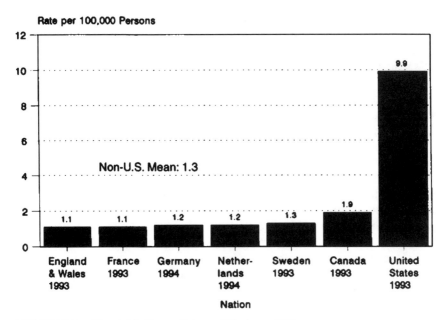

FIGURE 7.2   Homicide Rates, Selected Nations, 1990s
SOURCE: WHO (1996).

International Dimensions

Figure 7.2 presents murder rates for eight Western industrial nations. All of them display a low incidence, around one homicide per 100,000 persons. In comparison, the U.S. rate is nearly ten times higher. Thus, even when U.S. rates are low, as in the years 1940–1960, and even when they are declining, as in recent years, the base is very high. The United States is a much more violent society.

Consequences of Homicide

The impact of all this violence—not only murder but also robbery, assault, and rape—is enormous. We focus on three consequences.

(1) The most important effect is that people who should be alive are now dead. Since murder victims tend to be younger than those who die of other causes (about half are under age 30), the loss of "potential life" is high (BJS, 1996). Homicide is the twelfth leading cause of death in the United States, but the relative youth of victims means it is the fourth leading cause of the loss of potential life. And some segments of U.S. society bear the brunt of this slaughter more than others. Homicide is the

leading cause of death among young black men (Roth and Moore, 1995). Thus, even though the rate has declined recently, the 20,000 or so murders represent a tremendous scale of carnage, year after year. And society loses: inventions not made, works of art not finished, talent left bleeding in the street. There is a void where people used to be.

(2) In addition, many of those who survive are also victims, especially children, and the impact of their trauma affects the rest of us over the long term. About 45 percent of first and second graders in Washington, D.C., have witnessed a mugging, 31 percent a shooting, and 39 percent have seen a dead body in the street (APA, 1993). In some public housing complexes, every child knows a victim of homicide (Garbarino, 1992). These children do not make up monsters, and parents need not worry about violence on television; the streets provide the real thing. The title of Alex Kotlowitz's book suggests the impact of such experiences: *There Are No Children Here*. In the quotation earlier, the two children crawled home—a survival skill that does not bode well for their future. In the book, LaJoe Rivers says that her sons, Lafeyette and Pharaoh, have "seen too much to be children" (1991:x). Thus, when asked what he wanted to be, 10-year-old Lafeyette replied: "If I grow up, I'd like to be a bus driver."

"If I grow up." The wounds that follow from exposure to violence are rarely so obvious. They resemble Snowden's secret in Joseph Heller's novel *Catch-22* (1961). Snowden, a bomber navigator, seems to suffer from a minor wound. But when Captain Yossarian opens Snowden's flak jacket, he finds a hideous and indeed fatal injury. Similarly, the wounds of children, cheated of their childhood by violence, are deep and long-lasting, often fatal. Lodged in the psyche, such wounds haunt children, destroying their adulthood and redounding to the entire society.

The experience of trauma smashes the fundamental assumptions people make about themselves and their world, especially their sense of trust (Janoff-Bulman, 1997). Most people assume that the world is meaningful and benevolent and that they are decent and competent. When these (unconscious) beliefs are shattered, victims' inner security crumbles, and the world seems malevolent and meaningless. Most people manage to rebuild their lives; some cannot, especially when trauma occurs over and over. The impact can be described on a continuum. Although this strategy simplifies, it provides a way to highlight the way many victims of pervasive trauma react. At one end, some people retreat from society. They may abuse drugs. They may develop various forms of psychosis or clinical depression. You may recall from Chapter 3 that the term does not mean simply feeling bad. Depressed persons become immobilized, unable to function. This is probably one reason some poor parents neglect their children. Regardless of the form of retreat, it affects not only these individuals but everyone else as well. At the other end of the continuum, some people become enraged and violent themselves. Some belong to gangs who wage war on each other and anyone else who gets in the way. Others are freelance predators. Their numbers are unknown, but thousands exist in every city (Huff, 1991). Their impact on daily life is profound.

In *Do or Die*, Léon Bing talks to Faro, who is 17 years old, illiterate, and homeless (1991:40). His mother died from a drug overdose. His 8-year-old brother was killed during a holdup at a convenience store. He has been neglected all his life. Faro belongs to a gang.

> "See them two dudes? . . . I'm gonna look crazy at 'em. You watch what they do." He turns away from me. . . . The driver, sensing that someone is looking at him, glances over at my car. His eyes connect with Faro's, widen for an instant. Then he breaks the contact, looks down, looks away. And there is no mistaking what I saw there in his eyes: It was fear. Whatever he saw in Faro's face, he wasn't about to mess with it.
>
> Faro giggles and turns back toward me. He looks the same as he did before: a skinny, slightly goofy-looking kid. . . . I ask Faro to "look crazy" for me. He simply narrows his eyes. That's all. He narrows his eyes, and he looks straight at me and everything about his face shifts and changes, as if by some trick of time-lapse photography. It becomes a nightmare face, and it is a scary thing to see. It tells you that if you return his stare, if you challenge this kid, you'd better be ready to stand your ground. His look tells you that he doesn't care about anything, not your life and not his.

"Not your life and not his." Such youths, raised in violence, represent damaged, lost children; they are victims. Yet underlying the rage is an attempt to seek control and meaning in life. Where else but in a gang are children like Faro going to get love, attention, an income (through crime), and status? In a twisted, upside-down world, an anomic social structure, gang-related violence is a predictable consequence of widespread poverty. In a way, gang members are simply pursuing conventional goals in unconventional ways.[3] And everyone is affected. After all, if they grow up, children become adults.

(3) Finally, the economic costs of homicide are great. Consider Faro's little brother. We will call him Joey. Although we do not know how he was killed, it is easy to imagine the economic costs. At the first report of the robbery, a police dispatcher sent officers along with a team of paramedics. At this point, expenses began mounting that will be paid by taxes. Perhaps Joey was still alive when the paramedics arrived. These days trauma victims are usually transported to a hospital by ambulance (or sometimes by helicopter). This costs more money. The trauma team at the hospital did their best, but Joey died. In 1992 U.S. hospitals treated more than 75,000 gun injuries related to intentional assault. In about one-fourth of those incidents, the victims died of their wounds. It has

been estimated that violent crime in general (homicide, assault, robbery, and rape) causes 14 percent of the U.S. medical spending on the treatment of injuries (BJS, 1996; NIJ, 1996). This huge outlay continues year after year.

Even as Joey was being taken to the hospital, detectives were beginning an inquiry. It is plausible that uniformed officers, including a specially trained K-9 unit, were tracking the suspect. All this work costs money. Assume the suspect was subsequently arrested. Reports, interviews, expert witnesses, and depositions occurred. This work includes an assistant state attorney and staff and a public defender and staff. A medical examiner does an autopsy to determine the exact cause of death. The suspect is incarcerated, fed, supervised, and given medical treatment while awaiting court hearings. Expenses mount each day. On average about 65 percent of the 20,000 homicides result in an arrest, which means costs described here must be multiplied by about 13,000. About one-third of all homicide prosecutions lead to a jury trial, and nearly all defendants (93 percent) go to prison either as the result of a trial or plea bargain. This leads to more long-term outlays (BJS, 1996:393, 447). For example, in Florida, those sentenced to prison for homicide average ten years in prison at a cost of about $17,000 per year (FDC, 1996:29).

The impact of murder on friends and relatives of victims also must be considered, and these redound to the larger society as well. Their trauma often leads to drug abuse, other crimes, and mental health problems. It has been estimated that about one-fifth of expenditures on mental health care is due to violent crime. In addition, of course, there are funeral expenses, and a family may be without a breadwinner. The estimated annual cost to the families of homicide victims is about $184 billion (NIJ, 1996). Finally, there are costs, both psychological and economic, to the family and friends of the perpetrator, and, again, these redound to the larger society.

These consequences result from murder. Consider the impact (in lives, trauma, and costs) of robberies, assaults, rapes, and property crimes—all of which are much higher in the United States than other countries. The nation bears a terrible burden for all this violence.

Individuals and Homicide

Under the wrong circumstances, anyone can take another person's life. Moreover, under the wrong circumstances anyone can become a homicide victim. But there are some personal characteristics and experiences that increase the probability that one will become either a murderer or a victim.

Before proceeding, however, a caveat is necessary. Sociologists argue, correctly, that if we know something about individuals' socialization it is often possible to predict their behavior and to understand why they act as they do. Remember, though, that the empirical generalizations reported here simplify reality: "More likely" does not mean "will." People create their own lives; few ever assault or murder someone. That is the implication of Gurr's argument that there has been a long-term decline in violence in Western societies.

Offenders

Gender. *Males are more likely to commit homicide than females.* In 1994 about 90 percent of those arrested for homicide were males (BJS, 1996:363). Men's involvement has been stable over time and occurs with all violent crimes and most property crimes. Violence and physical aggression tend to be a "guy thing."

Age. *Young adults are more likely to commit homicide than any other age group.* Arrests rates show that the relationship between age and homicide is curvilinear in the form of an upside-down bowl (BJS, 1996:423). Thus, almost no one under 13 commits murder; the rate increases rapidly, however, to ninety-one per 100,000 persons aged 18–20; it then declines steadily to thirty at ages 25–29, and to three at ages 55–64. This same pattern occurs for other types of violent crime. So people (meaning men, mostly) become less aggressive as they get older.

Race and Ethnicity. *African Americans are more like to commit homicide than other racial and ethnic groups.* In 1995, 58 percent of those arrested for homicide were African American, 39 percent white, 2 percent Asian American, and 1 percent Native American (BJS, 1997b). (Data on Hispanics are unavailable.) The connection between race and homicide is well known and often leads whites to fear members of minority groups, especially young, African American males. This reaction is overwrought. The homicide arrest rate among African American males aged 18–24 is 201 per 100,000, which means the other 99,799 did not murder anyone. Moreover, 90 percent of all murders are intraracial, that is, white on white or black on black. And most are committed by the poor on the poor.

Social Class. *The lower the person's social class, the more likely he or she is to commit homicide.* Data on state prison inmates show that in 1991 70 percent had prearrest incomes of less than $15,000 (BJS, 1993). Moreover, most homicides occur in poor neighborhoods (BJS, 1997b).

Victims

Victims are usually similar to offenders in age, gender, race and ethnicity, and social class. For example, when young African American males commit murder, the victim is usually another African American male. This parallel occurs because 87 percent of victims know the perpetrator (BJS, 1996:354). More generally, this finding means that although a few people die in muggings or robberies, if you are afraid of being murdered, watch out for your loved ones, friends, and neighbors.

Why Do Individuals Kill?

The answer is painfully banal. Nearly all homicides involve arguments: over family matters or sex, drug deals gone awry, barroom scrapes, and differences between friends or neighbors. Even murders that appear to be instrumental (slaying a robbery victim) often have an emotional component as well: venting hostility toward others. Given these ordinary motives, the answer to the question "Why do individuals kill?" can be phrased like this: *The greater a person's frustration and the more the person has been socialized to violence, the more likely he or she is to commit murder.*[4]

Frustration and Aggression.   Consider a case of road rage: It is nighttime after a long day, and you are in your car and in a hurry. The person in front of you is driving slowly for no apparent reason in an area where it is hard to pass. Do you honk your horn, flash your headlights, scream, make an obscene gesture, or even pass recklessly? Motorists have been known to shoot at (and kill) other drivers in such situations. Or do you wait patiently because your mother is with you?

   People become frustrated when their goals are blocked, especially when this blockage appears to be intentional, unjustified, and unexpected (Berkowitz, 1963, 1989). One result is aggression. For example, in "The Code of the Streets," Elijah Anderson describes young African American males living in areas plagued with poverty, drugs, and violence (1994). In these environs, people prey on one another, and the appearance of weakness raises the danger of being victimized. Thus, a small sign of public disrespect can trigger great frustration. After all, people without psychological and social resources to maintain their self-esteem have few options and know that the threat of violence is a powerful source of control. (Think about Faro's "crazy look.") Sometimes the result is homicide, at other times only assault. But not always; not even most of the time. Everyone becomes frustrated and angry at others, as the road rage example suggests. Even among those with few resources, it usually takes more than goal blockage to trigger violence.

Socialization and Aggression. Aggressive problem solving is learned behavior. It is usually learned in childhood, often in primary groups (such as one's family), in interaction with others who are emotionally significant, and via long-term interaction (in one's neighborhood, for example).[5] Think about Lafeyette and Faro (referred to earlier). These are people who as children had to crawl home to avoid gunfire. Whose siblings were killed. Who witnessed violence in the streets. Who were subjected to violence at home and at school. Who have been poor all their lives. Who know their chances of getting a good job are zero. Who have suffered persistent racial discrimination. Who joined gangs as a mode of survival. They have formed long-term behavior patterns based on such experiences. They see others and are themselves reinforced for violence (Bandura, 1983; Akers, 1995). Put more simply, the "lesson of the streets" is that "survival itself, let alone respect, cannot be taken for granted; you have to [literally] fight for your place in the world" (Anderson, 1994:86). In this context, when people become frustrated, violence—and homicide—sometimes result.

Thus, murder is usually inflicted by and on marginal persons, often members of minority groups. But it seems probable that both the banal motives of individuals and this explanation for why they kill also apply to the nations shown in Figure 7.2. The data presented earlier raise a different question: Why are there so many more homicides in this country? An answer to this question, of course, requires changing the level of analysis.

Social Structure and Homicide

With modernization, all Western nations except the United States display a long-term decline in crime, homicide being the example used here. Although, as shown in Figure 7.1, the U.S. rate has fluctuated over time, this variation occurs above a high and stable base. The mean U.S. rate is 6.6 compared to 1.3 for those nations shown in Figure 7.2. Thus, the lowest levels of U.S. homicide during this century are much greater than the highest levels in other nations. This same pattern occurs with other crimes: Even at their lowest level, U.S. rates far exceed those in other Western nations. As Louise Shelley observes in *Crime and Modernization,* U.S. crime patterns are unique because they are so high, pervasive, and serious: "The country has not benefitted from the stabilization of crime patterns that appears to accompany the maturation of the developmental process" (1981:76).

Why is this so? Our hypothesis is: *The high base rate of homicide in the United States compared to other Western societies reflects the impact of (1) the high rate of gun ownership, (2) the acceptance of violence, (3) drug policy failure, (4) high income inequality, and (5) racial and ethnic discrimination.*

Before explaining the logic of this hypothesis, we want to remind you that the goal of a structural analysis is to interpret variations in rates of behavior, not why individuals act. Each item in the hypothesis explains part of the difference in murder rates between the United States and Western European nations. The argument, like most structural analyses, constitutes a logical experiment of the sort Max Weber conducted.

Gun Ownership

In most nations, people do not own guns. Of those shown in Figure 7.2, none has a handgun ownership higher than 7 percent (van Dijk, 1990). Less than 1 percent own guns in England and Wales, where (not accidentally) the homicide rate is lowest. By contrast, Americans are armed and ready, with guns in about 40 percent of U.S. households (BJS, 1997b). But this armament does not protect them, since the United States displays the highest rate of homicide.

Guns are used in 70 percent of homicides. Other weapons, usually knives or fists, are used in the other 30 percent (BJS, 1996:337). The homicide rate in 1996 was a very low (for the United States) 7.9. Thus, 70 percent of 7.9 equals 5.5 gun-related deaths per 100,000 people. By subtraction, other weapons accounted for 2.4 homicides per 100,000. This exercise suggests that the homicide rate would be far lower—assuming that many of those who were both frustrated and socialized to violence would not kill (since death is less likely when fists and knives are used). Thus, the paradox: If we magically eliminated all the guns, we would be much safer. Yet this solution is unlikely because of the millions of guns in circulation; besides, the public opposes banning guns (more on this later). Note, however, that the remaining 2.4 homicides are still higher than the average of 1.2 in the nations shown in Figure 7.2. So other factors must be involved.[6]

Acceptance of Violence

Violence, it seems, is as American as apple pie. The existence of all these weapons symbolizes an acceptance of violence in social life in the United States that is unique among Western nations.

Crime, homicide, and a citizen's right to self-defense are intrinsic to U.S. history, as are vigilantism (Brown, 1989). The Civil War desensitized a generation of people, mainly men, to violence. Moreover, as waves of immigrants appeared on these shores, violence rose until they were assimilated. So the United States was a violent place in the nineteenth century. Not much has changed, as violence continues to be glorified. Think about the movies. Those made in the United States are more violent than those made in Western Europe, and witnessing violence leads to aggression by increasing hostile feelings and making such behavior seem acceptable (C. Anderson, 1997).

But violence is not only symbolic; it is used by the state as well. For example, the public overwhelmingly supports capital punishment: 77 percent in 1995 (Gallup, 1995). Yet capital punishment has no deterrent effect (Sellin, 1980). Moreover, violence goes up after executions occur (Stack, 1987). Even more striking, each of the four military campaigns engaged in by U.S. armed forces during the 1980s was followed by an increase in criminal violence (Bebber, 1994). Thus, the message of executions and military campaigns is that there is a connection between using force and getting what you want; in short, violence works. This finding is not new. In general, the acceptance of violence increases a nation's homicide rate (Kposowa and Breault, 1993; Cutright and Briggs, 1995).

Finally, there are groups for whom violence is not only acceptable but expected and encouraged. In a classic work, *Delinquent Boys*, Albert Cohen found this value among youth gangs (1955). Subsequent research showed the existence of "subcultures of violence" wherein people learn that the willingness to use violence is one of the most important measures of self-worth (Wolfgang and Ferracuti, 1967). For example, it is pervasive among members of both outlaw motorcycle gangs and urban street gangs (Danner and Silverman, 1986; Bing, 1991).

Thus, the impact of so many guns combined with acceptance of violence in our society leads to a high rate of homicides. This situation is made worse by the failure of drug policy.

Drug Policy Failure

Drug policy in the United States is designed to reduce the supply of illegal substances by eradicating them in foreign nations, interdicting them as they are smuggled in, and arresting sellers and buyers. As shown in Chapter 6, this policy has failed; illegal drugs are readily available. Paradoxically, however, it has succeeded in creating markets regulated by violence. And where people shoot, people die—especially the young (NIJ, 1995).

It is now common to compare the terror and danger of living in drug-related areas of U.S. cities to war zones. A soldier sent to Somalia to suppress drug warlords assumed he would find it to be an exotic place. Not so. "The fear of walking the streets without a gun, the fear of someone shooting at you, these are things I go through every time I go back to D.C." (Messner and Rosenfeld, 1997:32).

This reaction is not unique. Consider the Englewood section of Chicago (Messner and Rosenfeld, 1997:33). During the early 1980s, it was a stable residential area to which many residents had moved, fleeing drug dealing and violence in other sections of the city. Then dealers invaded the area (note the term "invaded"), and it became one of the most violent neighborhoods in the United States—a war zone. Its homicide rate of eighty-nine per 100,000 is nine times the overall level in this country, shown in Figure 7.1; it is also higher than that of Northern Ireland. The streets of this community are empty during the day. Schoolchildren cannot play outside. There are no grocery stores, hardware stores, restaurants, movie theaters, laundromats, or newspaper vending machines—all the elements of life that people take for granted. There is no police protection. The result, as one police officer put it, is that "nothing is worth anything in the area because you open up and you get knocked off, and you get knocked off, and you get knocked off until you give up" (Messner and Rosenfeld, 1997:34). But the drug dealers thrive, and they regulate their business by violence. Although this example is an extreme case, something like it happens in some area of most cities in America. Whatever one thinks about U.S. drug policy, it results in an increase in the homicide rate.

This increase exacts a huge price. Its impact is amplified, of course, when combined with the effects of guns and the acceptance of violence. It is further amplified by inequality.

High Income Inequality

The United States displays much more income (and wealth) inequality than do other Western nations. Moreover, it has risen to an all-time high in recent years (Beeghley, 1996a). Such inequality means that many people endure persistent poverty—with debilitating consequences. In addition, as Chapter 5 revealed, poor persons in this country find it difficult to express their interests politically in legitimate ways, for example, by voting. Such a context produces high rates of violence and murder (Cutright and Briggs, 1995; Nijboer, 1995). In one study of homicide rates in Detroit over fifty years, people who were poor for long periods displayed significantly higher rates of homicide (Loftin, 1989). This finding follows from the level of segregation typical of cities: Poor people live apart, and their neighborhoods are relatively violent. We are describing an anomic social structure.

In a classic article, "Social Structure and Anomie," Robert K. Merton points out that although American culture emphasizes the importance of economic success and people judge others by this criterion, a large segment of the population is denied the ability to achieve this goal—using legitimate means (1968a). In effect, people's location in the class structure determines their range of opportunities. Remarkably, most people with few opportunities persevere in a ritualistic way, believing (against the facts) that with hard work they will eventually succeed and believing (rightly) that even if they do not, they will be judged honorable.[7] Some people, however, adapt in other ways. As Merton puts it, some retreat, which means rejecting both the goal of success and means to achieve it. More prosaically, this alternative refers to withdrawing from society, via psychopathology (e.g., depression) or drugs (as discussed in Chapter 6). Some rebel, that is, they try to change society. The violence directed against school buildings is an inchoate form of rebellion, and (as suggested in Chapter 4) the uprisings of minority groups can be interpreted as rebellions. Finally, some innovate: They develop deviant but effective strategies for economic success (such as drug dealing). This is, of course, another way of talking about crime and violence—and murder. A reasonable guess is that many homicides are attempts at solving disputes when legal options are not available, either because the police will not respond or because the behaviors (drug sales) are illegal.

Racial and Ethnic Discrimination

The impact of inequality on homicide is made worse by pervasive discrimination against minorities, especially African Americans. Immigrant groups historically displayed very high rates of crime, including homicide, because so much of the population comprised rootless young males, adrift in a new country. Over time, however, as they found jobs, developed skills, married, and melded into the society, the level of violence dropped. Many African Americans, however, had much different experiences. As Roger Lane observes in *Roots of Violence in Black Philadelphia, 1860–1900,* African Americans were largely excluded from participating in the industrializing economy in the North (1986). Moreover, the long-term increase in residential segregation that has occurred during the twentieth century (described in Chapter 4) has isolated this group more than others. Finally, as noted in Chapter 6, drug policy creates (illicit) opportunities and stimulates violence in impoverished African American neighborhoods. As a result, many have adapted in other ways. So the rate of homicide by and against African Americans, not only in Philadelphia but in all U.S. cities, has been high for much of this century. And the carnage continues today.

Some observers argue that issues like those considered here are not adequate explanations of the high U.S. homicide rate (e.g., Messner and Rosenfeld, 1997). They point out the rate is higher in this country even after the impact of guns is subtracted out. They also point out that excluding African Americans, the level of homicide among whites is higher than in Western Europe. Although both assertions are correct, we believe this approach is wrongheaded (see note 6). The task, as shown here and in other chapters, is logically to parcel out the effects of each of the factors that, taken together, produce a high U.S. rate.

Implications

The great debate over crime and what to do about it centers on front-end versus back-end strategies. Front-end strategies, which usually appeal to liberals, focus on preventing crimes, mainly from a sense (often formless) that everyone's daily life would be better. Back-end strategies, which usually appeal to conservatives, focus on punishment, partly for its presumed deterrent effect but also (we suspect) for its own sake. From this point of view, bad people should be disciplined for their misdeeds. Homicide seems like an archetypal example of such misdeeds.[8]

Since the 1970s, back-enders have dominated the debate. And politicians have responded with an increasing emphasis on punishment, mainly by raising sentencing requirements in a conscious attempt at jailing more people for longer periods. Hence, the number of convicts in state and federal prisons has risen steadily, to 1.2 million in 1996, a 135 percent increase since 1985 (BJS, 1997a:1). Executions of convicted murderers have also increased; they averaged twenty-seven per year from 1990 to 1994 (BJS, 1996:615). Hence, costs for operating the criminal justice system have skyrocketed. California and Florida, for example, now spend more money keeping persons in jail than educating their college-age population (Butterfield, 1997a). We wonder whether the political will exists for further cost increases.

Even though rates of homicide have fallen in recent years, it is not clear whether this change is due to the emphasis on punishment. The argument supporting this relationship is that more violent people are dead or in prison. Well, maybe. But most homicides are crimes of passion (this is the simple way of saying that people who become frustrated and have been socialized to violence are more likely to commit murder). Deterrence probably has little effect. In addition, as mentioned earlier, homicides tend to increase in frequency after executions. More generally, only a few crimes come to the attention of the police, and only a small percentage of those that do are "cleared" by arrest and jail. As noted in Chapter 6, a high proportion of prisoners have committed nonviolent drug offenses. In any case, most violent people who go into prison eventually come out: socialized to crime (and violence). These days, the number of people released from prison each year nearly equals the number convicted and sent to prison (D. Anderson, 1997).

Regardless of cause, however, it seems likely that the United States has taken the emphasis on punishment as far as it can (both in terms of cost and effectiveness). In this context, we would like to suggest some street-smart front-end strategies for consideration (D. Anderson, 1997). We focus on practical front-end approaches because although it would be nice to the eliminate anomie and reduce inequality, espousing such "policies" leads nowhere politically. In our view, the nation should strive for less vengeful but more effective policies about crime.

First, the United States should consider increasing the size of police forces and assertively enforcing laws against low-level offenses. The analogy goes like this: When police ignore a building where the landlord has neglected to repair a broken window, people realize they can get away with breaking more windows. The process continues until the building is either destroyed or taken over by lowlifes (drug dealers or gangs). Violence escalates in this context. There is some (not a lot) of evidence that such enforcement strategies work. In New York City, for example, police in 1990 began enforcing laws against "quality-of-life" offenses, such as drinking in public. They also began using these laws and traffic stops as a legal way to look for illegal guns. A decline in homicides followed: from 2,262 in 1990 to 985 in 1996 (D. Anderson, 1997:53). In addition, the proportion of murders committed with guns outdoors fell more than those that took place indoors and involved other weapons. We should emphasize, however, that correlation is not causation (i.e., just because enforcement of quality-of-life offenses was followed by a fall in homicide does not mean the former caused the latter). Other factors may be at work. Even so, it seems reasonable to argue that a focus on low-level offenses and preserving a neighborhood's quality of life is a way of creating stability—and reducing crime.

Second, the United States should consider taking gun control seriously. Although a majority of the population, 60 percent, opposes banning the possession of handguns, even greater majorities favor requiring a permit to buy them (80 percent) and then registering them after purchase (83 percent) (BJS, 1996:193). In effect, the public supports laws for gun ownership similar to those for owning and driving a car. Thus, it also makes sense to require gun owners to pass written and practical tests on gun handling and safety and to carry liability insurance. These policies are normal for automobile owners; they would make it harder for crooks to possess guns and easier to jail people who fail to obey these laws. In addition, the technology is available to make guns easier to trace (with computer chips) and to build in safety devices permitting use only by the registered owner. Although an underground market for firearms would continue to exist, such policies would be designed to reduce the free flow of armaments. It makes sense to suggest that the homicide rate would fall as a result.

Third, the United States should consider using the courts, probation departments, and other intervention programs more aggressively to divert people from criminal "careers." Those who end up in state prisons have usually committed many low-level crimes and have not been dealt with effectively. Heavy workloads and lack of coordination among agencies often prevent attention to youthful offenders' real problems: family, drugs, school. It may be possible to divert many young persons (like Faro and Lafeyette, mentioned earlier) from committing crimes of violence, including homicide, when these issues are confronted. Again, there is some (not a lot) of evidence that such strategies might work. For example, in Jacksonville, Florida, representatives of the school board, police, child protective services, and other agencies meet weekly to identify children aged 6–15 who have either committed crimes or had serious trouble in school. Intervention programs are then devised to deal with the sources of their behavior (Butterfield, 1997b). When older children commit crimes in Jacksonville, the policy is to prosecute them in adult court. When convicted, however, they are not sent to state prison; instead, they are housed in a local facility separate from adults and provided special services: education, drug treatment, and sex education, among others. Those completing their stay without bad conduct reports have their convictions withheld. The idea is that locking up a 25-year-old man for life for murder will cost a huge amount of money (say, $600,000 to $700,000), whereas confining an older teenager for one year and successfully diverting him from future crime costs about $25,000. Since these strategies have been implemented, the rate of homicide (along with other crimes) fell. Moreover, they fell earlier and farther in Jacksonville than in other areas of the country. Recall, however, our earlier caveat: Correlation is not causation; there could be other factors at work. In addition, even if such strategies are successful with some people, others (perhaps like Faro) have been so damaged and make such poor decisions that they will end up in jail. Nonetheless, it makes sense to suggest that an intervention strategy might reduce that number.

Fourth, the United States should consider making drug treatment easily available. As observed in Chapter 6, even if motivated abusers find it difficult to stop using drugs and even if it often takes several attempts for treatment to succeed, those in treatment usually reduce their consumption and thus the crime that goes with it. But affordable treatment resources are limited, with long waits for admission. Treatment facilities should be accessible so that any person voluntarily seeking help could get it right away and so that judges can realistically make treatment part of a sentencing package. This goal could be reached by amending the Medicaid law so that freestanding clinics (rather than hospitals) can be reimbursed for providing such care (D. Anderson, 1997). Although Medicaid costs would increase, no new bureaucracy would be created. As before, the evidence on this issue is mixed. Nonetheless, it makes sense to suggest that even if current drug laws are not changed, making treatment easily available might reduce (it will not eliminate) the violence connected to drugs.

These strategies are not panaceas. Not all may work; as indicated, evidence remains tentative. We offer them as a way to begin discussing how to reduce homicide and, more generally, the level of violence in this country. The alternative is to live in fear. Even when this fear is not realistic, it affects everyone. Industries arise to provide security; parks are not used at night; street life declines; gated communities with private police forces proliferate. Freedom is lost.

Perhaps it was accidental, but shortly after returning from the Olympics Charles Barkley left Philadelphia to play for Phoenix, a far less violent city. Even though he subsequently moved on to Houston (professional athletes change teams a lot), he continues to live in Phoenix. Perhaps Barkley is like most people: He prefers living in a safer environment. The question is how to achieve this goal.

Notes

1. Note that the data on robbery and assault refer to crimes reported to the police. Because such acts are underreported, real victimization rates are higher.

2. Recall the discussion of modernization in Chapter 1.

3. You should recall that the term "anomie" refers to a disjunction between conventional values, such as economic success, and the legitimate means to achieve them (Merton, 1968a).

4. I am simplifying (some would say oversimplifying) the theories explaining why individuals kill. For an overview, see Steven Messner and Richard Rosenfeld, *Crime and the American Dream* (1997).

5. These are the elements of the socialization process presented in Chapter 1.

6. In looking at the impact of guns on homicide (and other forms of violence), it is important to be clear about what is being explained. If we wished to explain fluctuations in the U.S. homicide rate over time, guns would be a minor part of the analysis because firearms have been a (relatively) constant part of the U.S. scene over the past century. What produced fluctuations in homicide rates, then, are social and demographic factors, for example, the size of the young adult population. In contrast, we wish to explain why the base rate of U.S. homicides is so much higher than in other Western nations. Given this goal, logic points directly at the size of the arsenal in private hands in this country.

7. Recall from Chapter 5 how an exaggerated version of a Monopoly game served as a metaphor for describing how difficult it is for poor people to obtain economic success—let alone security.

8. This section has benefited from a provocative analysis by David C. Anderson, "The Mystery of the Falling Crime Rate" (1997).

Recommended Reading

Bing, Léon. *Do or Die* (New York: HarperCollins, 1991).

Gurr, Ted Robert. "Historical Trends in Violent Crime: Europe and the United States." Pp. 21–55 in T. R. Gurr (ed.), *Violence in America,* Vol. 1 (Newbury Park, CA: Sage, 1989).

Merton, Robert K. "Social Structure and Anomie." Pp. 185–215 in R. K. Merton, *Social Theory and Social Structure* (New York: Free Press, 1968).

Messner, Steven F., and Richard Rosenfeld. *Crime and the American Dream,* 2nd edition (Belmont, CA: Wadsworth, 1997).

8 *An Aging Population*

Outline of Chapter 8

I. Dimensions of the Aging Population
  A. Historical Dimensions
  B. International Dimensions

II. Consequences of an Aging Population
  A. When to Retire
  B. How to Support the Aged
  C. How to Care for the Aged

III. Individuals and an Aging Population
  A. Adapting to Old Age
  B. Adapting to Illness and Disability
  C. Adapting to Death

IV. Social Structure and an Aging Population
  A. Declining Fertility Rates
  B. Declining Infant Mortality Rates
  C. Declining Immigration Rates
  D. Advances in Medical Technology

V. Implications
  A. Limiting Medical Treatment
  B. Suicide and Euthanasia

It is, in a way, the ultimate gift—the luxury of aging—and it is now shared by many. As a result, the U.S. population will soon comprise as many old as young persons. Yet this gift, which is historically unique, also creates social problems. The wording here is important. In other chapters, the title indicates the harmful condition being discussed; this chapter, however, concerns the impact of a present we have given ourselves. Put bluntly, we must face the consequences of an aging population squarely, without blinking. This task will not be easy.

Here is a story, a legend really, about Siddhartha Gautama that illustrates the difficulty (Bradley, 1963:103). He lived in northern India or Nepal some 2,500 years ago. His wealthy father shielded him from misery in the world by maintaining a palace surrounded by a huge park. Thus, he grew up in splendor and ease, without concern for others. One day, however, Gautama ventured outside the palace and saw a leper covered with sores, an aged beggar, and a corpse being carried to its grave. In this transforming moment, the sheltered reality he knew crumbled and he recognized the existence of sorrow, aging, illness, and death. Shortly thereafter he attended a great feast accompanied by the usual drunken revelry. Only Gautama remained sober. He surveyed the scene, revolted by its meaninglessness, and renounced his life of self-indulgence and material comfort. With his newfound awareness of suffering, he eventually developed a set of principles for living and dying. We know him today as the Buddha.

Until recently, most Western people have been like the young Gautama, shielded from the reality of old age, illness, and death. After all, among those who are not poor early death has become rare, and few people die at home anymore; most die in hospitals, attended to only by their immediate family. Moreover, this means that physicians and hospitals control the conditions of death, and they do so quite naturally in terms of their own values and economic interests. One of these values is preserving life, which is usually an easy decision when patients are 20 or 40 or 60. But is it so easy at 80? At 90? Do we wish to preserve life at every age, no matter how old, no matter what its quality may be? Ultimately, who should control the circumstances of death? And what values should guide decisionmaking?

Simply raising these questions indicates how difficult the task of examining the impact of long life will be. Other questions come to mind. At what age should people retire? What is a fair (and moral) allocation of public resources to the aged, such as income support and medical treatment? Who should care for the frail and disabled elderly? That these queries are increasingly salient to the public suggests that we are no longer shielded from the reality of old age. Like Gautama, then, we must come to understand the meaning of aging and develop ethical standards to guide decisions about life and death.

Dimensions of the Aging Population

The origin of the dilemma we face goes back to the early years of the nineteenth century, when a demographic transformation began. In *Growing Old in America*, David Hackett Fischer compares this change to one of those enormous Pacific waves the Japanese call *tsunami* (1978:113). The seafloor moves slightly, causing a huge current to rise to the surface that spreads out and destroys everything in its path. In much the same way, a great demographic wave set in motion nearly 200 years ago has produced a fundamental historical shift in population distribution. People began living long lives, and the aged gradually became a significant proportion of the population. The result has been a number of social problems, ethical questions really, which are altogether new in history. Before dealing with them, however, it is useful to know more about the dimensions of this wave of aged people.

Historical Dimensions

Although survival into old age was rare in the past, it did occur. In colonial New England, old age was loosely defined as living into the sixth decade. The Puritan spiritual leader Cotton Mather, for example, expressed wonderment at those who crossed "the borders . . . of old age" by "out-living three score winters," or 60 years (Fischer, 1978:27). Such longevity seemed like a miracle when most of the population was young. The median age in the United States in 1790, when the first census was taken, was only about 16. At that time, only 2 percent of the population was over 65 years old (USBC, 1975:15). The collection of this datum suggests a definition, one still used today: The *aged population* comprises those over 65. Thus, although this age seems like an arbitrary cutoff point, it is in fact very old (pun intended).

The population began to get older after about 1800, slowly at first but at an increasing rate over time. Thus, Figure 8.1 shows that the aged population had doubled a century later, to 4 percent. Although this level still seems small, it signified the beginning of the demographic transformation. The figure shows that a steady upward trend in the aged population has occurred over the past 100 years, about 1 percent each decade between 1910 and 1980. Today 13 percent are over 65, roughly 30 million persons. Old people have become common and are destined to become more so. In fact, if the population projections included in the figure are correct, a temporary stability in the proportion of aged people will give way in the next two decades to an accelerated rate of increase during the next century. The elderly now constitute the fastest-growing segment of the population (USBC, 1996c:2–3). As a result, by the year 2050 the aged will constitute about 21 percent of the population, or 69 million people. In comparison, children less than 17 years will make up only 20 percent of U.S. inhabitants. Thus, in just a few years there will be as many old as young people in the United States. These data mean that in less than 200 years the age structure will have changed from resembling a pyramid,

Percentage

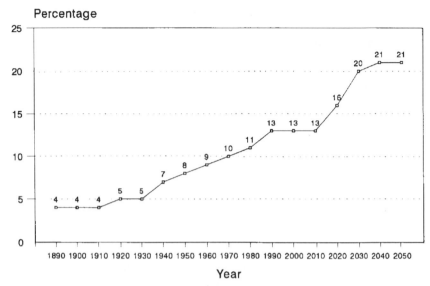

Year

FIGURE 8.1   U.S. Population over Age 65, 1890–2050
NOTE: Years 2000–2050 are projections reflecting midlevel assumptions about
fertility, mortality, and immigration.
SOURCE: USBC (1975:15, 1996c:2–3).

with children making up the large base, to resembling a rectangle, with
few differences in the number of persons at various ages.

   Not only are there more old people in the population, but the composition of the aged has changed. At the turn of the century, nearly all of the
aged were between 65 and 74 years (USBC, 1996c:2–3). This is when most
deaths among the aged occurred. Today, however, 7 percent of the U.S.
population is between 65 and 74 years, now called the young-old, whereas
4 percent are between 75 and 84 years, the middle-old, and 1 percent are 85
or over, the old-old. These changing proportions constitute all-time highs,
a trend that will continue. The old-old constitute the fastest-growing segment of the elderly population (USBC, 1996c:2–3). In the future, an increasing proportion of deaths, perhaps most, will occur in this age category.

   These demographic data reveal that Americans can no longer shield
themselves from the political, economic, and moral implications of an
aging population. Moreover, the United States is not unique. Other
Western nations display a comparable population profile.

International Dimensions

Figure 8.2 presents data on the current and projected population over 65
years for six nations. The left portion of each panel reveals that all these

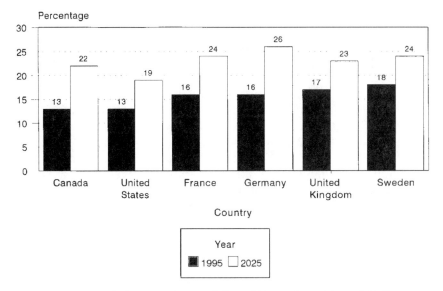

FIGURE 8.2   Population over Age 65, Selected Countries, 1995 and 2025
NOTE: Data for 2025 are projections reflecting midlevel assumptions about
fertility, mortality, and immigration.
SOURCE: USBC (1995c:A-1).

Western countries currently display a large percentage of aged inhabitants. Although not shown in the figure, the data represent all-time
highs in every case. Hence, the demographic change described above for
the United States has happened in each of these societies. Moreover, as
the right portion of each panel shows, the size of the aged cohort will increase significantly in all these nations over the decades to come. Such
facts suggest that similar structural changes are taking place in all Western countries.

Before continuing, I should mention that population counts typically
understate the total inhabitants of a nation, missing some of the poor, illegal aliens, and the like. These errors were probably greater in the past.
Nonetheless, the data in Figures 8.1 and 8.2 constitute the most accurate
that are likely to become available. The population projections given in
the figures are conservative guesses. I would bet on higher increases because Census Bureau projections have been low in the past (Preston,
1993). If this hunch is correct, the impact of an aging population described below will be more difficult to resolve. In any case, there is no
question that the proportion of the population that is aged will continue
rising, like an enormous wave.

Consequences of an Aging Population

This demographic *tsunami* means that daily life will be different in the future. In a society dominated by an aged population, for example, entertainment often will be pitched to their interests. This is simply because they will constitute a large and wealthy market. (I envision Mick Jagger and the Stones creaking onstage to sing "Let's Spend the Night Together" to thousands of screaming geriatrics. Their children and grandchildren, of course, will mutter disapproval.) The impact of an aging population, however, will go beyond entertainment. The United States faces a moral crucible: What ethical standards are appropriate when most people live long lives and choose when to die?

Such standards exist in every society as part of the implicit "contract" between generations (Rossi and Rossi, 1990). The idea is that parents provide support and care for children, who constitute a legacy for the future. In return for this gift of life, when children become adults, they in turn support and care for their parents. In the past, this obligation was limited; since most people did not survive into old age, few 50-year-old adults had elderly parents. Those who did survive, however, were often venerated (not necessarily loved), and if they possessed land or some other form of wealth, they exercised great power within both the family and community. This situation meant that adult children in their 30s and 40s were kept economically dependent for much of their lives. Nonetheless, when people lived into old age, families could care for parents prior to their death, usually without help. In modern societies, however, so many people live long lives and the economy has changed so much that these obligations cannot be fulfilled on a family-by-family basis. Thus, government now serves as the agent, regulating the terms of the "contract" for the common good. In this context, three issues become salient: when to retire, how to support the aged, and how to care for the aged.

When to Retire

At the turn of the century, nearly all individuals worked until they died, men at paid jobs and women at home, and few lived into old age. Today, in contrast, the average man lives 74 years, the average woman 78. Thus, those living beyond the average can expect to spend one-fourth of their lives, twenty years or more, out of the labor force. One aspect of the luxury of aging, then, is retirement from paid work. (Women never retire from housework.) An assumption underlies the notion of retirement: When they become old, people have a right to the economic support and care of non-aged people; they no longer must work until they die.

But the point at which people ought to retire remains unclear. At the least, people receive contradictory messages. This inconsistency reflects confusion about the role of the aged and the mutual obligations of the generations to each other (Hareven, 1994).

On the one hand, people are told they ought to delay retirement (Kramer, 1995). Thus, the age at which they can receive full Social Security benefits was recently raised from 65 to 67 for those born after 1960. Similarly, amendments to the Age Discrimination in Employment Act now prohibit mandatory retirement at age 65, which means that companies cannot (legally) force people to leave their jobs simply because of their age. These changes represent an initial attempt at recognizing the problems posed by a large population of elderly persons with no assigned role: They should remain in the labor force longer. And some people do, especially those with relatively high status, earnings, and power—who often wish to retain them. (Power is like a drug. It produces a far greater euphoria than the chemicals discussed in Chapter 6.) This pattern suggests that the "Prince Charles phenomenon"—waiting around, often resentfully, for an elderly person to retire—might become widespread in the future.

On the other hand, people are asked to retire early. And some do (USBC, 1996c:3–4). At age 50, nearly all men, 88 percent, are employed or looking for work. The proportion falls steadily with age, however, until only 28 percent remain in the labor force at 65 and 10 percent after 75. The pattern for women is similar, although the percentages are lower because of historical differences in gender relations (see Chapter 3).

One way people are asked to retire early is by the offer of economic support—from both public and private sources (Henretta, 1994). The public sources are disability and Social Security income. About 65 percent of those who become disabled are over age 50. Labor, especially assembly-line labor, devours people. Regardless of cause, many persons become physically unable to work during their fifth decade, obtain disability benefits and, if they live to age 65, then convert to Social Security. In addition, people can retire at age 62 and receive 80 percent of full Social Security benefits. The private source of economic support is pensions. In recent years, about 40 percent of firms with more than 1,000 employees have offered special incentives for early retirement with pensions. Such public and private inducements partially account for the tendency to leave the labor force after age 50.

In addition, however, people are coerced into leaving the labor force, which subsequently leads to early retirement. For example, the duress behind a company's proposal that employees over age 50 take "early retirement" is often thinly veiled, mainly because the alternative is to simply lay off or fire older individuals. Although such actions are illegal, employers can and do find ways around this problem. The result is unemployment. When an older worker does find a job, it is often in a different industry and at a lower wage. The new occupation becomes a "bridge job," an (often) unwanted transition to retirement.

Although there are other reasons for leaving the labor force as people age, these constitute the major ones. When they are juxtaposed with pressures to continue working, it becomes clear that the issue of an appropriate time to retire remains unsettled. This fact has important implications for the cost of income support and medical treatment for elderly persons.

How to Support the Aged

Old age is a luxury of modernity, and like most luxuries, it has a price. All Western industrial nations have implemented society-wide provisions for income support and medical treatment for the aged (Williamson and Pampel, 1993). Yet how to pay for these items has become controversial.

A century ago, there were no pensions. As a result, the few people who lived past three score and five years were often poor. Fischer, for example, reports that in Massachusetts in 1910, 23 percent of those over 65 were public paupers, and many more were clearly impoverished (1978:161). And Massachusetts was a wealthy state; imagine what it was like to be aged (and not rich) on the frontier in the 1890s. During the early years of the twentieth century, widespread poverty among the aged led to proposals for "old-age pension plans" in many states and Congress. Finally, the Social Security Act, passed in 1935, taxed the working-age population to supply income support for the elderly. Note the phrasing: This is not an insurance plan; it is, rather, a pay-as-you-go operation. Although other income programs, such as Supplemental Security Income (SSI) and veterans' benefits, also help the aged, Social Security remains the primary government transfer to the elderly population.

In addition to income support, the cost of providing medical treatment for the elderly must be considered. A century ago, such costs were minimal, since the ability to heal was limited. As this skill increased over time, legislation to provide treatment for the aged population was introduced in Congress. Today Medicare, enacted in 1965, constitutes the main source of money for medical treatment of the aged. In addition, the Medicaid program provides funds for nursing home care for the elderly poor.

Major federal expenditures for income support and medical treatment for the aged are estimated below, as of 1994 (CEA, 1995:369):

Income support (Social Security only)	$276 billion
Medical treatment (Medicare only)	$189
Other benefits (estimated)	$ 50
Total	$515

This is a lot of money, about 48 percent of the federal budget. Moreover, current policies producing such outlays will lead to inexorable—and unsustainable—increases (CBO, 1996).

Even if policies are changed, future generations will bear a greater burden because differences in the "elderly dependency ratio," the proportion of employed to retired persons, means that each worker's taxes will support a growing number of retirees (CBO, 1996:70). For example, today there are 4.8 persons between the ages of 20 and 64 for every person over age 65. In about 2010, when the huge baby boom generation begins retiring, however, the situation will change radically. By 2030, there will be only 2.8 non-aged persons for everyone over age 65. These changes pose inescapable economic, political, and moral dilemmas.

The problem of income support was supposedly confronted by 1983 increases in Social Security taxes paid by currently employed persons, which were designed to build up trust fund reserves. As a practical matter, however, this money is used to reduce the current federal budget deficit via the purchase of government bonds. This strategy allows current federal expenditures—such as the cost of the military and failed savings and loan associations—to be met. As a result, when these bonds are redeemed over the next half century, the economic burden on employed people will increase. Over the long term, the only alternatives are to raise Social Security revenues or decrease benefits. My guess is that both strategies will be used. The main choices for increasing revenues include higher (and more progressive) Social Security taxes and higher (or more progressive) income taxes. The main choices for reducing benefits involve increasing the age of retirement, reducing yearly cost-of-living adjustments, and taxing benefits that go to high-income persons. Obviously, these policy decisions will be difficult, and it is not possible to know which ones will be made. Social Security, however, provides only part of the income support aged people need. The remainder is supplied by programs like SSI, the elderly themselves (via savings and private pensions), and their families. These costs will also escalate, and choices about whether and how to limit benefits will have to be made.

Similar problems exist with funding the Medicare and Medicaid programs. Politically, it is becoming clear that the cost of providing treatment for the aged must be reduced. Yet all the available choices raise significant moral questions. I discuss this issue in the concluding section.

No matter how they are resolved, provisions for income support and medical treatment are necessary but not sufficient for the aged. People obtain psychological sustenance, intimacy, and a sense of meaning from those closest to them: family members.

How to Care for the Aged

The luxury of aging also carries a social price because most people eventually find it difficult to perform daily tasks on their own. So someone must help. Such assistance is often instrumental: running errands and providing transportation. Other help involves intimate tasks: bathing, toileting, and dressing. The need for some form of personal care varies by age (USBC, 1996c:3–21). For example, less than 10 percent of 65-year-old people need any aid. By 85 years, however, about 40 percent find at least one task difficult and require assistance. With age, then, people become dependent, and the number who need care will increase in the future. During the next half century, the growing proportion of the population that is aged means that most 50-year-old adults will have retired parents and many people at retirement age will also have elderly parents. Who will care for them?

In the past, Fischer reports, it was the custom for the youngest daughter to remain at home, caring for her parents until they died. It was a wretched obligation, often (depending on the age of parental death) requiring that she sacrifice her chance for marriage (1978:150). One of the most famous examples is Emily Dickinson. She cared for her father for many years and after he died became a recluse who found sustenance in her poetry, which is filled with melancholy dreams (Sewell, 1975). Although the custom has changed, assisting the aged remains women's burden.

Today, women provide more care, more difficult care, and for longer periods of time than ever before in history (Dwyer and Coward, 1992). Although caregiving is often hard, I would like to pause to note its intrinsic value. Looking after others, young or old, can teach us about ourselves: our ability to tolerate those who are difficult, our capacity to be patient, and our willingness to postpone our own needs. Caregivers become transcendent in the process. Moreover, the connection between generations that results from providing care is a legacy to the future (Boyd and Treas, 1995). It is important, however, not to romanticize family caregiving. Not all aged parents are endearing. Some are simply not very likable persons. Some were abusive to their children. For many reasons, then, the ties between generations can be strained.

Regardless of the nature of the relationship, however, caregiving usually has two negative results. First, nurturing an elderly parent rarely counts as doing productive work. This issue is important because in modern societies useful work is usually defined as paid work in which a product or service results. Women engaged in caregiving are thus sacrificing a great deal. For example, it is hard to hold a job and look after another, since a frail elderly person can require several hours of attention each day. Thus, the economic value of caregiving is enormous. But because it is done for free, out of moral obligation, it carries no status and receives little social support. And because it is done primarily by women, it is another example of gender inequality.[1]

Second, family caregiving produces stress in the caregivers (Dwyer and Coward, 1992). In the ideal setting mentioned above, providing care for an elderly parent is mutually nurturing. I am inclined to believe, however, that this ideal rarely happens. It is especially infrequent when caregiving obligations become extreme. Even when giving assistance is rewarding, stress occurs because of the many roles adults have: to job, spouse, children remaining at home, and volunteer activities. Adding care for parents to this list produces role conflict. When the ties to parents are strained, the stress becomes even greater. Now I am aware that the notion of role conflict does not sound serious. After all, people should tough out their difficulties. Maybe. Some, however, collapse under the pressure.

Most children believe that they are obligated to sustain their parents. Normally, these expectations exist regardless of the nature of the relationship or economic situation (Rossi and Rossi, 1990). But I wonder whether Americans sometimes ask more than is realistic or possible. As Daniel Callahan observes, "A good society is one that finds ways to avoid requiring too much heroism; it will seek to match needs to strengths" (1987:106). Leaving people to their own resources in providing care for their aged parents strikes me as shortsighted.[2]

The examples in this section illustrate some of the problems posed by an aging population. A new stage in the life cycle has been created, and the resulting difficulties suggest that neither the obligations between generations nor the appropriate role of the aged in our society has been resolved. For individuals who are aging, however, these problems take on a different dimension. They must cope with the personal dilemmas associated with becoming old. But coping is especially hard in a context where people shield themselves from these realities.

Individuals and an Aging Population

Old age. Illness. Death. One follows the other in inevitable progression. These facts mean that each individual must adapt, must find meaning and satisfaction in life in a context where few guidelines exist.

Adapting to Old Age

During the last stage of life, most people eventually give up the master role with which they identified. Bricklayers stop building. Lawyers quit arguing cases. Retirement is thus a "roleless role" in the sense that people's place in society disappears (Riley and Riley, 1994). Yet the majority of people are glad to retire (Palmore, 1985). They see their jobs as boring, feel caged up, or become physically unable to work. Some, however, retire with difficulty, mainly because their sense of self is tied to their occupations. If I am not a lawyer, then what am I? To arrive at an answer, each person must, like the young Gautama, discover some principles for living and dying. Most find this issue hard to confront.

In *Threshold: The First Days of Retirement,* Alan Olmstead describes how he looked forward to leisure, and then how the endless days without formal duties left him morose. Like most people, he found that work not only produced an income, it filled the day, provided contact with others, and gave life meaning. Work was the glue that tied him to the community, a bond lost upon retirement. Olmstead, in fact, comes to a surprising conclusion (1975:212):

> Leisure, the freedom, is like all freedoms in that it cannot exist except in relation to fixed occupations, duties, and obligations. . . . Leisure ceases to exist unless it keeps bumping itself against and reinforcing itself through contact and conflict with things that must be done. To begin to plan for leisure time, then, one aims first to make sure of a continuing context of chore or obligation. . . . To find leisure, look for work.

The trick, then, is to "look for work." If I read him correctly, however, Olmstead does not necessarily mean full-time employment (although that is one option); rather, he means that people should remain involved in the society and develop meaningful obligations. But since there are few external guidelines, they must construct their own roles. The alternative is to be adrift.

It appears that most people begin by doing fewer things they have to do and more they want to do. Some become involved in politics, community service, or volunteer work. Others may read, work in the yard, and keep a busy social life. Still others travel. What makes these strategies "work," in Olmstead's sense, is that people remain psychologically and physically active. In general, the "use-it-or-lose-it" phenomenon applies to both intellectual abilities and muscle tone. Those who "use it" usually display satisfaction with their lives: *The more aged individuals maintain active ties to the community and society, the greater their life satisfaction* (Atchley, 1995:375).

It is much easier to preserve such bonds when people enjoy relatively high income and good health. It follows, then, that these factors also predict life satisfaction among the aged: *The higher the income and the better health aged individuals have, the greater their life satisfaction* (Atchley, 1995:375). These characteristics, of course, reflect inequality established prior to old age, since people at each class level usually remain in their relative positions after retirement (Crystal and Shea, 1990). In addition, people's health also varies by social class (see Chapter 9). What these differences mean in practice is that the range and quality of each person's choices differ by class. For example, individuals who were middle class prior to retirement usually have more and better options in their daily lives after retirement than do working-class individuals. But such differences do not mean that working-class persons cannot have a satisfying old age. Again, involvement with the community usually indicates how individuals adapt during this last stage of life. It remains the key to psychological and physical well-being at all class levels.

Some people, however, do end up adrift. As Olmstead emphasizes, although leisure is necessary to both psychological and physical health, too much of it can seem hollow. What exactly is one to do with all this time?

When the answer to this question is unclear, some aged people try to escape (Atchley, 1995:371). One reaction is to consume too much alcohol. Another is to sleep as much as possible. It is common, however, for the slumber of aged individuals to become more fragmented, with less deep sleep and more wakeful periods during the night. Hence, they turn to sleeping pills and other drugs, even though it is rare for aged persons to require such medication. With the help of physicians who overprescribe, elderly people frequently take such drugs in doses that are too high and for too long a period of time. For example, in one study of Halcion, a sleeping pill, a review of over 14,000 prescriptions to aged persons revealed that 85 percent of the recipients exceeded the recommended cumulative dosage and 70 percent exceeded the recommended duration (Kahn, 1994:46). One need not be unduly psychodynamic to suggest that sleep seems better than boredom, than the gnawing meaninglessness of life. Such strategies can have serious consequences. For example, the side effects of some drugs (especially combinations of them) can cause excessive anxiety, loss of coordination, dementia, and psychosis in various forms. To ordinary observers, these symptoms indicate senility or Alzheimer's disease. People who display such traits sometimes end up in nursing homes, more unhappy than ever.

Now escapist behavior takes many forms, and I have noted only some examples here. Those most prone to escapism live alone or become isolated regardless of their living arrangements. Such persons display significantly lower levels of life satisfaction. Once again, the key is to maintain ties to the community. Such bonds also help people cope with illness and disability.

Adapting to Illness and Disability

As people age, they often develop chronic illnesses and disabilities. Some are only slightly incapacitating, such as mild forms of arthritis; others involve more serious infirmities, such as heart disease. In any case, most people eventually become disabled in some form and dependent not just for a short time but more or less permanently.[3]

Becoming dependent is not easy for most individuals. Indeed, 78 percent of the population say they fear the loss of freedom that can result from illness and disability (AAR, 1991). Instead of driving to the store the way ordinary adults do, they must ask for help. Instead of bathing or cooking for themselves as ordinary adults do, they must ask for help. It is difficult for people who have been responsible for themselves and others over many decades to adjust to needing assistance. This situation suggests one reason elderly individuals talk about the past so much: to maintain self-esteem by referring to a time when they were independent. It also suggests why aged people sometimes do not admit they need assistance and resent it when given: to maintain self-esteem and independence. Dependency returns aged persons to the condition of childhood. (It has been said that one reason grandparents and young children become so close is that they have a common enemy . . .) Most aged people try to avoid becoming dependent for as long as possible.

In the aftermath of his father's death in 1952, the poet Dylan Thomas wrote the following lines (1988:148):

> Do not go gentle into that good night,
> Old age should burn and rave at close of day;
> Rage, rage against the dying of the light.

I think Thomas is saying that the issue is not old age but the maintenance problems that result. Phrased more simply, the trick is to admit needing help, accept it gracefully, yet maintain as many choices as possible for as long as possible. In so doing, a certain good-humored irascibility is useful, even though this can wear on caregivers. In any case, the ability to make meaningful choices, to control one's life, even as one becomes frail, suggests independence. It keeps individuals committed to their well-being, tied to the community, and more satisfied with their lives.

Eventually, however, every individual will die. This is bluntly put, I know. But even though old age and illness signal impending death, many wish to deny it—to themselves and others. This orientation makes coming to terms with death difficult.

Adapting to Death

In the past, most deaths occurred at home. They were public or quasi-public events in which the dying person said good-bye to family and friends. Remember, until recently death could not be avoided; when people stopped breathing, they died. Moreover, indicators of death frequently presented themselves ahead of time. People knew. So did their families and friends. And since death occurred often, it was accepted as a normal part of life. It could not be denied.[4]

Today the situation is altogether different. Death is like sex was to the Victorians: It is fascinating and frightening, inevitable, but we do not speak of it. One reason for this reticence is that death is now concentrated in old age. Since 72 percent of all deaths occur after age 65, there are fewer relatives and friends who are touched by them (USBC, 1996c:3–6). Death is not seen as an everyday event. A second reason for our reluctance to speak is that people sometimes deny death is pending. This includes caretakers and medical personnel, as well as individuals about to die. Today medical treatment prevents the symptoms of death from showing. So people do not necessarily know. Moreover, physicians and indeed the general population are oriented to "beat" death (as a variation on the old football cheer states, "Push it back, push it back, push it way back"—indefinitely). In this context, family members, physicians, and others do not always level with the dying person. So a meaningful death, one in which people say good-bye to one another, come to terms with life, prepare practical affairs, and mourn together, has become difficult. This problem is especially severe in hospitals and nursing homes, where organizational imperatives, such as avoiding legal liability, dominate.

In *On Death and Dying,* based on some remarkable interviews with dying persons, Elizabeth Kübler-Ross inferred a five-stage process of adapting to death (1969). (1) Some people react at first by refusing to believe they are going to die. (2) Some then become angry at the unfairness. (3) Some next begin bargaining, which might mean asking God to postpone death in exchange for better behavior or changing lifestyle and hoping for the best. (4) As reality sinks in, some people become depressed and focus on all they are losing. (5) Finally, most accept their fate. Not everyone goes through these stages, of course. A previously healthy 65-year-old will probably react differently than an 88-year-old. A person isolated from family and friends may act differently than one actively engaged. Thus, these "stages" represent some typical responses to dying that many individuals display in some form. Yet much depends on people's awareness of their pending death. They cannot adapt to that which they are unwilling to confront. Such a confrontation can be terrifying. In his poem "Aubade," Philip Larkin captures the sense of panic—indeed, terror—that death inspires (1988:208):

> *This is what we fear—no sight, no sound,*
> *No touch or taste or smell, nothing to think with.*
> *Nothing to love or link with,*
> *The anesthetic from which none come round.*

Yet the terror must be faced, precisely because most people now live long lives and death is concentrated in old age. In facing an uncomfortable issue, it is usually helpful to understand how structural changes have produced the dilemma.

Social Structure and an Aging Population

Until the past 200 years or so, every society displayed high birth- and death rates, and this balance produced little population growth. Today, in contrast, societies like the United States display low birth- and death rates. I earlier described this fundamental change as a *tsunami*, but in sociological jargon the term is *demographic transition* (Thompson, 1929). The concept refers to rapid total population increase and a change in its composition: a rising percentage of aged people. The empirical generalization is: *The long-term increase in the size of the population and the proportion that is aged in Western industrial societies reflects (1) declining fertility rates, (2) declining infant mortality rates, (3) declining immigration rates, and (4) advances in medical technology.* The wording here is important. Unlike many structural arguments, the demographic transition has been analyzed many times, and the results are stable (Sen, 1994). Hence, I label it an empirical generalization.[5]

Declining Fertility Rates

The population grew older because of the declining fertility rate, the average number of children each woman has (Coale, 1956). In Fischer's graceful prose, "Changes in fertility and age composition have run together in American history. Fertility has changed first, with changes in age composition coming close behind, like a statistical shadow" (1978:105). Thus, the average woman born in the early 1800s had seven to eight live children. Today she has about two. Low fertility narrows the population pyramid's base and leads to a relative increase in the number of aged people.

Declining fertility reflects the transformation of the family. As Chapter 2 showed, the value of bearing children fell when the significance of rearing them rose, and their number was reduced in order to provide a nurturing environment. Childhood became, for the first time in history, a distinct stage in life. This change is related, of course, to industrialization, which requires a more highly skilled workforce. It is also related to the increasing proportion of children who survive infancy.

Declining Infant Mortality Rates

The second factor producing an aging population is the declining infant mortality rate, the number of live babies who die within the first year of life. Over the past century, the infant mortality rate has fallen from 170 per 1,000 live births to nine (USBC, 1975:57; NCHS, 1995:2).

The main reasons for this decline are improvements in nutrition and sanitation (McKeown, 1976). They help to prevent the onset of short-term diseases that used to kill people, especially infants: influenza, pneumonia, tuberculosis, typhoid, measles, and the like. In addition, advances in medical technology reduce infant mortality because some diseases can now be cured after they are contracted.[6] The result is an increase in life expectancy at birth. In 1790 only 11–14 percent of those born alive lived to age 60. In comparison, 43 percent of those born in 1890 lived to age 65, and (it is projected) 86 percent of those born in 1990 will live to retirement age (Fischer, 1978:105; NCHS, 1995:17).

As with declining fertility, the falling infant mortality rate produces an aging population by changing the ratio of the old and young. In effect, elderly people today constitute the first cohorts in history that had a reasonable chance of living through infancy and thus reaching old age.

Declining Immigration Rates

The third factor producing an aging population is the decline in immigration. As noted in Chapter 4, the United States is a nation of immigrants. From 1880 to 1930, about 28 million persons entered this country, which meant that immigrants made up a high proportion of the inhabitants (USBC, 1975:97). Since most were young, the age of the population was low, even as fertility and infant mortality rates declined. Today immigration has decreased and has little demographic effect. Thus, the impact of declining fertility and infant mortality has become even greater.

Advances in Medical Technology

The final factor producing an aging population is advances in medical technology. The increasing ability to apply scientific knowledge to the practical problem of preventing death means that many diseases can be cured and physiological problems repaired. Death can be pushed back.

I would like to illustrate the impact of medical treatment by mentioning some of the life-sustaining technologies that now exist. The term refers to drugs, surgical procedures, and medical devices that keep alive individuals who would otherwise die within a foreseeable but usually uncertain time (OTA, 1987:4).

Drugs are one form of life-sustaining technology. Antibiotics combat all sorts of bacterial infections. For example, an outbreak of Spanish flu just after World War I killed about 250,000 people. Today the use of antibiotics keeps the death toll from influenza minimal at every age. Recently developed antihypertensive drugs reduce blood pressure. For the 40-year-old, such drugs add decades to life. For the 85-year-old, they add years. New drugs are invented all the time.

Surgical procedures constitute another life-sustaining technology. Some are now simple operations; appendicitis, for example, is easily diagnosed and treated today, so deaths from this condition are rare. Again, decades are added to people's lives. In the past, they just died. Other operations are more difficult, albeit common. Coronary artery bypass procedures, for example, mend the heart. When combined with modern drugs, the operation repairs the body, prevents death, and extends life.

Medical devices constitute the final life-sustaining technology. They are used as substitutes for normal bodily functions; for example, mechanical ventilation assists or replaces normal breathing. For many patients, such help buys time—a few hours or days—during which physicians can try other therapies. Again, lives are saved. Among the aged, however, permanent dependence commonly develops when medical devices are used (OTA, 1987). Such dependence is sometimes an obvious good. For example, a heart pacemaker allows a person to lead an active, engaged lifestyle. With other devices, however, I wonder. For example, mechanical ventilation produces significant physical discomfort. Basically, patients feel chronically miserable. They also experience eating difficulties, speech deficiencies, and decreased mobility, among other afflictions. Obviously, the nature of the problems that develop depends upon the technology used.

Implications

Consider certain aspects of the medical history of a fictional person I call Harriet James. Between the ages of 20 and 50, Harriet had the flu four times (one developed into walking pneumonia) and an appendectomy. Each time she was treated with antibiotics and other modern medical procedures, and her chance of recovery was essentially 100 percent. So treatment probably prevented death and added many decades of productive life. At age 53, Harriet found a lump in her breast and had a partial mastectomy. Her recovery was complete. Note that her life span would have been much shorter if the cancer had not been treated. Thus, as before, medical treatment allowed her to survive for many additional years.

Over the next twelve years, Harriet contracted several colds and the flu once. Again, medical treatment meant that survival into old age was not an issue. At age 65, however, she suffered a heart attack. With the help of modern drugs, Harriet recovered completely. Note again that in the past she would have died. Once retired, she continued to be as independent as before, traveling to Europe on two occasions.

At age 75, Harriet developed cancer of the colon. Although the odds of full recovery were only 50 percent, she was mentally alert and eager to go forward with the procedure. Alas, she did not return to health after the operation. Her days of foreign travel were over, and she needed her daughter's help with a variety of instrumental tasks, such as errands and house maintenance. Nonetheless, she remained reasonably active.

At 80, Harriet suffered another heart attack. A coronary bypass allowed her to recover but left her more disabled and dependent. Although Harriet remained mentally alert, her daughter began providing a variety of personal as well as instrumental forms of care.

Two years later, Harriet had a stroke. Treatment saved her life, but within a week she developed pneumonia. Antibiotics again saved her life. Unfortunately, she was left partially paralyzed and only semicompetent. At this time, she was placed in a nursing home. She did not choose this abode. In fact, she could no longer make such basic decisions.

During her mid-80s, Harriet declined steadily, both physically and psychologically. She suffered a series of strokes that left her incontinent and bedridden. She also had pneumonia several times. Each time antibiotics saved her life. Harriet James died at 89. She spent her last years debilitated and demented.

This vignette raises a fundamental issue: At what point was Harriet James dying? It seems to me that no straightforward answer exists. Without the benefit of medical technology, she might have died as a young woman. Her life expectancy was increased by treatment. The vignette makes clear, however, that the impact of medical therapy differs with age. By preventing death at age 20 or 40 or 65, it often restores people to fully functioning adulthood; their quality of life is as it was before. For people like Harriet James, however, treatment at age 85 did little more than keep her physically alive in a humiliating condition. There is nothing magic about 85; I merely suggest that preventing death among the old-old has different consequences than at earlier ages.

Limiting Medical Treatment

These considerations lead to a profound ethical issue: At what point, if any, should treatment of people like Harriet be withheld or withdrawn? It is reasonable to ask whether coronary bypass operations should be paid for by the government and performed on aged people, especially the old-old. In some circumstances, as the vignette shows, it is even reasonable to ask whether such basic treatment as administering antibiotics ought to occur. This ethical issue must be considered, of course, along with the economics of medical treatment for the elderly. A high proportion of the cost of Medicare goes to people in the last two years of life, much of it high-technology medicine (Callahan, 1987). More generally, as indicated earlier, the escalating cost of treatment for the aged under the Medicare and Medicaid programs is not supportable in the future. The choice involves how to limit costs yet act ethically.

In thinking about this choice, it should be recognized that medical treatment is withheld or withdrawn all the time, often in accordance with living wills or the decision of someone with power of attorney for medical treatment (OTA, 1987). My impression, however, is that hospital deaths often reflect the withholding or termination of treatment even in the absence of explicit guidance. This is one of the (many) secrets of modern medicine. Yet no one knows how often such decisions are made, what criteria are used, or who participates. And it often happens after the use of painful and expensive procedures. This sequence occurs because no societal consensus exists as to how these determinations ought to be made.

In order to develop such a consensus, the proper goals of medical treatment must be discussed. In so doing, it is useful to distinguish between active and disabled life expectancy (Olshansky et al., 1991, 1993). The major diseases afflicting elderly people today are often symptoms of aging, which is why being saved from death does not have the same impact for the old as it does for the young. Instead of raising active life expectancy, treatment can simply lead to long years of disability. Nonetheless, if the extension of life is deemed the most important goal of medicine, then the tools for doing this are readily available today—albeit at great (and growing) cost. From this angle, then, treatment should rarely be withheld or withdrawn. And this is so even if the disability is extreme, as in Harriet James's last years.

It is reasonable to ask, however, whether simply being alive is worth it. Was Harriet's quality of life toward the end sufficiently satisfying to justify a moral stance in which life-sustaining technology always ought to be used? Now the notion of "quality of life" is difficult to define, and it is probable that people see it in different ways. But at a minimum, almost everyone would agree that it involves the capacity to reason, to have emotions, and to enter into relationships. It might also involve living without great pain and being mobile to some degree. These are key elements of being a person, as opposed to merely being alive. If the sanctity of life involves a sense of personhood defined in this way, then perhaps appropriate goals for medical treatment involve a greater emphasis on caring for people rather than curing sickness. From this angle, situations will arise in which treatment might be limited.

In *Setting Limits: Medical Goals in an Aging Society,* Daniel Callahan makes this argument explicit and in so doing opens a discussion that the nation needs to have (1987). He says that the proper goals for medicine should be the avoidance of premature death and the relief of suffering in old age. He makes several proposals for implementing these goals: (1) The elderly, like everyone else, should have access to universal medical treatment. (2) The goal of treatment should be to help everyone avoid premature death. (3) There should be a "better balance" between curing and caring, with greater emphasis on the latter (e.g., more stress on nursing, physical therapy, and home support). (4) Assuming the above reforms, age should be used as a categorical standard for cutting off life-sustaining technology. Callahan's logic is that at some point, usually in a person's 80s, it becomes morally appropriate to withhold (public payment for) treatment because people have lived out their natural lives by then. Whether you agree with his proposals or not, Callahan believes that these issues need to be debated in order to develop ethical guidelines about life and death, about the obligations of the generations to each other.[7]

It is easy to see why developing a consensus about limiting medical treatment is going to be difficult. As Callahan observes, aged people have two fears: They dread dying alone, demented, in a nursing home, and they worry about dying in a hospital with tubes sticking out of every orifice (AAR, 1991). Yet many elderly patients believe that "the doctor knows best." This orientation does not change when patients are faced with tough choices near the end of life. Physicians have a bias to treat.

This bias occurs partly because they are paid for services performed. (One needs to be appropriately cynical. Physicians, like other entrepreneurs, do consider their own economic benefit in making treatment decisions.) It occurs partly because they are afraid of lawsuits if treatment is withheld. It occurs partly because physicians, like other competitors, do not like losing: to death. And it occurs partly because they are trained to preserve life. This goal has always been intrinsic to the practice of medicine. A frequent result is that life-sustaining technology gets used even for terminally ill patients who specifically oppose aggressive (often painful) medical treatment (Knaus, 1995). Aggressive treatment is administered even to people in their 90s (Hosking, 1989). When people die after suffering a great deal, physicians may say something like, "We did all we could." They do not say, "We put them through hell, made a lot of money, and then let them die," even though that may be a more accurate description of what actually happened. And aged people's fears come true.

Suicide and Euthanasia

Limiting medical treatment is also difficult because it implies that human beings decide when life should end. Yet this happens a lot, as the vignette shows. If nature had taken its course, Harriet James would probably have died at a young age. She and her doctors used technology to interfere with the "natural" order of events. And what if Harriet, while fully competent, had decided to commit suicide after her second heart attack? This is, of course, another way of interfering with the "natural" order of events. Given the options, some people in her situation make this choice because they wish to control their own demise. In addition, many aged people do not want to become burdens on their children (AAR, 1991). And what, moreover, if Harriet had asked for assistance in carrying out this task? This is called euthanasia, or mercy killing. It places family, friends, and physicians in a very difficult position, both morally and legally. Although evidence about the frequency with which events like this occur is anecdotal, they often happen.

One indicator is changing attitudes toward suicide. In 1947 only 38 percent of the population agreed that suicide would be acceptable when a person had an incurable disease; by 1996, however, 64 percent agreed (GSS, 1996). Given these data, it should not be surprising that suicide rates increase considerably among the aged (USBC, 1994:94). And this datum includes only known suicides; they are significantly underreported.

Another indicator is changing attitudes toward euthanasia. In 1977 only 38 percent of the population agreed that physicians might hasten death for people with incurable diseases who want to die; in 1996, however, an astonishing 71 percent agreed (GSS, 1996). These responses lend credence to news reports suggesting that mercy killing (direct or indirect) is increasing, although the rate is a complete unknown. Because such behavior can lead to a murder indictment, it tends to happen circuitously. Sometimes, it appears, terminal patients are informed of the proper dosage for pain-killing or sleep-inducing drugs and warned to take only a limited number of tablets because an overdose can be fatal. A sort of dance of death takes place. Knowing the lethal dose, patients can choose the time and place of their death. Again, how often this or some other mode of assistance occurs remains unclear. But physicians, nurses, or family members sometimes risk acting overtly to assist people's deaths (Asch, 1996). Dr. Timothy Quill, for example, chose to assist his dying patient's suicide (1991). The patient wanted to say good-bye to her family and end her life with some dignity. After writing about the experience, Quill was brought before a grand jury and threatened with indictment for murder. The jury refused to indict (Altman, 1991). This has been the pattern in similar cases.

Yet the issues surrounding the end of life are not always clear-cut. Those opposed to allowing physicians (or anyone else) help people die argue that the public will lose confidence in doctors as healers. They worry that aged people will be manipulated to end their lives for selfish reasons: to save money, to reduce stress on caregivers, or to salvage an inheritance. Since even a small inheritance (a few thousand dollars) can motivate people to wish an aged person dead, this concern is realistic.

Despite this apprehension, the problems of limiting medical treatment, euthanasia, and suicide among the elderly will not go away. Dying can be a lonely event, the stuff of nightmares. This is especially likely in a hospital setting, where people feel isolated and helpless. It seems to me that so much is taken in death that asking to leave one's dignity intact is not asking a great deal. People should not have to die the way Harriet James did. It could be argued that she was sentenced to life at the end because she no longer had enough of the organ of consent, the brain, to choose death. One way of preventing this result is to get people out of hospitals and into either hospices or their own homes. A hospice provides care for terminal patients by alleviating pain and enhancing their quality of life prior to death. The idea is that death should occur "naturally." Yet neither entering a hospice nor returning home obviates the problems discussed here. The moral crucible remains, simply because choices about death exist. They cannot be avoided. So we must fashion a moral tradition in a historical context where new choices are possible. Like Gautama, we must develop a new vision of life and death—and life.

Despite the terror that death poses, Philip Larkin concludes "Aubade" with a vision of life's mundane continuity (1988:208):

> *Work has to be done.*
> *Postmen like doctors go from house to house.*

I think it is significant that the poem's title, "Aubade," refers to a song (in French, of course) in which lovers separate at dawn.

Notes

1. Given the gendered nature of elder care, it is amazing that most studies of the division of labor in families fail to mention it (Seccombe and Dwyer, 1995).

2. For example, how are families to care for an elderly person with Alzheimer's who needs twenty-four-hour supervision? Only extremely affluent families may be able to hire someone. In such cases, a woman becomes a manager supervising others, who are often poor women.

3. Dependency does not always occur. In "The Oldest Old," Thomas Perls shows that long-lived people, over age 90, are often more healthy and agile than those in their 70s and 80s (1995). They appear to benefit from luck, "longevity genes," and adaptive behaviors (e.g., exercise, not smoking). Their existence suggests that illness and disability can sometimes be compressed into a relatively short time prior to death (Fries, 1980).

4. I am simplifying a complex and very interesting historical process here. See Philippe Ariès, *The Hour of Our Death* (1981).

5. This finding is limited to Western industrial societies. Whether it applies to developing countries today has been questioned because the historical context differs (Teitelbaum, 1975).

6. The order of these variables is important. Advances in medical technology have been far less significant than improvements in nutrition and sanitation for the health of the population. I discuss this (contentious) issue in Chapter 9.

7. Callahan's argument is controversial. For critical views, see Gerald Winslow and James Walters, *Facing Limits: Ethics and Health Care for the Elderly* (1993). For Callahan's reply to his (many) critics, see "Setting Limits: A Response" (1994).

Recommended Reading

Ariès, Philippe. *The Hour of Our Death* (New York: Knopf, 1981).
Callahan, Daniel. *Setting Limits: Medical Goals in an Aging Society* (New York: Simon & Schuster, 1987).
Fischer, David Hackett. *Growing Old in America* (New York: Oxford University Press, 1978).
Olmstead, Alan. *Threshold: The First Days of Retirement* (New York: Harper & Row, 1975).

9 *Health*

Outline of Chapter 9

I. Dimensions of Health
   A. Historical Dimensions
   B. International Dimensions

II. Consequences of Ill Health and the Emphasis on Treatment

III. Individuals and Health
   A. Age
   B. Gender
   C. Race and Ethnicity
   D. Social Class

IV. Social Structure and Health
   A. The Long-Term Improvement in Health
      1. Improvements in Nutrition
      2. Improvements in Sanitation
      3. Improvements in Medical Technology
   B. The Relative Ill Health of the U.S. Population
      1. Degree of Income Inequality
      2. Low Emphasis on Prevention
      3. Lack of Access to Treatment and Preventive Care

V. Implications

In *Past and Present,* his indictment of mass poverty in England written in the 1840s, Thomas Carlyle tells the story of a poor Irish widow who goes with her three children from one charitable institution to another (1977:151). At each of them she appeals: "Behold I am sinking, bare of help. You must help me. I am your sister, bone of your bone, one God made us." The response, predictable at that time, was: "Thou art no sister of ours." Ultimately, the woman dies of typhus, infecting seventeen of her neighbors, who also die. At the end of the story, a physician asks the obvious question: "Would it not have been economy to help this poor widow?"

The spread of this kind of deadly disease is unlikely today, although not because we have become more charitable and not because epidemics no longer arise (HIV-AIDS is an obvious example). Rather, people are less exposed to such acute diseases as typhus, tuberculosis, whooping cough, measles, scarlet fever, diphtheria, cholera, typhoid, and bubonic plague. *Acute diseases* are health problems of less than three months' duration that restrict activity. The lessened impact of acute diseases is a new phenomenon in history. In Carlyle's time—and indeed for most of human existence—high exposure to toxins and pervasive malnourishment (which increased susceptibility) meant that typhus, tuberculosis, and other illnesses swept through towns, killing large numbers. Most people lived hard lives and, like the Irish widow, died young. Yet as described in Chapter 8, this age-old pattern began changing in the nineteenth century. People are healthier now and live longer. Today we do not fear epidemics of tuberculosis, the leading cause of death 100 years ago, since it is now easily prevented.

This chapter examines the health of the U.S. population.[1] *Health* is often defined as the absence of illness, a useful definition because it leads to quantifiable data. But it is also limited, for there is more to health than not being ill; it is better to feel well, to live fully, to be able to realize one's potential. These more subtle indicators suggest that health involves more than treating illness.

This suggestion is important because medical treatment is only one factor influencing population health. And it may not be the most effective. Carlyle's physician had it half right: It would have been both humane and wise to help the poor widow. It would have been even wiser, however, to promote health so that her illness did not occur. Typhus, for example, is caused by rickettsia carried by fleas and lice. Such simple and now common public health measures as clean water and indoor plumbing prevent this disease from developing by lowering exposure, thus obviating the need for treatment. This example is generalizable.

Yet the United States rejects its implications, emphasizing the treatment of illness rather than the promotion of health. Moreover, the United States does a poor job of treating illness in the population because many people do not have access to treatment. Despite the long debate over "health care," millions have no insurance; so, like the poor widow, they endure illness more often than they should and must beg for help (e.g., at hospital emergency rooms). Although those with insurance are better off, their situation has changed greatly in recent years. It used to be that on becoming ill, they saw physicians who were paid on a fee-for-service basis, a system that encourages high costs and unnecessary treatment. Increasingly, however, those with insurance see physicians in health maintenance organizations (HMOs), who are paid on a capitation system (a yearly fee for each patient a physician has), a system that discourages treatment. Although costs have stopped rising as fast, is the focus on providing treatment wise? Would it not be wiser to need physicians less often?[2]

Dimensions of Health

The overall health of the population can be seen by examining *vital statistics*, which provide data about births and deaths in a society. The term "vital" comes from the Latin word meaning "life," implying that such information indicates a society's level of illness and death. Typical vital statistics are infant mortality and life expectancy, which are used in this section.

Historical Dimensions

Figure 9.1 reveals the historical improvement in the health of the population by showing changes in the infant mortality rate since 1870. You should recall that the *infant mortality rate* refers to the number of live babies who die in the first year of life. The figure reveals that about 16–17 percent (160–170 per 1,000) of all babies born in the later years of the last century failed to live until their first birthday. This high rate meant that most families experienced the death of a newborn child. Beginning about 1900, however, the infant mortality rate fell steadily, from about 141 per 1,000 in 1900 to twenty-eight in 1950. Put differently, after World War II only about 3 percent of all babies died in their first year. Since that time, the rate has fallen even further (albeit at a slower pace), to about eight per 1,000 in 1996. An infant death has become rare today, and most people do not know anyone who has had a newborn baby die.

Although this emphasis on infant deaths may seem morbid, such data are useful because deaths are countable and their number has been collected for a long time. More important, the infant mortality rate indicates (inversely) the overall health of a population because it is sensitive to the degree of nutrition, sanitation, and medical treatment in a society. In fact, the quality of a child's early environment influences its health risks throughout life (Barker, 1992; Hertzman, 1994). As will become clear, this fact has enormous implications for health policy.

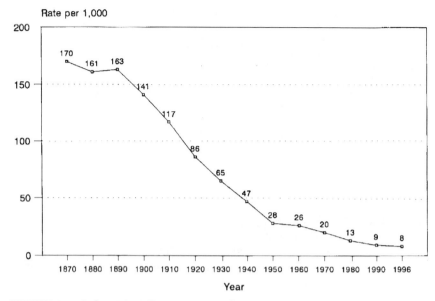

FIGURE 9.1   Infant Mortality Rate, United States, 1870–1996
NOTE: Data for 1870–1910 are for the state of Massachusetts.
SOURCE: USBC (1975:57, 1996d:93); NCHS (1996b:26).

One indicator of the improvement in health is that the major causes of death have changed from acute to chronic diseases such as cancer, heart disease, and cerebrovascular disease leading to strokes.[3] *Chronic diseases* are long-term health problems that restrict activity, often causing death. The tuberculosis death rate dropped from about 3.7 per 1,000 in 1860 to nearly zero in 1995 (USBC, 1975:58; NCHS, 1996c:15). In contrast, the death rate from all forms of cancer rose from 0.6 per 1,000 in 1900 to 201 in 1995. Such illnesses typically develop during middle age or later, and their increasing rate indicates that people live longer today. This change has come about in all economically developed nations (see Chapter 8).

International Dimensions

Many people assume, as common sense, that the United States is healthier than other nations. It is not so. Table 9.1 illustrates this fact by displaying infant mortality rates and life expectancy for seven Western nations and Japan. The United States has the highest rate of infant mortality and Japan the lowest. The small differences among nations (tenths of a point) are substantively significant; they reflect many deaths. Similarly, the United States has the shortest life expectancy among the na-

TABLE 9.1   Infant Mortality and Life Expectancy by Nation, 1996

	Infant Mortality (per 1,000)	*Life Expectancy (years)*
Japan	4.4	79.6
Sweden	4.5	78.1
Netherlands	4.9	77.7
Germany	6.0	76.0
Canada	6.1	79.1
France	6.2	78.4
United Kingdom	6.4	76.4
United States	6.7	76.3

SOURCE: USBC (1996c:831, 834).

tions being compared and Japan the longest. Again, small differences mean a lot.

Although not displayed in the table, the U.S. position in international comparisons of health has worsened over the years. Japan, in fact, is now the healthiest nation in the world. The United States, in comparison, ranked seventh among all nations in infant mortality rate in 1950; it now ranks sixteenth (USBC, 1996d:831). This change suggests there are more effective ways of reducing infant deaths than those the United States pursues. By inference, it also suggests there are more effective ways of promoting the health of the entire population than those the United States pursues. I confront these issues momentarily; for now, simply note that although vitality in the United States has improved over time, it has become even better in other societies.

Before continuing, the usual caveat about viewing these data cautiously must be mentioned. No nationwide data on infant mortality exist prior to 1900. Thus, as indicated in Figure 9.1, I have relied on information from the state of Massachusetts for years prior to the turn of the century. Such data may understate the prevalence of acute diseases at that time, and it is possible that infant mortality was higher than indicated. Nonetheless, they offer the best information available.

Consequences of Ill Health and the Emphasis on Treatment

The data in Tables 9.1 and 9.2 show that the United States is not a very healthy nation compared to others. Nonetheless, the United States pays a lot for its relative ill health: about $950 billion each year in order to

TABLE 9.2   Differences by Nation in Outlays for Health, 1994

	(1) **Total** *Percent* *GDP Spent* *on Health*	=	*(2)* *Percent* *GDP Spent* *on **Medical*** ***Treatment***	+	*(3)* *Percent* *GDP Spent* *on **Public*** ***Health***	*(4)* *Column 3* *as Percent* *of* *Column 1*
United Kingdom	6.9	=	1.1	+	5.8	84%
Japan	7.3	=	2.0	+	5.3	73%
Sweden	7.7	=	1.3	+	6.4	83%
Germany	8.6	=	2.6	+	6.0	70%
France	9.7	=	2.1	+	7.6	78%
Canada	9.8	=	2.8	+	7.0	71%
United States	14.2	=	7.5	+	6.7	47%

NOTE: Data for Germany are for 1993.

SOURCE: USBC (1996c:834).

treat illness. About 44 percent of this amount comes from government outlays, with the remainder from individuals and private industry, mainly insurance companies (USBC, 1996d:112). As shown in column 1 of Table 9.2, these costs amounted to 14.2 percent of the GDP in 1994. In comparison, the United Kingdom spent only 6.9 percent, Japan 7.3 percent, and Sweden 7.7 percent. Thus, the United States spends almost twice what Sweden does, which has an infant mortality rate 30 percent lower. Tables 9.1 and 9.2 show a pattern of higher outlays and worse health outcomes.

The reason for these differences can be seen in columns 2–4 of Table 9.2: Other nations spend less on treatment and more on public health— which provides a rough indicator of health promotion. Although the United Kingdom, for example, spends relatively little compared to other Western nations, about 84 percent of the total goes to public health. Sweden, which spends more, uses 83 percent of its outlays for public health and gets much better results than either the United States or the UK.

To get a sense of the advantages and disadvantages of health promotion versus treatment, I want to focus on infant mortality. In so doing, it is useful to distinguish between neonatal mortality, deaths in the first twenty-seven days of life, and postneonatal mortality, deaths in the remainder of the first year. The key factor causing postneonatal mortality is disease, such as the acute conditions mentioned earlier. Look again at Figure 9.1. Nearly all the decline from 141 to 28 per 1,000 from 1900 to

1950 occurred in postneonatal deaths (Budiansky, 1986). This decline reflects the degree to which disease became less widespread because of improvements in sanitation and nutrition. Sanitation is important because babies living in relatively clean environments are less exposed to toxins. Nutrition is important because well-fed infants display greater resistance to illness when exposed. These environmental improvements affect everyone, of course, so not only are infants more likely to survive, but the vitality of the total population is better, too. Such improvements did not happen by accident; they reflect advances in medical technology and public health policies that implemented such insights. For example, the decision to add small amounts of chlorine to the water supply in the 1880s was based on knowledge about how cholera is transmitted (Page, 1987). Thus, prevention results not only in fewer deaths but lower costs. Cholera can now be treated, but it would cost far more (in both money and human suffering) to cure this disease than to prevent it.

In contrast to postneonatal mortality, the key factor in neonatal mortality is low birth weight, mainly because babies born weighing less than 5.5 pounds often do not have fully developed immune systems and have difficulty breathing, among other problems. Although genetic factors, the quality of the pregnancy and delivery, and gestational age also influence neonatal mortality, most of these factors act through low birth weight. Many die, more in this country than in other nations. But fewer die than in the past. Nearly all of the decline in infant deaths between 1950 and 1995 occurred in neonatal mortality, primarily because of improvements in medical treatment—not prevention of low birth weight (Budiansky, 1986; Hack, 1995).

Such treatment is enormously expensive. About 274,000 babies were born low birth weight in 1996, 7 percent of total births (NCHS, 1996b:13). Most were placed in neonatal intensive care. The estimated average cost of treatment in the first year of life was $25,000 for each neonate, totaling about $6.9 billion annually. For the survivors, expenditures for medical treatment during years 1–4 total several billion dollars more. Medical expenses in the remainder of childhood are also significant, as low-birth-weight babies are more likely to display chronic health problems and need treatment (Lewit, 1995). These continuing difficulties illustrate my previous comment that the quality of a child's early environment affects its health throughout life.[4]

In addition, such treatment is traumatic and has a long-lasting impact on survivors' quality of life. Thus, they are more likely to perform poorly in school, require special education classes, and repeat grades (which also costs money). They are also more likely to drop out of school, become poor as adults, and receive public aid (costing yet more money). Finally, both the infants and their families endure pain and trauma. For example, being connected to a mechanical ventilator for a long period (weeks, months) means being chronically miserable during perhaps the most important period of development. Low-birth-weight babies who do not survive are traumatized as well, for they often undergo invasive and painful treatment before dying.[5] As a result, there is much debate among medical ethicists and parents as to the wisdom of treating and saving infants with only marginal chances at a healthy life (Tyson, 1994; Hack, 1993).

The emphasis on treating low-birth-weight babies epitomizes a fundamental characteristic of medicine in the United States: Risks are understated because people want to do something, preferably with high-technology equipment (Payer, 1988). Note, however, that the ability to treat does not mean that the cause of neonatal mortality—low birth weight—has changed. The key to preventing low birth weight and thus reducing the infant mortality rate to levels seen in other nations is prenatal care. The empirical generalization is: *The later in the pregnancy prenatal care begins, the worse the birth outcome* (e.g., low birth weight leading to infant mortality).

In the low-technology task of prenatal care, nearly all the risks associated with pregnancy can be identified in a pregnant woman's first visit to an obstetrician. This visit should include a complete physical examination and start a process of encouraging healthy behavior about nutrition, weight gain, safe sex, the dangers of drugs, and other issues. Yet only about 80 percent of pregnant women receive prenatal care in the first trimester, when it is most important (NCHS, 1996f:9). Moreover, there are notable racial and ethnic differences in the odds of getting prenatal care, its quality, and the results; more on this later.

For the moment, I simply want to point out that prenatal care costs little. Current medical protocol indicates about ten visits, which probably cost around $500 (less if the woman is seen by a nurse practitioner and no complications are revealed by the examination, more if she is seen by a physician and complications exist). It is important, however, especially for low-income people, that prenatal care be more comprehensive than just a medical examination. It should involve, for example, providing vitamin and food supplements (due to the relatively high level of malnutrition that occurs in this country), psychosocial risk assessment, and counseling. Comprehensive prenatal care works; it is associated with about a 27 percent reduction in low-weight births, which would lead to far fewer deaths and much lower costs for treatment (Henderson, 1994; Limpson, 1997). It also means that the early life of many children would be less traumatic, their development more normal, and their health throughout life better. Moreover, the impact of comprehensive prenatal care is long term. After fifteen years, a group of low-income mothers who received home visits from nurses while pregnant and during their children's infancy displayed far fewer arrests, reports of child abuse, and other problems (Olds, 1997; Kitzman, 1997). So the impact of prenatal care goes far beyond just avoiding illness; it helps people to live fully, to realize their human potential.

The barriers to starting prenatal care in the United States are usually monetary: lack of insurance, transportation, and child care (CDC, 1996). In addition, women who do not want to be pregnant often delay beginning prenatal care, suggesting another obvious strategy for reducing the number of low-weight infants: preventing unwanted pregnancy by contraception (recall Chapter 2). In contrast, other Western nations have fewer low-birth-weight babies and thus less infant mortality because virtually all women have insurance, financial incentives encourage them to seek prenatal care, and outreach programs exist for high-risk pregnancies (Chaulk, 1994). These differences help to explain why such nations are healthier: They emphasize promoting public health rather than treating illness.

The data presented so far raise several questions. Why has the health of populations improved so dramatically over the past century or so? Why does the United States, one of the richest nations in the world, display more ill health than societies like it but with far fewer resources? The answers to these questions must be structural. Before pursuing that line of inquiry, however, I want to look at individuals and health.

Individuals and Health

So who gets sick? And who dies? As Figure 9.1 implies (using infant mortality as an example), most people in the United States are reasonably healthy, and the overall health of the population is far better than it was just a short time ago. But *epidemiologists*, researchers who study the incidence and control of illness in a population, have shown that age, gender, race and ethnicity, and social class are associated with illness and death.

Age

Age is correlated with illness and death among individuals in a curvilinear way: *The younger and older people are, the greater their likelihood of illness and death.* Data on heart disease, the leading cause of death in the United States today, illustrate the finding (NCHS, 1996a:37):

Age in Years	Deaths per 100,000
<1	18
1–4	2
5–14	1
15–24	3
25–34	9
35–44	32
45–54	113
55–65	330
65–74	817
75–84	2,093
≥85	6,495

To "see" the curve described by these data, imagine that it has the form of a bowl with the edge on the left lower than that on the right. A similar pattern is revealed by data on other chronic and acute conditions, admissions to nursing homes, visits to physicians, and the like. Younger and older people are more likely to become ill and die.

Gender

Although the stereotype is that women are physiologically weaker than men, their health situation is actually more complex. With regard to mortality: *Males are more likely to die at every age than females.* Men and women, however, die from different causes, mainly because of lifestyle differences. For example, although heart disease is the leading cause of death among women over age 65, it becomes the most important cause of death among men as early as age 40 (NCHS, 1996a). This disparity, along with differences in deaths from lung cancer, reflects the variation in cigarette-smoking habits between men and women.

The relationship between gender and morbidity differs as well: *Females are more likely to become sick at every age than males.* This difference remains even if problems due to pregnancy and childbirth are discounted. Although it can be argued that morbidity variations indicate women's greater tendency to report symptoms of illness, studies show that gender differences are real (Verbrugge, 1989). The only acute condition in which men's incidence is higher is injuries, mainly because of occupational differences. Thus, although men die sooner, they often feel better than do women.

Race and Ethnicity

Significant variations exist in illness and death by race and ethnicity. For example, African and Hispanic Americans are infected with HIV at rates greater than their proportion of the population (CDC, 1996). These differences exist with a wide variety of illnesses. Data on infant mortality for 1994 illustrate the overall health of various groups (NCHS, 1996e:99).

	Group Deaths per 1,000
African American	17
Native American	11
Puerto Rican American	10
Mexican American	7
White (non-Hispanic)	7
Cuban American	5
Chinese American	5
Japanese American	4

As implied earlier, African and Hispanic American women are less likely to obtain prenatal care and obtain it later in the pregnancy, and its quality varies. For example, women of color are less likely to receive information about the dangers of smoking and alcohol use and less likely to learn about the advantages and disadvantages of breastfeeding. These differences in access to and quality of prenatal care extend to many forms of treatment. African Americans are less likely to receive treatment for heart attacks (even controlling for ability to pay) than are whites; they are also less likely to have access to kidney transplants. Similarly, Hispanic persons, especially those who speak little English and lack insurance, have less access to treatment of all sorts. Obese Latina women, for example, are less likely to be properly classified as overweight and hence less likely to understand or be treated for the risks of obesity during prenatal care, leading to poor birth outcomes. It thus appears that the tendency to treat occurs more often with whites.[6]

The hypothesis that best explains these differences is this: *The health of racial and ethnic minority groups is reduced by (in order of importance): (1) the stress associated with discrimination, (2) inferior access to and quality of medical treatment, and (3) genetic differences.* A good example is high blood pressure among African Americans, a possibly fatal condition because it leads to heart attacks (Krieger, 1996). African Americans are about twice as likely to suffer from this disease as whites. Research shows that although African Americans may have a predisposition to high blood pressure, its occurrence is strongly affected by the stress produced by discrimination along with less access to treatment (Jackson, 1996). It is probable that this example is generalizable to other racial and ethnic groups.

Social Class

Just after the Civil War, fewer than one-fourth of the citizens of Providence, Rhode Island, paid taxes. This distinction provides a simple indicator of social class differences in health at that time. Those who paid taxes constituted the most affluent segment of the population and displayed mortality rates less than half that of nontaxpayers (Chapin, 1924). Since that time, all data show a social class gradient in health (Smith, 1996b; Gregorio, 1997): *The lower the social class, the greater the likelihood of illness and death.*

Please note that this finding describes a linear relationship; it does not distinguish between the poor and nonpoor. Put simply, persons with a large house and two cars usually live longer than persons with a small house and one car. Put in social scientific terms, a rich person will (on average) live longer than a middle-class person, a middle-class person will live longer than a working-class person, and a working-class person will live longer than a poor person. For example, death rates among white women vary by education, one indicator of social class (Pappas, 1993:106).

Education	Deaths per 1,000
Less than a high school degree	3.4
High school degree	2.5
Some college	2.1
College degree	1.8

This finding applies to all racial and ethnic groups (Smith, 1996a, 1996b). It holds across all societies (Kunst and Mackenbach, 1992; Wilkinson, 1997). And it has been true throughout this century, even though the causes of death have changed significantly.

The usual explanation of class differences in health focuses on access to treatment, mainly due to low income and lack of insurance coverage. But these factors, though real and important, are concentrated among the poor. They do not help much in understanding the gradient of health (as opposed to treatment). In order to deal with this issue, we must examine how the social structure influences the health of the population.

Social Structure and Health

Epidemiologists, like most people, tend to look at individuals in order to understand the causes of illness. Thus, studies of the "risk factors" associated with heart disease focus on cigarette smoking, high blood pressure, and high cholesterol. If only, it is believed, we could get individuals to change their behavior, the incidence of heart disease could be reduced. Yet these "risk factors" account for only about 40 percent of the incidence of this illness. In addition, even when a significant proportion of smokers and fat eaters reduce their consumption, they are replaced by new persons entering the "at risk" population (as adolescents begin smoking, for example). These details ought to suggest that structural phenomena underlie this disease. Indeed, as Leonard Syme observes in his essay "The Social Environment and Health," focusing on individuals "can have only limited success because it does nothing to alter those forces in society that cause" heart disease and other health problems (1994:81).

Syme cites Durkheim's observation that the rate of suicide differs from one group to another (1895). As noted in Chapter 1, Durkheim reasoned that structural differences among groups lead to varying rates of suicide. So it is with population health. I am concerned here with two issues. First, why has there been a long-term improvement in health? This process, illustrated in Figure 9.1, is typical of Western industrial societies—implying certain common structural changes. Second, why do international comparisons, shown in Table 9.1, reveal that societies similar to the United States are healthier? The usual argument is that the United States needs to spend more money for more and better (meaning high-tech) treatment. Well, maybe. The problem with this analysis is that this country already directs more resources to treatment than do other nations (Table 9.2). There must be structural reasons for both the long-term improvement in health and Americans' current relative ill health.

The Long-Term Improvement in Health

The improvement in population health over the past 150 years is one of the great triumphs of human history. Common sense, U.S. style, dictates that this change is due to the impact of medical advances. As is often the case, however, reality differs. *The long-term increase in population health reflects (1) improvements in nutrition, (2) improvements in sanitation, and (3) improvements in medical treatment.*

Two aspects of this finding should be emphasized. First, unlike many structural analyses, the evidence in this case is so strong that it constitutes an empirical generalization. Second, the order of the variables is important. In his now classic book *The Modern Rise of Population*, Thomas McKeown shows that the most important factors producing better population health have been improvements in nutrition and sanitation (1976). Medical treatment played a small role in this process.[7]

Improvements in Nutrition. As McKeown explains, the long-term increase in population required better nutrition. This change required, in turn, an increase in the food supply, which occurred just a short time ago. Here is the background:

The first agricultural revolution about 10,000 years ago, in which human beings learned how to cultivate crops, set the conditions for the relationship between social structure and health until very recently. Although knowledge is sketchy, it appears that most people were relatively healthy prior to this time, mainly because they lived in small bands rather isolated from one another. Crop cultivation changed that situation because it led to increases in food supplies and thus in population size. The growth and concentration of human populations, however, meant that infection was more easily transmitted. For a long time, then, the relationship between population size and food supplies remained close. The evidence reveals that until lately no human society has been able to limit births voluntarily (McKeown, 1976:19–43). Hence, population always tended to outstrip food supply, and the twin scourges of famine and disease reduced the number of people. Most people were relatively malnourished most of the time anyway, even in times of plenty. Hence, they were more susceptible to disease and its deadly impact (Frank and Mustard, 1994).

Nutrition influences resistance to disease at all stages: (1) the human host's susceptibility to the initial invasion of the infection, (2) the impact of the infection once established in the host, (3) the host's susceptibility to secondary infection, and (4) recovery from the disease. Quite simply, malnourished people display higher illness and death rates. Moreover, the long-term impact of malnourishment on children is devastating: It stunts both growth and intellectual development.

U.S. data on agricultural productivity illustrate how McKeown's argument proceeds. During the first half of the nineteenth century, each worker could supply only about four persons with food (USBC, 1975:458). Productivity began rising steadily, however, so that today each farmworker feeds about eighty persons. Although these data understate the increase in productivity, since many tasks performed on the farm in the nineteenth century are now part of the manufacturing process, they demonstrate the pattern of rising food supplies. What happened is that improvements in both farming methods and technology took place, such as crop rotation, fertilization, seed production, winter feeding, farm implements, and transportation (Langer, 1975). The resulting second agricultural revolution assured the ability of societies to feed themselves.

The impetus for rising farm productivity was not altruism in the sense of a quest for health. Farmers in the nineteenth century were driven by two forces: the need to survive and the desire for profit. The by-product of the latter was better nutrition, and therefore health, for the population as a whole.

Improvements in Sanitation. McKeown shows that the second factor in the decline in the death rate from acute conditions was reduced exposure to infection caused by better sanitation (1976:110–27). As with nutrition, these changes occurred recently. It is probable that at least in Western Europe sanitation during Roman times was rather good but became steadily poorer over the next 1,000 years (Tuchman, 1978). Industrialization and capitalism made a bad situation worse. Cities, newly grown and without adequate local government, were often giant cesspools. People lived amid their own bodily filth, exposed to infection.

The impact of attempts at reducing exposure depend upon the way a disease is transmitted. Airborne diseases are difficult to control because they are passed from person to person via close contact, such as sneezing or touch. Water- and food-borne diseases, however, can be cheaply and effectively prevented via sanitation. The establishment of clean water supplies and sewage disposal in all cities in the latter part of the nineteenth century affected the transmission of cholera, nonrespiratory tuberculosis, typhoid, and typhus, significantly reducing the death toll from these diseases. Indoor plumbing also stimulated personal cleanliness and thereby contributed to the decline of disease. The passage and enforcement of sanitation laws affected food-borne diseases as well. The decline in the infant mortality rate, for example, was influenced by the increasing safety of milk through pasteurization.

Improvements in sanitation reduced people's exposure to infection and, along with improved nutrition, led to better health. Yet the effect of sanitation was unintended. It may seem bizarre today, but the origins of the sanitation movement in cities involved aesthetic concerns, not health. Cities were dirty and smelled bad. Water was foul and odorous. At least initially, the existence of unseen and dangerous microorganisms appeared far-fetched. Rather, it was the ugliness that bothered people. The health impact of sanitation did not become clear until later.

Improvements in Medical Technology. Advances in medical technology aided in the prevention of illness, as knowledge about modes of transmission advanced and, later, when immunization and effective treatment became available. As mentioned earlier, medical treatment prior to the nineteenth century was often ineffective, typically involving folk medicines and questionable—indeed, harmful—procedures. By the beginning of the twentieth century, however, treatment was increasingly based on scientific knowledge. Thus, in about 1840 a vaccine for smallpox was developed that reduced the impact of the disease in subsequent years. In addition, an antitoxin against diphtheria was discovered in about 1890. Although the scientific nature of medical treatment today is often overstated (Payer, 1988), proven ways now exist to treat illness.

McKeown shows, however, that these advances had only a marginal impact on the long-term fall in the mortality rate (1976:91–110). Figure 9.2 illustrates the type of data McKeown uses by charting the death rate

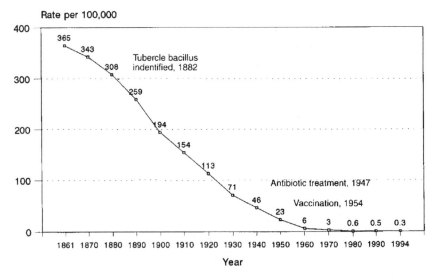

FIGURE 9.2   Death Rates from Tuberculosis, 1861–1994, with Years When
Medical Interventions Became Available
NOTE: Data for 1861–1890 are for the state of Massachusetts.
SOURCE: USBC (1975:58, 63; 1996d:93); NCHS (1996a).

from tuberculosis along with the years in which medical interventions
became available. The figure reveals that deaths from this disease were
falling even before knowledge of how it is transmitted became clear in
1882. McKeown infers that this initial improvement was due to increasing nutrition. After discovery of the tubercle bacillus, however, prevention became more systematic as cities became cleaner. Hence, the decline in tuberculosis accelerated. An effective medical treatment for
tuberculosis became available only in 1947 and a preventive vaccination
in 1954, by which time about 92 percent of all the decline in deaths had
already occurred. The pattern shown in Figure 9.2 resembles that for all
other acute conditions except smallpox and diphtheria. Thus, medical
treatment cannot have had much effect on the fall in the mortality rate
over time.

   Now I do not want to be misleading about the significance of science.
As shown in Figure 9.2, scientific advances led to accurate diagnoses of
acute diseases, identified how they are transmitted, and showed the importance of sanitation. Moreover, in everyday life diagnoses are made,
bones are set, sutures inserted, and people recover from illness and injury with the help of physicians. I do want to emphasize, however, that
physicians' impact on the population's health is more limited than com-

mon sense suggests. The long-term improvement in health has been due mainly to better eating and living in a cleaner environment, and only marginally to advances in medical treatment. Intuitively, McKeown observes, "we believe we are ill and made well: It is nearer the truth to say that we are well but made ill" (1976:162). The remark suggests that health must be supported, that focusing on medical treatment is misguided.

The Relative Ill Health of the U.S. Population

Despite the tremendous improvement in health over the past century, the United States is not as healthy as other nations. My hypothesis is: *The relative ill health of the U.S. population reflects (1) the degree of income inequality, (2) the low emphasis on prevention, and (3) lack of access to treatment.*

Degree of Income Inequality. By *degree of income inequality,* I mean the distance from the highest to the lowest incomes. Richard Wilkinson has shown that economic growth (industrialization and capitalism) underlies the improvements in health described above. But after a certain level of economic growth occurs, the degree of income inequality becomes more important in determining population health (1994). In practical terms, nations displaying the greatest vitality are those with the smallest spread of income.

For example, income inequality in various Western nations is shown below by the Gini coefficient, a number ranging from zero to one; closer to zero represents a low and to one a high level of income inequality (Smeeding, 1996:48).

Sweden (1982)	.229
Netherlands (1991)	.249
Canada (1991)	.285
France (1984)	.294
United Kingdom (1986)	.303
United States (1991)	.343

As before, small differences are significant. Among the nations compared, the United States displays the most income inequality and Sweden the least. You should recall from Chapter 5 that these differences represent clear policy choices; nations today can control the extent of inequality. Comparing these data to those shown in Table 9.1 reveals that an association (although not a perfect one) exists between inequality and infant mortality, between inequality and life expectancy. By extrapolation, of course, the population's health reflects the level of inequality.

Why this is so remains unclear. Wilkinson suggests the importance of the psychosocial links between income distribution and health, especially in the form of stress (1994, 1997). In engineering, stress is a force that deforms structures. In biology, the term refers to how the body adapts to demands in the environment. Not all stress is bad. The trick is to avoid stress in the engineering (i.e., deforming) sense. For example, people who feel they have some control over their conditions of work may be pressured—and thrive. Others who feel they have little control over their working conditions may be pressured—and wither, become deformed. They may smoke or drink excessively. Their blood pressure may go up, leading to strokes. The argument Wilkinson and others make is that deforming stressors mirror the distribution of income and that reducing inequality affects both the level of stress and the sense of relative deprivation that exists. Although this analysis is speculative and other variables may link inequality and health, their connection is not in doubt.

Low Emphasis on Prevention.   The following metaphor suggests the relationship between prevention and treatment (Evans, 1994:21): Imagine that becoming ill or injured is like the failure of a weight-bearing structure—say, a beam. The failure is often due to an external stress, perhaps one that acts quickly (like an acute disease), perhaps over time (like a chronic disease). Although some stress can be useful (exposure to a disease can inoculate), when it becomes too much the beam collapses. Two strategies exist for dealing with such a problem. One is prevention: using supports to make the beam more resistant to stress. A horizontal beam can carry more weight if it is supported at many points along its length than if it is simply fastened at one end and left projecting into empty space. Another is treatment: fixing the beam each time it breaks. Obviously, this strategy will cost more time and money, not to mention lowered productivity while the beam is being repaired. Of course, those who make their living fixing and replacing beams benefit a great deal. This is precisely the strategy the United States uses in dealing with ill health.

The existence of health maintenance organizations complicates but does not change the deemphasis on prevention. There is often confusion about who benefits from outlays for treatment. Those receiving services benefit as they are cured of illness, operated on, and so forth. But those providing services also benefit: Every dollar of spending becomes a dollar of income for doctors, administrators, shareholders of HMOs, and others.

The players in this game—physicians, hospitals, drug companies, and now HMOs—have an uncanny ability to protect their interests (i.e., their incomes). The expansion of HMOs reflects a recognition that costs in a fee-for-service system were rising beyond the nation's ability to pay (see Table 9.2). About 74 percent of those who obtain insurance through their employers are now in HMOs of some sort (Toner, 1996). HMOs often pay physicians a set price per client that varies by age (Rosenthal, 1996). Thus, a company may pay $480 yearly for infants less than 1 year old, $78 yearly for children 5–18, $99 for adults 19–39, with payments rising as people get older. The idea is that physicians are paid such fees regardless of whether clients become sick or injured. The HMOs garner income by covering as many healthy people as possible, setting capitation fees as low as possible, offering physicians extra money to avoid referring patients to expensive services, and hindering access to aggressive treatment (Anders, 1996). To the extent they can, managers in HMOs will manage treatment in their interests: Instead of "managed care," it might be more accurate to refer to it as "profit care."

In response, physicians are organizing themselves into large practices so that a few very sick persons do not overwhelm them. In so doing, they have incentives to avoid taking patients (those infected with HIV, for example) who are likely to need lots of treatment. Moreover, they have incentives to limit "unnecessary" contact with patients. For example, since earaches are almost always infectious, why not simply prescribe antibiotics over the phone without seeing the patient? But this may not be good medicine. In the past, when physicians were paid on a fee-for-service system, the incentive was to treat and indeed to overtreat. But now the incentive is to avoid treating. Either way, physicians will act to protect their incomes.

Sadly, and despite all the rhetoric, neither HMOs nor physicians are oriented to protecting the health of the population, except as it is in their economic interest to do so (Wolinsky and Brune, 1994). For example, HMOs will encourage prenatal care and immunizations among those they cover because it is, indeed, cheaper. Surprisingly, however, other forms of prevention are not cheaper—to an HMO—and so will not be emphasized (Rosenthal, 1997). For example, diagnosing and treating high cholesterol (which can lead to heart attack) costs a great deal, and the results will not show up for a decade or more. Similarly, screening for HIV can be expensive since drugs to combat it can cost more than $10,000 per year. Such expenses cut into the profits HMOs need to show each year. So they market prevention programs that are without substance to potential subscribers. In reality, as with beams, it is often more beneficial for both HMOs and physicians to fix health problems than prevent them.

Fixing health problems, of course, requires access to a physician. Unfortunately, those without insurance usually find it hard to see a doctor.

Lack of Access to Treatment and Preventative Care.   Today's version of Carlyle's poor Irish widow might be a woman who becomes pregnant and does not have access to prenatal care: Her child is born weighing less than 5.5 pounds and is placed in neonatal intensive care. The child's life is saved, but at great cost and increased odds of long-term suffering. This woman is not unique. It is estimated that 41 million persons, about 15 percent of the population, are not covered by either private or government insurance (Medicaid or Medicare) (USBC, 1996a). In addition, millions more are underinsured. It appears that the sickest persons are the most likely to either lack insurance or be underinsured, a finding that follows from the interest of HMOs and physicians affiliated with them to avoid becoming entangled with high-cost (i.e., sick) patients.

People lacking insurance coverage tend to be working class and poor, members of racial and ethnic minorities, and those with less education (USBC, 1996e). People lacking insurance also tend to be medically disadvantaged; they are less likely to receive treatment when needed (Paulin and Dietz, 1995; Donelan, 1996). For example, they are less likely to visit a doctor in any one year and less likely to be hospitalized (USBC, 1995b). But once they see a physician, they have more visits and are more likely to be hospitalized. This difference occurs because those without insurance usually do not have an ongoing relationship with a physician. Hence, they are sicker when they visit a doctor, often in the emergency room of a public hospital. When sick and dying people appear at private hospitals without insurance or cash, they are nearly always transferred to public institutions. At the latter, conditions are more crowded, patients are more likely to be seen by a graduate of a foreign medical school or a physician in training, therapies and procedures are decided on by physicians without much personal knowledge of patients' characteristics, and follow-up after release from the hospital is less systematic.

Although equalizing access to prevention and treatment would not mean equal health (because of the impact of inequality on health), it would reduce suffering and death enormously. It would also reduce costs. For example, as mentioned earlier, other nations work actively to prevent low-birth-weight babies rather than relying on treatment. In the United States, in contrast, individuals must bear a great deal of responsibility for buying insurance, preventing illness, and obtaining medical treatment.

Implications

Although individuals care about their health, they are often, like an unsupported weight-bearing beam, forced to bear stress that either originates elsewhere or could be prevented or both. As Evans and Stoddart remark, public health policies in the United States are "dominated by health care policy" (1994:27). And "health care, in turn, is over-whelmingly reactive in nature"; that is, it reacts to illness with treatment. This emphasis means that even when preventive care occurs, it consists of identifying and treating departures from health—at the individual level. High cholesterol or blood pressure, for example, are treated as "diseases."

It is clear, however, that many factors unrelated to medical treatment affect population health. For example, instead of changing drug policy to reduce violence in poor (often African American) neighborhoods, the United States treats victims of gunshot wounds. Yet reducing the violence would do more to increase life expectancy than any conceivable improvement in medical technology. Even with regard to issues that are health-related, the United States focuses on treatment rather than prevention. Instead of immunizing children who are without insurance, the United States treats them for disease. Of course, such children are often members of racial and ethnic minorities. Instead of preventing low-birth-weight babies, the United States places them in neonatal intensive care units. Are such strategies wise?

In thinking about this question, it is worth considering whether the country is spending too much money on the wrong things. Perhaps resources ought to be directed at reducing drug dependency. In this case, as noted in Chapter 6, expansion of treatment would be useful—compared to the cost of jail. But drug treatment can only be palliative; getting people work at meaningful jobs and reducing inequality would have even greater long-term benefits. Perhaps resources ought to be directed at immunizing all children and providing all women with prenatal care. Perhaps, in other words, the goal ought to be to need physicians and hospitals as little as possible. Redirecting resources will not be easy. As Paul Starr observes, "The dream of reason did not take power into account" (1982). The emphasis on treatment in the United States reflects not only the application of knowledge but also power: the power of providers over consumers, of the rich and middle class (who have insurance) over the working class and poor. Reason, it seems, can be perverted, can be used to exploit.

Nonetheless, the United States is less healthy than other nations and spends more money. In reaction, the past five presidents have declared a "health crisis" and offered legislation to deal with it. President Clinton, for example, proposed a "health security plan" modeled after Social Security that was designed (albeit very imperfectly) to solve many of the problems noted above. The failure of this (or some other) plan to pass means that fundamental changes in the way people obtain medical treatment have been left to the marketplace. One result has been the rise of HMOs. A marketplace solution raises important issues: Should health and medical treatment be commodities, like cars, that are purchased according to ability to pay, or should they be part of a basic set of collective needs? The other nations considered in this chapter all have national insurance (oriented to prevention). Thus, health—the ability to feel well and to live fully, the ability to realize one's potential—is defined as a right of citizenship. The United States, by contrast, downplays prevention and rations medical treatment by income and occupation. In the past the treatment of indigent persons depended on the generosity of physicians and charitable institutions. Are we returning to those days? I am haunted by Carlyle's story of the Irish widow.

Notes

1. The focus in this chapter is on physical health, ignoring (unfortunately) the problem of mental health.

2. Note my language. Although it is convention to refer to "health care" in describing what doctors do, they generally do not promote health in the sense of preventing sickness. Rather, they provide treatment when we become ill. In that context, the dedicated efforts of physicians are extremely important. When successful treatment results, as it has for me over the years, one ought to be appropriately thankful. But it is medical treatment that has occurred, not health promotion.

3. HIV-AIDS will be added to this list, of course, as the death toll mounts.

4. The word "estimate" in this paragraph should be taken seriously. Lewit (1995) provides data for 1988, which I adjusted for the impact of inflation in the cost of medical services as of 1996 (USBC, 1996d:119). The best way to think about these data is to note that it requires a great deal of money to treat low-birth-weight babies and costs have been rising steadily. There is no end in sight.

5. The literature on these issues is long; see Saigal (1996), Gemke (1995), Hack (1994), and McCormick (1992).

6. On racial and ethnic differences in the likelihood of prenatal care and its timing, see NCHS (1996f). On differences in its quality, see Kogan (1994a, 1994b), Collins and Shay (1994). On treatment differences by race and ethnicity, see Mitchell and Khandker (1995), Eggers (1995), and Schur (1995).

7. McKeown's work is quite readable and deserves a look. Subsequent scholars have added to his insights. The most important is probably Robert Fogel, "The Conquest of High Mortality and Hunger in Europe and America: Timing and Mechanisms" (1991); but see also Reves (1985) and Szreter (1988).

Recommended Reading

Fogel, Robert W. "The Conquest of High Mortality and Hunger in Europe and America: Timing and Mechanisms." Pp. 156–89 in David Landes, Patrice Higgonet, and Henry Rosovsky (eds.), *Favorites of Fortune: Technology, Growth, and Economic Development Since the Industrial Revolution* (Cambridge: Harvard University Press, 1991).

McKeown, Thomas. *The Modern Rise of Population* (New York: Academic Press, 1976).

McNeil, William H. *Plagues and People* (New York: Anchor Books, 1976).

Syme, S. Leonard. "The Social Environment and Health," *Daedalus* 123(Fall, 1994):79–86.

Wilkinson, Richard G. *Unhealthy Societies: The Afflictions of Inequality* (London: Routledge, 1997).

10 Reflections on the Study of Social Problems

Nicholas Kristoff, a *New York Times* reporter, opens his article "I Lived to Tell About Japan's Medical Miracle" by describing a paradox: Japan has the longest life expectancy in the world, eighty years, yet spends only about half as much as the United States on medical treatment (1997). His assumption, of course, is that "the Japanese medical system is one of the best in the world" and that this fact explains why the population is so healthy. After arriving in Tokyo from a trip to Africa, Kristoff displayed the symptoms of malaria and thus had an unintended opportunity to assess this idea.

Among his experiences were the following: Japanese ambulance crews have little training or equipment; they transport and that is all. Although access to physicians is relatively equal, it is usually impossible to make an appointment; the custom is to go to a doctor's office and wait. And wait. And wait some more. Japanese physicians usually do not tell patients very much; in Kristoff's case, he was told without explanation to come back in two days for a blood test. The physician denied Kristoff's assertion that he might have malaria and that waiting might kill him. With the help of his office, Kristoff was able to get a malaria specialist to see him, and he immediately hospitalized him. Although the Japanese national health insurance system covers everyone and access to a hospital is relatively equal, conditions differ from those Americans are used to. There are no private rooms. Patients must bring their own personal supplies: cups, utensils for eating, and towels. More important, common medicines (even Tylenol) are not available. Thus, the drug that is standard (in the rest of the world) for treating Kristoff's form of malaria could be obtained only from his physician's private stock. The good news was that Kristoff recovered and was charged less than $1,000 for five days in the hospital. His conclusion, though, is strange: "Ultimately, I was treated as well as I would have been in the United States—for a fraction of the cost. In the end, I came to see Japan's medical system . . . not as a new Mercedes but an old Volkswagen: a 'people's car' that is cranky and slow but gets you where you want to go."

This conclusion is strange because despite his negative experiences, he still opts for the commonsense explanation: Like an old Volkswagen, the system of medical treatment in Japan "gets you where you want to go"—that is, it determines population health. Actually, my guess is that the good health of the Japanese people is not a "medical miracle" at all; rather, it results from other factors. Although I know essentially nothing about Japanese social structure, if I were to study this issue my preliminary hypothesis (based on the analysis in Chapter 9) would be something like this: *The better health of the Japanese population compared to that in the United States reflects (1) a superior diet (2) less malnutrition, (3) less inequality, (4) greater emphasis on prevention, and (finally) (5) greater access to treatment.* There are probably other factors contributing to the health of the Japanese population, but this preliminary hypothesis offers a logical argument as a means of starting an investigation.

I want to pause here for a moment to consider the importance of asking questions. Much education focuses on learning facts. This task involves the so-called hard skills: identifying formulas, people, events, and other information, things we memorize. Life expectancy in Japan is eighty years. Knowing this nugget of data is obviously better than knowing nothing. And it leads quite naturally to attempts at explanation: The health of the Japanese population reflects their system of medical treatment. In reality, I would like to suggest, such arguments are often wrong. But whether right or wrong, whenever empirical assertions seem like common sense you ought to look again—closely.

As it turns out, the most valuable form of education emphasizes the so-called soft skills: critical thinking, asking the right questions. The key to developing these "soft skills" is an intellectual framework that provides a mechanism for establishing meaning and understanding. Perhaps, compared to the United States, the Japanese system of medical treatment is actually not very good. This was certainly Nicholas Kristoff's experience.

But if this is so, Japanese health must result from something else. The hypothesis above provides a preliminary way of identifying that "something else." Whether it is correct is less important at the beginning; in the process of asking questions about how the Japanese situation differs from that in the United States, a logical account will (one hopes) eventually emerge.

The hypothesis poses a question, the answer to which requires a plan of action. In this book, I have tried to teach you a two-step strategy for asking and answering questions about social problems (and other issues as well). Ideally, this approach will enable you to see social life clearly, understand its various dimensions, and do so as objectively as possible. Note that this is the definition of sociology offered in Chapter 1.

The first step is to identify the facts, a process that has two parts. (1) I have tried to show that the best place to start is by obtaining historical and international data. Again: A fact by itself—that life expectancy in the United States is seventy-six years—is not very useful. Historical trends show how these conditions have changed over time. Thus, it is more useful to know that life expectancy has increased steadily over the previous century. International comparisons show how these conditions vary across societies. Thus, it is even more useful to know that although life expectancy is high in the United States, it is even higher in Japan and other nations. (2) It is also important to assess the consequences of social problems, not based on stereotypes but in terms of the most objective data possible. Otherwise, the nature and extent of harm will remain unknown. For example, as shown in Chapter 8, the fact that people now have long lives raises problems about when to retire, how to provide economic support, and how to care for the elderly. In addition, moral issues arise because when people live a long time they often want to choose how and when to die. But if the facts—trends and comparisons along with consequences—lend perspective, they do not provide an explanation. Rather, they tell us what needs to be explained.

The second step is to distinguish between individual and structural levels of analysis. Each is important because the answers to questions depend on one's angle of vision. At the individual level, everyone wants to know how some problem affects people like them. Am I more or less likely to die young, whether of malaria or some other disease? Will I be able to control my demise? So identifying the factors affecting individuals is an important task. Indeed, industries of people exist—social workers, therapists, psychologists, and some sociologists, among others—who attempt to understand how individuals affect and are affected by groups. But, as I have tried to show, for my purposes in this book the answers to such questions are limiting: Individuals are neither the cause nor the solution to social problems.

These issues must be considered at the structural level. Thus, based on the analysis in Chapters 8 and 9, the hypothesis posed above constitutes a structural question. Throughout this book, I have tried to show that the social structure exists externally to individuals and influences their range of choices. At the same time, of course, the social structure changes over time. In Chapter 1, I used the metaphor of a house to illustrate these characteristics. In thinking about a preliminary hypothesis to account for Kristoff's experience, I drew on material in Chapter 8: Farmers produced more food in the nineteenth century in order to make a profit, whereas urban dwellers wanted clean water and air for aesthetic reasons. But the impact of better nutrition and sanitation along with improvements in medical treatment was to make the population healthier, leading to longer life. My guess is that this process is generalizable, that it occurred in Japan as well. Only further research can establish whether this guess is correct. In any case, this observation suggests a more general point made throughout this book, that modernity has meant an increase in people's range of choices.

The nature of modernity and its relationship to social problems remains a misunderstood issue, about which I want to comment at some length. In his lecture "Science as a Vocation," Max Weber mused about the modern "disenchantment of the world" (1918:139). It is a marvelous phrase, suggesting that human beings have passed from an enchanted world into a colder, heartless world, devoid of morality. And it is true that modernity has meant the passing of old ways of thinking and acting, mainly because of the dominance of science and its practical results. Science teaches people to use reason based on knowledge. Thus, the pervasiveness of modern technology stimulates in most people a rational, practical approach to the problems of everyday life. This orientation means that modern life is characterized by a mindset that is impatient with mystery, that looks for scientific rather than supernatural explanations. Nonetheless, as I note just below, some observers still engage in wishful thinking, glorifying (a mythical version of) the past, when values seemed clear and unambiguous.

Georg Simmel, however, was not one of them. Like Weber, he was also interested in the origin and nature of modern life. He suggested how the change to modernity occurred in his essay "The Web of Group Affiliations," originally published in 1908. Simmel's general argument is that the social structure in which individuals participate influences how they interact regardless of their purposes. More specifically, he showed in his essay that the number of groups individuals belong to and the principles on which those groups are organized affect behavior. As it turns out, this argument has implications for understanding both modernity and social problems.[1]

One of the most important factors affecting people's webs of group affiliations is the degree of *social differentiation*. This term is jargon, of course, referring to how complex a society is. For example, in a hunting and gathering society, almost all tasks are done in and by the family (gathering and producing food, educating children, worshiping gods, making law, and the like). Thus, people have only few roles in an undifferentiated society, and this simplicity means that everyone they know is just like them; they do not interact with others different from themselves. By contrast, in an industrial society many important tasks are divided up. This increase in complexity, which is another way of describing modernization, affects interaction. People still produce goods, worship, educate, and make laws, but they do so differently. They play a far greater number and variety of roles and, in so doing, meet others who differ from themselves.

The process of social differentiation produced, Simmel said, two fundamental changes in social structure. First, the principles underlying group formation changed, in his words, from "organic" to "rational" criteria. As Simmel used it, the term "organic" is a biological metaphor suggesting that a family or village is like a living organism in which the parts are inherently connected. Thus, when groups have an "organic" basis, people belong to them based on birth—into a family, a religion, a village—and they are so strongly identified with the group to which they belong that they are not seen as individuals in their own right. In Shakespeare's play *Romeo and Juliet,* written about 1595, Romeo did not have an identity apart from his family and village; they constituted who he was (1980). This is why his banishment was so devastating. Shakespeare's development of this theme and its resonance with his audience suggest that group formation in England was based mostly on "organic" criteria as recently as at the turn of the seventeenth century—and that it was changing. This change, to what Simmel called "rational" criteria, involves the use of reason and logic. Thus, when groups are formed on a "rational" basis, people belong by choice. This is the modern orientation, where people decide whom to marry, what religious beliefs to adhere to, and where to live, among many other choices.

Second, social differentiation also leads to an increase in the number of groups that people can join. When groups have an "organic" basis, people can belong only to a few primary (i.e., small, intimate, face-to-face) groups: their family, their village, and that is about it. Romeo, for example, had no job, did not play on a softball team, did not correspond (via E-mail) with anyone in another town; he was isolated in family and faith. By contrast, when groups have a "rational" basis, people can join a greater number and variety of them, depending on their skills, mutual interests, income, and other types of commonality. Moreover, many of these groups are larger and more formal than primary groups. As often occurs, what people can do, they in fact do: Simmel observed a trend in modern societies for people to join lots of groups and for such affiliations to be based on conscious reflection. And this latter tendency applies even to intimate relationships, such as marriages.

Simmel's argument can be summarized in the following way: *The greater the social differentiation, the more choice people have in group affiliation and the more groups to which they belong.* I would like to suggest that this simple theory leads to new insights about the nature of modern societies. Simmel proposed, for example, that when groups are formed by choice and people belong to a large number of them, the possibility of role conflict arises because groups place competing demands on people. Thus, it is now common for an individual to have multiple obligations: as spouse, parent, employee, club member, student, and so forth. Sometimes these duties create hard choices, as, for example, when sorority, fraternity, or other social commitments conflict with studying for an examination. Usually, Simmel said, people try to balance their competing responsibilities by keeping them spatially and temporally separate. Nonetheless, the impact of structurally induced conflicting expectations can result in psychological stress and therefore influence behavior.

One example of the impact of role conflict and the resulting stress occurs in gender relations—although this is not a topic about which Simmel had much to say. Recall from Chapter 3, for example, that husbands do not like doing housework; this fact shows the continuing salience of traditional (i.e., nineteenth-century) norms about men's and women's roles. In Chapter 3, I used the comic's assertion that "a man around the house is an inanimate object" as a way of satirizing this situation. More to the point, employed wives usually have two jobs (roles) that are often incompatible: keeping house (defined broadly to include nurturing family relationships) and earning a living. One way married women resolve this conflict is by sacrificing career ambitions, working part time, and devising other stratagems to make their lives a little easier. Another way is to get a divorce. After all, Simmel's analysis implies that a marriage is simply one group among many in modern societies; it remains special to be sure, and intimate, but one that people choose to form and sometimes choose to leave, just as they do other groups (Beeghley, 1996b). Some inanimate objects are not worth keeping around the house.

The problem of role conflict (and divorce) in gender relations seems to be a negative consequence of modernity, a perception that leads some observers to wishful thinking. If, it is said, we could return to a time when men's and women's roles were assigned at birth and expectations were clear, we would not have so many problems today. There might be fewer divorces, for example. Gertrude Himmelfarb makes this kind of argument in *The De-Moralization of Society* (1995). The title has a double meaning, of course, suggesting that modern societies are disenchanted and de-moralized in two senses: We lack moral guidance and we lack morale. As the poet William Butler Yeats put it, "Things fall apart; the centre cannot hold; Mere anarchy is loosed upon the world" (1933:185). Regardless of whether you agree with such judgments (I do not), the source of the role conflict we all sometimes experience lies in changes in the social structure.

As an aside, unlike either Himmelfarb or Weber, I find it hard to imagine an enchanted nineteenth-century society. After all, couples could not control fertility, men's and women's roles were highly restricted, racial and ethnic discrimination was pervasive, poverty was rampant, and life was short, among many other problems. The paradox is that although this book focuses on harmful conditions, we are actually much better off today than our forebears were in the past.

Simmel's theory leads to other important insights about modern societies, insights that reveal some of the positive consequences of modernity. For example, if the theory is accurate, people now play many different roles in contexts that are spatially and temporally separated. I am a husband, parent, son, (erstwhile) athlete, employee, and political activist. This list, which could be extended, gives me a distinct identity in relationship to other people. And these others also have a discrete set of characteristics that make them distinct. Thus, Simmel's theory implies that the changes produced by social differentiation lead to greater individuality (what he called a "core of inner unity") that makes each person unique. Unlike the situation in Verona, where Romeo and Juliet lived, the group no longer absorbs the whole person, and geographical mobility is more frequent. In Simmel's words, "The objective structure of society provides a framework within which an individual's non-interchangeable and singular characteristics may develop and find expression" (1908:150). Such a result is impossible when everyone resembles everyone else. It is an irony, then, that modernity not only produces role conflict and psychological stress but also creates the conditions under which individuality emerges.

It emerges precisely because people in modern societies can, indeed must, make choices. Moreover, they must adjust their behavior to different people in different situations—an insight that carries many implications. For example, as people make choices and become aware of their uniqueness, they enjoy greater personal freedom. In Simmel's words, although "the narrowly circumscribed and strict custom of earlier conditions was one in which the social group as a whole . . . regulated the conduct of the individual in the most varied ways," such regulation is not possible in differentiated societies because people belong to so many different groups (1908:165). It is not accidental, from this point of view, that the twin values of personal freedom and equality of opportunity as inalienable rights of every adult arose during the past two centuries. Their structural basis, Simmel said, lies in social differentiation.

The argument that we are demoralized, then, rings hollow. Anarchy is not loosed upon the world when women and men (and racial and ethnic groups) are more equal. Rather, equality recognizes the inherent dignity of each human being—a fundamental Western value. The argument that the past was better is, implicitly, an argument in favor of inequality, an argument that women like Gertrude Himmelfarb should stay at home and bear children. But she is a respected scholar (the fact that I happen to disagree with her is irrelevant to this judgment). Arbitrarily confining people like her to the home would be wrong.

Other insights follow from Simmel's theory. In *Social Theory and Social Structure,* for example, Robert K. Merton notes that when people play many roles and face conflicting expectations, they develop the capacity for empathy, the ability to identify with and understand another's situation or motives (1968b:436). This capacity can sometimes reduce the level of conflict between people; it can also stimulate a recognition of their inherent worth. Thus, the increasing complexity of modern societies provides a structural basis for an important personality characteristic. Note two important implications of Simmel's and Merton's arguments: First, the existence of role conflict actually constitutes a positive feature of modern societies. Second, the distribution of psychological characteristics typical in a modern society, such as people's sense of individuality and empathy, did not develop by chance; it reflects changes in the social structure.

Rose Laub Coser elaborates on these implications in her book *In Defense of Modernity.* She observes that although role conflict burdens individuals, it also forces them to make choices and thereby encourages creativity (1991). After all, in a complex society, roles cannot be taken for granted; they must be negotiated. So people have to consider both their own and others' situations and think imaginatively and originally. This aptitude for creativity extends to all arenas of life as people confront problems. Thus, as Coser puts it, "The development of mental ability [in modern societies] takes place together with the grasp of the complexity of social roles" (1991:7). The logic of this analysis suggests that modernity results from and, at the same time, produces a spiral effect such that as societies become more complex, more people become creative; and as more people become creative, societies become more complex. One impact is the expansion of scientific knowledge. This is of course one basis of our disenchantment and the cause of so many social problems.

We live in an uneasy time, surrounded by harmful conditions. And we are handcuffed to history, a metaphorical way of restating Durkheim's dictum that "social facts are things." But we have keys now that were unavailable in the past, which means that (within limits) we can alter the course of history. We do not need to live with so many abortions, great inequality, the destructive impact of drugs, continuing discrimination, a high level of violence, the suffering associated with dying, and unnecessary illness. We can reduce their impact. In trying (and, inevitably, sometimes failing) to achieve such goals, it is important to recognize that modernity requires subtle judgments about right and wrong. This fact does not mean we are demoralized. Rather, it means we must focus on the core value: the dignity of each human individual. Chapter 1 closed with the comment that the one thing we cannot do is choose to be people who do not have choices. In a way, the remainder of this book has been a meditation on this theme.

Notes

1. The following paragraphs elaborate on an analysis originally developed in my essay "Demystifying Theory: How the Theories of Georg Simmel (and Others) Help Us to Make Sense of Modern Life" (Beeghley, 1997).

Recommended Reading

Coser, Rose Laub. *In Defense of Modernity* (Stanford, CA: Stanford University Press, 1991).

Himmelfarb, Gertrude. *The De-Moralization of Society* (New York: Knopf, 1995).

Merton, Robert K. "Social Structure and Anomie." Pp. 185–215 in R. K. Merton, *Social Theory and Social Structure* (New York: Free Press, 1968).

Simmel, Georg. "The Web of Group Affiliations." Pp. 65–128 in Georg Simmel, *Conflict and the Web of Group Affiliations* (New York: Free Press, 1955; original 1908).

Weber, Max. "Science as a Vocation." Pp. 129–58 in Hans Gerth and C. Wright Mills (eds.), *From Max Weber: Essays in Sociology* (New York: Oxford University Press, 1947; original 1918).

Glossary

Note: Page numbers indicate where the term is first used.

Acute diseases: Health problems of less than three months duration that restrict activity (p. 190).

Affirmative action: Public policies designed to give advantages to members of one group over others (p. 90).

Aging population: People over age 65 (p. 167).

Alienation: People's belief that they have little control over their lives, that trying to improve their situation is futile, and the development of strategies for coping with this situation (p. 80).

Anomie: A lack of connection between valued goals and the means to achieve them (p. 80).

Casual drug users: People who consume drugs occasionally, often in social settings (p. 121).

Chronic diseases: Long-term health problems that restrict activity, often leading to death (p. 192).

Clinical depression: Psychological incapacity; people lose interest in daily activities for an extended period, have little energy, feel worthless, and find it difficult to concentrate. Depressed persons often consider suicide and are prone to drug use and abuse (p. 53).

Controlled drug users: People who consume drugs frequently but in moderate amounts, often at home (p. 121).

Degree of income inequality: The distance between highest and lowest income in a society (p. 205).

Demographic transition: A historical process in which a society with high birth and death rates changes to low birth and death rates and displays rapid population growth (p. 180).

Discrimination: People's unequal treatment due to their personal characteristics, such as gender or race (p. 73).

Drug: Any chemical substance that, when ingested, changes a person's physiological or psychological functioning (p. 120).

Drug abusers: People who become dependent, consume large quantities of a drug over a long period, and experience a variety of life problems as a result (p. 121).

Drug dependence: The compulsive craving and use of drugs, often in increasing amounts over time (p. 121).

Epidemiologists: Researchers who study the incidence and control of illness in a population (p. 197).

Ethnic group: Aggregates of people with distinct social attributes, such as their customs, language, and religious heritage (p. 72).

Family instability: Families broken by separation or divorce. Also, families that are disorganized such that parental guidance is unclear or nonexistent, abuse occurs, or one or both parents abuses drugs (p. 129).

Feminism: An ideology of equality between women and men and the social movement supporting that goal (p. 37).

Frustration-instigated behavior: Behavior that is not goal-oriented or a means to an end, but is an end in itself (p. 133).

Gross domestic product: The total value of all goods and services produced in a nation (p. 135).

Health: In narrow terms, the absence of illness. More broadly, feeling well, living fully, realizing one's potential (p. 190).

Homelessness: Lacking access to a conventional dwelling, such as a house, apartment, mobile home, or rented room (p. 103).

Homicide: Human death purposely and illegally inflicted by another (p. 146).

Human capital: People's skills (education, work experience, and tenure on current job), and employment priorities (labor force continuity, choosing part-time employment, absenteeism due to a child's illness, and leaving a job due to a spouse's mobility) (p. 56).

Hunger: The chronic under-consumption of nutrients (p. 104).

Infant mortality rate: The number of live babies who die within the first year of life (p. 75).

Industrialization: The transformation of the economy as new forms of energy were substituted for muscle power, leading to advances in productivity (p. 34).

Institutionalized discrimination: The unequal treatment of people with different characteristics, such as gender or race, that is embedded in the social structure (p. 61).

Learned helplessness: An individual's belief that her or his behavior will not affect outcomes (p. 54).

Leisure-centered Values: Beliefs that people should pursue self-expression, enjoy pleasure, and consume goods and services (p. 136).

Macroeconomic policy: The way the government regulates the economy, especially inflation and unemployment (p. 113).

Motivated-instigated behavior: Behavior that is a means to an end rather than an end in itself (p. 132).

Neonatal mortality: Death in the first 27 days of life (p. 194).

Opinion leaders: People who bring issues to people's attention and teach them where their interests lie (p. 5).

Post-neonatal mortality: Death in days 28–365 of life (p. 194).

Post-traumatic stress disorder: Refers to the impact of trauma, as indicated by intense anxiety, inability to concentrate, becoming easily startled, nightmares, flashbacks, and insomnia (p. 53).

Poverty: An income level below which persons or families have difficulty surviving (p. 98).

Prejudice: People's hostile attitudes toward others in a different group or toward other groups as a whole (p. 73).

Race: Groups identifiable by their physical traits, such as skin color (p. 72).

Reference group: Collectivities of people whose values, tastes, and patterns of action become significant in the development of one's own attitudes and behavior. p. 14

Religiosity: A person's identification with and attachment to a faith group (p. 130).

Social class: People's location in the stratification structure, as shown by their jobs, income, and education (p. 29).

Social problem: A harmful condition identified by a significant number of people and recognized politically as needing improvement (p. 4).

Social psychology: The study of how people act, interact, influence groups to which they belong, and are influenced by groups (p. 13).

Social structure: The networks of relationships and values connecting people to one another and to the society (p. 16).

Socialization: The life-long process by which individuals learn norms and values, internalize motives and needs, develop intellectual and social skills, and enact roles in everyday life (p. 13).

Sociology: A systematic attempt at seeing social life as clearly as possible, understanding its various dimensions, and doing so without being swayed by one's personal hopes and fears (p. 2).

Underclass: People who are persistently poor, residentially homogeneous, and relatively isolated from the rest of the population (p. 80).

Vital statistics: Data about births and deaths in a society (p. 191).

Work-centered Values: Beliefs that people should work hard, organized their lives methodically, delay immediate gratification, and earn money (p. 175).

References

AAR (Alliance for Aging Research). 1991. Americans View Aging. Washington, DC: Alliance for Aging Research.

Acker, Joan. 1990. "Hierarchies, Jobs, Bodies: A Theory of Gendered Organizations." Gender and Society 4:139–58.

AGI (Alan Guttmacher Institute). 1997. Facts in Brief: Induced Abortion. New York: Alan Guttmacher Institute.

Aguirre, Adalberto, and Jonathan H. Turner. 1993. American Ethnicity: The Dynamics and Consequences of Discrimination. New York: McGraw-Hill.

Ahn, Namkee. 1994. "Teenage Childbearing and High School Completion: Accounting for Individual Heterogeneity." Family Planning Perspectives 26:17–21.

Akers, Ronald L. 1992. Drugs, Alcohol, and Society. Belmont, CA: Wadsworth.

_____. 1995. Social Learning Theory. Belmont, CA: Wadsworth.

Allport, Gordon W. 1954. The Nature of Prejudice. Cambridge, MA: Addison-Wesley.

Altman, Lawrence K. 1991. "Jury Declines to Indict Doctor Who Said He Aided in Suicide." New York Times, national edition. July 27:1.

_____. 1995. "AIDS Is Now the Leading Killer of Americans from 25–44." New York Times, national edition. January 31:B8.

AMA (American Management Association). 1996. Sexual Harassment: Policies and Procedures. New York: American Management Association.

Anders, George. 1996. Health Against Wealth: HMOs and the Breakdown of Medical Trust. Boston: Houghton Mifflin.

Anderson, Craig. 1997. "Effects of Violent Movies and Trait Hostility on Hostile Feelings and Aggressive Thoughts." Aggressive Behavior 23:161–79.

Anderson, David C. 1997. "The Mystery of the Falling Crime Rate." American Prospect 32(May-June):49–55.

Anderson, Elijah. 1990. Streetwise: Race, Class, and Change in an Urban Community. Chicago: University of Chicago Press.

_____. 1994. "The Code of the Streets." Atlantic Monthly 273(May):80–110.

APA (American Psychological Association). 1993. Violence and Youth: Psychology's Response. New York: American Psychological Association.

_____. 1994. Diagnostic and Statistical Manual of Mental Disorders, 4th edition. Washington, DC: American Psychological Association.

Applebome, Peter. 1997. "Minority Law School Enrollment Plunges in California and Texas." New York Times, national edition. June 28:1.

Ariès, Philippe. 1962. Centuries of Childhood: A Social History of Family Life. New York: Vintage.

_____. 1981. The Hour of Our Death. New York: Knopf.

Asch, David M. 1996. "The Role of Critical Care Nurses in Euthanasia and Assisted Suicide." New England Journal of Medicine 334(May 23):1374–79.

Ascheim, Solomon. 1930. "Early Diagnosis of Pregnancy." American Journal of Obstetrics and Gynecology 19:118–24.

Ashley, Richard. 1975. Cocaine: Its History, Uses, and Effects. New York: St. Martin's Press.

Atchley, Robert C. 1995. Social Forces and Aging, 7th edition. Belmont, CA: Wadsworth.

Bandura, Albert. 1983. "Psychological Mechanisms of Aggression." Pp. 1–40 in R. G. Green and E. I. Donnerstein (eds.), Aggression: Theoretical and Empirical Reviews, Vol. 1. New York: Academic Press.

Barker, David J.P. 1992. Fetal and Infant Origins of Adult Diseases. London: BMJ.

Bassuk, Ellen L. 1991. "Homeless Families." Scientific American 265(December):66–74.

Bebber, Charles. 1994. "Increases in U.S. Violent Crime During the 1980s Following Four American Military Actions." Journal of Interpersonal Violence 9:109–16.

Becker, Gary S. 1975. Human Capital: A Theoretical and Empirical Analysis. New York: Columbia University Press.

Becker, Howard S. 1963. The Outsiders: Studies in the Sociology of Deviance. New York: Free Press.

Beckett, Samuel. 1954. Waiting for Godot: A Tragicomedy in Two Acts. New York: Grove Press.

Beeghley, Leonard. 1983. Living Poorly in America. New York: Praeger.

_____. 1989a. "Individual Versus Structural Explanations of Poverty." Population Research and Policy Review 8:201–22.

_____. 1989b. "Social Structure and the Rate of Divorce." Pp. 147–70 in James A. Holstein and Gale Miller (eds.), Perspectives on Social Problems, Vol. 1. Greenwich, CT: Jai Press.

_____. 1992. "Social Structure and Voting in the United States: A Historical and Comparative Analysis." Perspectives on Social Problems 3:265–87.

_____. 1993. "Social Problems." Pp. 605–7 in William Outhwaite and Tom Bottomore (eds.), Blackwell Dictionary of Twentieth Century Social Thought. London: Blackwell.

_____. 1996a. The Structure of Social Stratification in the United States, 2nd edition. Boston: Allyn & Bacon.

_____. 1996b. What Does Your Wife Do? Gender and the Transformation of Family Life. Boulder, CO: Westview Press.

_____. 1997. "Demystifying Theory: How the Theories of Georg Simmel (and Others) Help Us to Make Sense of Modern Life." Pp. 267–74 in Jon Gubbay, Chris Middleton, and Chet Ballard (eds.), The Student's Companion to Sociology. Malden, MA: Blackwell.

Beeghley, Leonard, E. Wilbur Bock, and John C. Cochran. 1990. "Religious Change and Alcohol Use: An Application of Reference Group and Socialization Theory." Sociological Forum 5:261–78.

Beeghley, Leonard, and Debra Van Ausdale. 1990. "The Status of Women Faculty in Graduate Departments of Sociology: 1973 and 1988." Footnotes 18(December):3–4.

Beeghley, Leonard, Barbara Zsembik, and Anna Campbell. 1996. "The Correlates of Religiosity Among African Americans, Latinos, and Non-Latino Whites." Paper presented at the annual meeting of the American Sociological Association, New York, August.

Berger, Peter L. 1963. Invitation to Sociology. Garden City, NY: Doubleday.

_____. 1977. Facing Up to Modernity. New York: Basic Books.

_____. 1986. The Capitalist Revolution. New York: Basic Books.

_____. 1992. A Far Glory. New York: Free Press.

Berkowitz, Leonard. 1963. Aggression: A Social-Psychological Analysis. New York: McGraw-Hill.

_____. 1989. "Frustration-Aggression Hypothesis: Examination and Reformulation." Psychological Bulletin 106:59–73.

Bing, Léon. 1991. Do or Die. New York: HarperCollins.

Binstock, Robert H., and Stephen G. Post (eds.). 1991. Too Old for Health Care? Controversies in Medicine, Law, Economics, and Ethics. Baltimore, MD: Johns Hopkins University Press.

Bird, Carolyn. 1968. Born Female: The High Cost of Keeping Women Down. New York: Van Rees Press.

BJS (Bureau of Justice Statistics). 1993. Survey of State Prison Inmates. Washington, DC: U.S. Government Printing Office.

_____. 1996. Sourcebook of Criminal Justice Statistics 1995. Washington, DC: U.S. Government Printing Office.

_____. 1997a. "Prisoners in 1996." Bureau of Justice Statistics Bulletin. June.

_____. 1997b. Sourcebook of Criminal Justice Statistics—Online. <http://www.albany.edu/sourcebook/>.

Blair, Sampson L., and Daniel T. Lichter. 1991. "Measuring the Household Division of Labor." Journal of Family Issues 12:91–113.

Blank, Rebecca M., and Alan S. Blinder. 1986. "Macroeconomics, Income Distribution, and Poverty." Pp. 180–208 in S. H. Danziger and D. H. Weinberg (eds.), Fighting Poverty: What Works and What Doesn't. Cambridge: Harvard University Press.

Blau, Peter M., and Otis Dudley Duncan. 1967. The American Occupational Structure. New York: Wiley.

Blossfeld, H. P., and G. Rohwer (eds.). 1997. Between Equalization and Marginalization: Part-Time Working Women in Europe and the United States. New York: Oxford University Press.

Bose, Christine E. 1987. "Devaluing Women's Work: The Undercount of Women's Employment in 1900 and 1980." Pp. 95–115 in Christine Bose, Roslyn Feldberg, and Natalie Sokoloff (eds.), Hidden Aspects of Women's Work. New York: Praeger.

Boyd, Sandra L., and Judith Treas. 1995. "Family Care of the Frail Elderly: A New Look at 'Women in the Middle.'" Pp. 262–68 in Jill Quadagno and Debra Street (eds.), Aging for the Twenty-First Century. New York: St. Martin's Press.

Boyer, Debra, and David Fine. 1992. "Sexual Abuse as a Factor in Adolescent Pregnancy and Child Maltreatment." Family Planning Perspectives 24:4–11.

Bradley, Bill. 1997. Foreword to Chester Hartman (ed.), Double Exposure: Poverty and Race in America. Armonk, NY: M. E. Sharpe.

Bradley, David G. 1963. A Guide to the World's Religions. Englewood Cliffs, NJ: Prentice-Hall.

Brecher, Edward M. 1972. Licit and Illicit Drugs. Boston: Little, Brown.

Bridges, J. S. 1989. "Sex Differences in Occupational Values." Sex Roles 20:205–11.

Brim, Orville G. 1966. "Socialization Through the Life-Cycle." Pp. 1–49 in O. G. Brim and S. Wheeler, Socialization After Childhood. New York: Wiley.

Brines, Julie. 1994. "Economic Dependency, Gender, and the Division of Labor at Home." American Journal of Sociology 100:652–88.

Brown, J. Larry, and H. F. Pizer. 1985. Living Hungry in America. New York: Macmillan.

Brown, Larry. 1992. Estimates of the Number of Hungry Americans Done for the House Select Committee on Hunger. Bedford, MA: Center on Hunger, Poverty, and Nutrition Policy, Tufts University.

Brown, Richard Maxwell. 1989. "Crime, Law, and Society: From the Industrial to the Information Society." Pp. 251–68 in T. R. Gurr (ed.), Violence in America, Vol. 1. Newbury Park, CA: Sage.

Browne, A., and K. R. Williams. 1989. "Exploring the Effect of Resource Availability and the Likelihood of Female-Perpetrated Homicides." Law and Society Review 23:75–94.

Buckley, William F., Jr. 1996. "The War on Drugs Is Lost." Part 1. National Review 48(February):34–36.

Budiansky, Stephen. 1986. "Public Health: A Measure of Failure." Atlantic 257:32–35.

Butterfield, Fox. 1997a. "Crime Keeps on Falling but Prisons Keep on Filling." New York Times, national edition. September 28, sec. 4, p. 1.

_____. 1997b. "System in Florida Intervenes to Ward off Juvenile Crime." New York Times, national edition. October 4:1.

Callahan, Daniel. 1987. Setting Limits: Medical Goals in an Aging Society. New York: Simon & Schuster.

_____. 1994. "Setting Limits: A Response." Gerontologist 34:393–98.

Campbell, Colin. 1987. The Romantic Ethic and the Spirit of Modern Consumerism. Oxford: Blackwell.

Carlyle, Thomas. 1977. Past and Present. New York: New York University Press.

Case, Charles E., Andrew Greeley, and Stephan Fuchs. 1989. "Social Determinants of Racial Prejudice." Sociological Perspectives 32:469–83.

Catalyst. 1996. The 1996 Catalyst Census of Women Corporate Officers and Top Earners. New York: Catalyst.

Cavilli-Sforza, Luca, Paolo Menozzi, and Alberto Piazza. 1995. The History and Geography of Human Genes. Princeton, NJ: Princeton University Press.

CBO (Congressional Budget Office). 1996. The Economic and Budget Outlook: Fiscal Years 1997–2006. Washington, DC: U.S. Government Printing Office.

CDC (Centers for Disease Control). 1996. HIV/AIDS Surveillance Report. Year-end edition. Atlanta, GA: Centers for Disease Control.

CEA (Council of Economic Advisers). 1969. Economic Report of the President. Washington, DC: U.S. Government Printing Office.

_____. 1995. Economic Report of the President. Washington, DC: U.S. Government Printing Office.

Chapin, C. V. 1924. "Deaths Among Taxpayers and Non-Taxpayers: Income Tax, Providence, 1895." American Journal of Public Health 14:647–51.

Chaulk, C. Patrick. 1994. "Preventive Health Care in Six Countries: Models for Reform." Health Care Financing Review 15:7–21.

Churchill, Ward, and Glenn Morris. 1992. "Key Indian Laws and Cases." Pp. 13–21 in M. Annette Jaimes (ed.), The State of Native America: Genocide, Colonization, and Resistance. Boston: South End Press.

Citro, Constance F., and Robert T. Michael (eds.). 1995. Measuring Poverty: A New Approach. Washington, DC: National Academy Press.

Clines, Francis X. 1992. "Ex-Inmates Urge Return to Areas of Crime to Help." New York Times, national edition. December 23:1.

Coale, Ansley J. 1956. "The Effects of Changes in Mortality and Fertility on Age Composition." Milbank Memorial Fund Quarterly 34:302–7.

Cockerham, William C. Medical Sociology, 6th edition. Englewood Cliffs, NJ: Prentice-Hall.

Cohen, Albert. 1955. Delinquent Boys. New York: Free Press.

Coles, F. S. 1986. "Forced to Quit: Sexual Harassment Complaints and Agency Response." Sex Roles 14:81–95.

Collins, John W., and Donna K. Shay. 1994. "Prevalence of Low Birth Weight Among Hispanic Infants with United States-Born and Foreign-Born Mothers: The Effects of Urban Poverty." American Journal of Epidemiology 139:184–92.

Collins, Randall. 1992. Sociological Insight: An Introduction to Nonobvious Sociology, 2nd edition. New York: Oxford University Press.

Coser, Rose Laub. 1991. In Defense of Modernity. Stanford, CA: Stanford University Press.

Courtwright, David T. 1982. Dark Paradise: Opiate Addiction in America Before 1940. Cambridge: Harvard University Press.

Crystal, Stephen, and Dennis Shea. 1990. "Cumulative Advantage, Cumulative Disadvantage, and Inequality Among Elderly People." Gerontologist 30:437–43.

CSO (Central Statistical Office). 1995. Social Trends 25. London: Her Majesty's Stationery Office.

Cutright, Phillips, and Carl Briggs. 1995. "Structural and Cultural Determinants of Adult Homicide in Developed Countries: Age and Gender Specific Rates, 1955–1989." Sociological Focus 28:221–43.

CWRIC (Commission on Wartime Relocation and Internment of Civilians). 1982. Personal Justice Denied. Washington, DC: U.S. Government Printing Office.

Danner, Terry, and Ira Silverman. 1986. "Characteristics of Incarcerated Outlaw Bikers as Compared to Non-Biker Inmates." Journal of Crime and Justice 9:43–70.

Degler, Carl N. 1980. At Odds: Women and the Family in America from the Revolution to the Present. New York: Oxford University Press.

Deloria, Vine, Jr. 1992. "Trouble in High Places: Erosion of American Indian Rights to Religious Freedom in the United States." Pp. 267–90 in M. Annette Jaimes (ed.), The State of Native America: Genocide, Colonization, and Resistance. Boston: South End Press.

DeMaris, Alfred, and Steven Swinford. 1996. "Female Victims of Spousal Violence: Factors Influencing Their Level of Fearfulness." Family Relations 45:98–107.

Des Jarlais, Don C., Cathy Casriel, and Samuel Friedman. 1989. "The New Death Among IV Drug Users." Pp. 205–18 in I. B. Corless and M. Pittman-Lindeman (eds.), AIDS: Principles, Practices, and Politics. New York: Hemisphere Publishing.

Des Jarlais, Don C., and Samuel Friedman. 1994. "AIDS and the Use of Injected Drugs." Scientific American 272(February):82–88.

Dickson, Donald. 1968. "Bureaucracy and Morality: An Organizational Perspective on a Moral Crusade." Social Problems 16:143–56.

Donelan, Karen. 1996. "Whatever Happened to the Health Insurance Crisis in the United States?" Journal of the American Medical Association 276:1346–50.

DuBois, Ellen. 1978. Feminism and Suffrage: The Emergence of an Independent Women's Movement in America, 1848–1869. Ithaca, NY: Cornell University Press.

Durkheim, Emile. 1893. The Division of Labor in Society. New York: Free Press, 1951.

_____. 1895. The Rules of the Sociological Method. New York: Free Press, 1982.

_____. 1897. Suicide. New York: Free Press, 1951.

Dwyer, Jeffrey, and Raymond T. Coward (eds.). 1992. Gender, Families, and Elder Care. Newbury Park, CA: Sage.

Easterlin, Richard A. 1976. "Factors in the Decline of Farm Family Fertility in the United States: Some Preliminary Results." Journal of American History 63:600–612.

Eggers, Paul W. 1995. "Racial Differences in Access to Kidney Transplantation." Health Care Financing Review 17:89–104.

Ellis, Joseph. 1997. American Sphinx: The Character of Thomas Jefferson. New York: Knopf.

Engelberg, Stephen, and Deborah Sontag. 1994. "Behind One Agency's Walls: Misbehaving and Moving Up." New York Times, national edition. December 21:A1.

England, Paula. 1992. Comparable Worth: Theories and Evidence. New York: Aldine de Gruyter.

ERC (Employee Relocation Council). 1992. "Relocation Trends Survey." Washington, DC: Employee Relocation Council.

Erikson, Erik. 1950. Childhood and Society. New York: Norton.

Evans, Robert G. 1994. Introduction to R. G. Evans, M. L. Barer, and T. R. Marmor (eds.), Why Are Some People Healthy and Others Not? The Determinants of Health of Populations. New York: Aldine de Gruyter.

Evans, Robert G., and G. L. Stoddart. 1994. "Producing Health, Consuming Health Care." Pp. 27–66 in R. G. Evans, M. L. Barer, and T. R. Marmor (eds.), Why Are Some People Healthy and Others Not? The Determinants of Health of Populations. New York: Aldine de Gruyter.

Falco, Mathea. 1994. The Making of a Drug Free America. New York: Times Books.

Faupel, Charles. 1991. Shooting Dope: Career Patterns of Hard Core Heroin Users. Gainesville: University of Florida Press.

FBI (Federal Bureau of Investigation). 1996. Crime in the United States. Washington, DC: U.S. Government Printing Office.

FDC (Florida Department of Corrections). 1996. 1995–96 Annual Report: The Guidebook to Corrections in Florida. Tallahassee, FL: Department of Corrections.

Feagin, Joe R. 1991. "The Continuing Significance of Race: Antiblack Discrimination in Public Places." American Sociological Review 56:101–16.

Featherman, David L., and Robert M. Hauser. 1978. Opportunity and Change. New York: Academic Press.

Fischer, David Hackett. 1978. Growing Old in America. New York: Oxford University Press.

Fitzgerald, Louise F. 1993. "Sexual Harassment: Violence Against Women in the Workplace." American Psychologist 48:1070–76.

Fix, Michael, and Raymond J. Struyk. 1993. Clear and Convincing Evidence: Measurement of Discrimination in America. Washington, DC: Urban Institute Press.

Fogel, Robert W. 1991. "The Conquest of High Mortality and Hunger in Europe and America: Timing and Mechanisms." Pp. 156–89 in David Landes, Patrice Higgonet, and Henry Rosovsky (eds.), Favorites of Fortune: Technology, Growth, and Economic Development Since the Industrial Revolution. Cambridge: Harvard University Press.

Francome, Colin. 1986. Abortion Practice in Britain and the United States. London: Allyn & Unwin.

Frank, D. A., M. Napoleone, A. Meyers., N. Roos, K. Peterson, and L. A. Cupples. 1992. Seasonal Changes in Weight for Age in a Pediatric Emergency Room: A Heat or Eat Effect. Boston City Hospital Pediatric Nutrition Surveillance Study. Boston: Boston City Hospital.

Frank, John W., and J. Fraser Mustard. 1994. "The Determinants of Health from a Historical Perspective." Daedalus 123(Fall):21–42.

Franklin, Benjamin. 1961. The Autobiography and Other Writings. New York: New American Library.

Fries, James F. 1980. "Aging, Natural Death, and the Compression of Morbidity." New England Journal of Medicine 300:130–35.

Fuchs, Stephen, and Charles E. Case. 1994. "A Grid-Group Theory of Prejudice." Research in Race and Ethnic Relations 7:37–54.

Fuller, Richard C., and Richard R. Myers. 1941. "The Natural History of a Social Problem." American Sociological Review 6:320–28.

Furstenberg, Frank F., J. Brooks-Gunn, and S. Philip Morgan. 1987. Adolescent Mothers in Later Life. New York: Cambridge University Press.

FVPF (Family Violence Prevention Fund). 1993. Men Beating Women: Ending Domestic Violence. San Francisco: Family Violence Prevention Fund.

Gallup, George. 1972. The Gallup Poll: Public Opinion 1935–1971. New York: Random House.

———. 1995. Gallup Poll Monthly 357(June).

Gans, Herbert. 1972. "The Positive Functions of Poverty." American Journal of Sociology 78:275–89.

Garbarino, James. 1991. No Place to Be a Child. Lexington, MA: D. C. Heath.

———. 1992. Children in Danger: Coping with the Consequences of Community Violence. New York: Jossey-Bass.

Garrett, Laurie. 1995. The Coming Plague: Newly Emerging Diseases in a World out of Balance. New York: Penguin.

Gemke, Robert J.B.J. 1995. "Long-Term Survival and State of Health After Paediatric Intensive Care." Archives of Disabled Children 73:196–210.

Glassner, Barry, and Julia Loughlin. 1987. Drugs in Adolescent Worlds. New York: St. Martin's Press.

Glendon, Mary Ann. 1987. Abortion and Divorce in Western Law. Cambridge: Harvard University Press.

Goldin, Claudia. 1990. Understanding the Gender Gap: An Economic History of American Women. New York: Oxford University Press.

Goleman, Daniel. 1995. Emotional Intelligence. New York: Bantam Books.

Goode, Erich. 1989. Drugs in American Society, 3rd edition. New York: Knopf.

Goode, William J. 1982. "Why Men Resist." Pp. 131–50 in Barrie Thorne (ed.), Rethinking the Family. New York: Longman.

Graham, Lawrence Otis. 1995. Member of the Club. New York: Harper & Row.

Gregorio, David I. 1997. "The Effects of Occupation-Based Social Position on Mortality in a Large American Cohort." American Journal of Public Health 87:1472–75.

Greven, Philip. 1991. Spare the Child: The Religious Roots of Punishment and the Psychological Impact of Physical Abuse. New York: Knopf.

Grieco, Margaret. 1987. Keeping It in the Family: Social Networks and Employment Chance. New York: Tavistock Publications.

Grossman, James R. 1989. Land of Hope: Chicago, Black Southerners, and the Great Migration. Chicago: University of Chicago Press.

GSS (General Social Survey). 1996. Cumulative Codebook. Chicago: National Opinion Research Corporation.

Gurr, Ted Robert. 1989. "Historical Trends in Violent Crime: Europe and the United States." Pp. 21–55 in T. R. Gurr (ed.), Violence in America, Vol. 1. Newbury Park, CA: Sage.

Gusfield, Joseph R. 1987. "Passage to Play: Rituals to Drink in American Society." Pp. 73–90 in Mary Douglas (ed.), Constructive Drinking: Perspectives on Drinking from Anthropology. Cambridge: Cambridge University Press.

———. 1990. "Sociology's Critical Irony: Countering American Individualism." Pp. 31–48 in Herbert Gans (ed.), Sociology in America. Newbury Park, CA: Sage.

Hack, Maureen. 1993. "Outcomes of Extremely Immature Infants: A Perinatal Dilemma." New England Journal of Medicine 329:1649–50.

_____. 1994. "School-Age Outcomes in Children with Birth Weights Under 750 Grams." New England Journal of Medicine 331:753–59.

_____. 1995. "Very-Low-Birth-Weight Outcomes of the National Institute of Child Health on Human Development Neonatal Network, November 1989 to October 1990." American Journal of Obstetrics and Gynecology 172:457–64.

Hall, Elaine. 1993. "Waitering/Waitressing: Engendering the Work of Table Servers." Gender and Society 7:329–47.

Hall, Trish. 1990. "After AIDS Diagnosis Some Embrace Life." New York Times, national edition. June 17:1.

Hareven, Tamara K. 1994. "Family Change and Historical Change: An Uneasy Relationship." Pp. 130–50 in Matilda White Riley, Robert L. Kahn, and Anne Foner (eds.), Age and Structural Lag. New York: John Wiley & Sons.

Harrington, Michael. 1962. The Other America. New York: Penguin.

Harrison, Roderick J., and Daniel H. Weinberg. 1992. "Changes in Racial and Ethnic Residential Segregation, 1980–1990." Paper presented at the annual meeting of the American Statistical Association.

Hartley, William B. 1969. Estimation of the Incidence of Poverty in the United States, 1870–1914. Ph.D. dissertation, Department of Economics, University of Wisconsin, Madison.

Hawthorne, Nathaniel. 1969. The Scarlet Letter. New York: Fleet Press.

Hayes, Cheryl D. (ed.). 1987. Risking the Future: Adolescent Sexuality, Pregnancy, and Childbearing, Vol. 1. Washington, DC: National Academy Press.

Hayghe, Howard V. 1997. "Developments in Women's Labor Force Participation." Monthly Labor Review 120(September):41–44.

Heilbroner, Robert L., and Lester C. Thurow. 1982. Economics Explained. Englewood Cliffs, NJ: Prentice-Hall.

Hein, H. A., L. F. Burmeister, and K. A. Papke. 1990. "The Relationship of Unwed Status to Infant Mortality." Obstetrics and Gynecology 76:763–70.

Heller, Joseph. 1961. Catch-22: A Novel. New York: Simon & Schuster.

Hellinger, Fred J. 1995. "The Lifetime Cost of Treating a Person with HIV." Journal of the American Medical Association 270(July 28):474–78.

Henderson, James W. 1994. "The Cost Effectiveness of Prenatal Care." Health Care Financing Review 15:21–33.

Henretta, John C. 1994. "Social Structure and Age-Based Careers." Pp. 54–79 in Matilda White Riley, Robert L. Kahn, and Anne Foner (eds.), Age and Structural Lag. New York: John Wiley & Sons.

Henshaw, Stanley K. 1990. "Induced Abortion: A World Review, 1990." Family Planning Perspectives 23:75–81.

Henshaw, Stanley K., and Kathryn Kost. 1996. "Abortion Patients in 1994–1995: Characteristics and Contraceptive Use." Family Planning Perspectives 28:140–47.

Henshaw, Stanley K, and Jennifer Van Vort. 1994. "Abortion Services in the United States, 1991 and 1992." Family Planning Perspectives 26:100–107.

Herman, Judith Lewis. 1989. "Wife Beating." Harvard Mental Health Newsletter 5(April):4–6.

_____. 1992. Trauma and Recovery. New York: Basic Books.

Hertzman, Clyde. 1994. "The Lifelong Impact of Childhood Experiences: A Population Health Perspective." Daedalus 123(Fall):167–80.

Hibbs, Douglas A. 1977. "Political Parties and Macroeconomic Policy." American Political Science Review 71:1467–87.

Himmelfarb, Gertrude. 1995. The De-Moralization of Society. New York: Knopf.

Himmelstein, Jerome. 1983. The Strange Career of Marijuana. Westport, CT: Greenwood Press.

Hodgson, Randy, and Robert L. Kaufman. 1982. "Economic Dualism: A Critical Review." American Sociological Review 47:727–39.

Hoekelman, Robert A., Saul Blackman, Stanford B. Friedman, Nicholas M. Nelson, and Henry M. Seidel (eds.). 1987. Primary Pediatric Care. St. Louis: Mosby.

Hosking, Michael P. 1989. "Outcome of Surgery in Patients 90 Years of Age and Older." Journal of the American Medical Association 261:1909–15.

Hout, Michael. 1988. "More Universalism, Less Structural Mobility: The American Occupational Structure in the 1980s." American Journal of Sociology 93:1358–1400.

Howard-Jones, Norman. 1971. "The Origins of Hypodermic Medication." Scientific American 255(January):96–102.

Huff, C. Ronald. 1991. Gangs in America. Newbury Park, CA: Sage.

Inciardi, James. 1986. The War on Drugs. Palo Alto, CA: Mayfield Publishers.

Innis, Leslie, and Joe R. Feagin. 1992. "The Black 'Underclass' Ideology in Race Relations Analysis." Social Justice 16:13–34.

Irving, John. 1985. The Cider House Rules. New York: William Morrow.

Jackson, James S. 1996. "Racism and the Physical and Mental Health Status of African Americans: A Thirteen Year National Panel Study." Ethnicity and Disease 6:132–47.

Jacobs, Janet Liebman. 1994. Victimized Daughters: Incest and the Development of the Female Self. New York: Routledge.

Jacobs, Jerry A. 1990. Revolving Doors: Sex Segregation and Women's Careers. Stanford, CA: Stanford University Press.

Janoff-Bulman, Ronnie. 1997. "Understanding Reactions to Traumatic Events." Harvard Mental Health Newsletter 14(October):8.

Joffe, Carole. 1995. Doctors of Conscience: The Struggle to Provide Abortion Before and After Roe v. Wade. Boston: Beacon Press.

Johnson, Bruce, D., Paul J. Goldstein, Edward Preble, James Schmeidler, Douglas S. Lipton, Barry Spunt, and Thomas Miller. 1985. Taking Care of Business: The Economics of Crime by Heroin Abusers. Lexington, MA: D. C. Heath.

Jones, Charisse. 1995. "Crack and Punishment: Is Race the Issue?" New York Times, national edition. November 28:1.

Jones, Elise, Jacqueline Darroch Forrest, Stanley K. Henshaw, Jane Silverman, and Aida Torres. 1989. Pregnancy, Contraception, and Family Planning Services in Industrialized Countries. New Haven, CT: Yale University Press.

Joshi, Heather (ed.). 1989. The Changing Population of Britain. London: Blackwell.

Joyce, Theodore, Stanley K. Henshaw, and Julia DeClerque Skatrud. 1997. "The Impact of Mississippi's Mandatory Delay Law on Abortions and Births." Journal of the American Medical Association 278:653–58.

Kahn, Robert L. 1994. "Opportunities, Aspirations, and Goodness of Fit." Pp. 37–56 in Matilda White Riley, Robert L. Kahn, and Anne Foner (eds.), Age and Structural Lag. New York: John Wiley & Sons.

Kallmuss, Debra S., and Pearila B. Namerow. 1994. "Subsequent Childbearing Among Teenage Mothers." Family Planning Perspectives 26:149–53.

Kane, Thomas J. 1997. "Racial and Ethnic Preference in College Admissions." Photocopy. Kennedy School of Government, Harvard University.

Kanter, Rosabeth Moss. 1978. "Some Effects of Proportion on Group Life: Skewed Sex Ratios and Responses to Token Women." American Journal of Sociology 82:965–90.

Kasarda, John D. 1990. "Structural Factors Affecting the Location and Timing of Urban Underclass Growth." Urban Geography 11:234–64.

Katz, Elihu, and Paul F. Lazarsfeld. 1955. Personal Influence: The Part Played by People in the Flow of Mass Communication. Glencoe, IL: Free Press.

Katz, Jack. 1988. The Seduction of Crime: Moral and Sensual Attractions in Doing Evil. New York: Basic Books.

Kelly, Rita Mae. 1997. "Gender Culture and Socialization." Pp. 19–32 in Dana Dunn (ed.), Workplace/Women's Place: An Anthology. Los Angeles: Roxbury Publishing.

Kennedy, Stetson. 1995. After Appomattox: How the South Won the War. Gainesville: University Press of Florida.

King, Mary C. 1992. "Occupational Segregation by Race and Sex, 1940–88." Monthly Labor Review 115(April):30–36.

Kitzman, Harriet. 1997. "Effect of Prenatal and Infancy Home Visitation by Nurses on Pregnancy Outcomes, Childhood Injuries, and Repeated Childbearing." Journal of the American Medical Association 278:644–52.

Knaus, William. 1995. "A Controlled Trial to Improve Care for Seriously Ill Hospitalized Patients." Journal of the American Medical Association 274:1591–8.

Kogan, Michael D. 1994a. "Racial Disparities in Reported Prenatal Care Advice from Health Care Providers." American Journal of Public Health 84:82–88.

_____. 1994b. "Relation of the Content of Prenatal Care to the Risk of Low Birth Weight: Maternal Reports of Health Behavior Advice and Initial Prenatal Care Procedures." Journal of the American Medical Association 27:1340–45.

Kohn, Melvin. 1987. "Cross-National Research as an Analytic Strategy." American Sociological Review 52:713–31.

Kohn, Melvin, and Carmi Schooler. 1983. Work and Personality: An Inquiry into the Impact of Social Stratification. Norwood, NJ: Ablex Publishing.

Kolata, Gina. 1996. "Boom in Ritalin Sales Raises Ethical Issues." New York Times, national edition. May 15:B8.

Kolb, Lawrence, and Andrew G. Du Mez. 1924. "The Prevalence and Trend of Drug Addiction in the United States and the Factors Influencing It." Public Health Reports 39(May 23):1179–1204.

Kolbert, Kitty, and Andrea Miller. 1994. "Government in the Examining Room: Restrictions on the Provision of Abortion." Journal of the American Medical Women's Association 49:153–64.

Konner, Melvin. 1991. Childhood. Boston: Little, Brown.

Koss, Mary P. 1993. "Rape: Scope, Impact, Interventions, and Public Policy Responses." American Psychologist 38:1062–69.

Kotlowitz, Alex. 1991. There Are No Children Here. New York: Doubleday.

Kposowa, Augustine, and Kevin Breault. 1993. "Reassessing the Structural Co-variates of U.S. Homicide Rates: A County Level Study." Sociological Focus 26:27–46.

Kramer, Natalie. 1995. "Employee Benefits for Older Workers." Monthly Labor Review 118(April):21–28.

Krieger, Nancy. 1996. "Racial Discrimination and Blood Pressure: The CARDIA Study of Young Black and White Adults." American Journal of Public Health 86:1270–79.

Kristoff, Nicholas D. 1997. "I Lived to Tell About Japan's Medical Miracle." New York Times, national edition. November 30:IV-7.

Kübler-Ross, Elizabeth. 1969. On Death and Dying. New York: Macmillan.

Kunst, Anton E., and Johan P. Mackenbach. 1992. An International Comparison of Inequalities in Mortality. Rotterdam: Erasmus University.

Kuznets, Simon. 1985. Modern Economic Growth, 1929–82. Washington, DC: Brookings Institution.

Lane, Ann J. (ed.). 1980. The Charlotte Perkins Gilman Reader. New York: Pantheon Books.

Lane, Roger. 1986. Roots of Violence in Black Philadelphia, 1860–1900. Cambridge: Harvard University Press.

———. 1989. "On the Social Meaning of Homicide Trends in America." Pp. 55–79 in T. R. Gurr (ed.), Violence in America, Vol. 1. Newbury Park, CA: Sage.

Langer, William L. 1975. "American Foods and Europe's Population Growth, 1750–1850." Journal of Social History 8:51–66.

Larkin, Philip. 1988. Collected Poems. Boston: Faber and Faber.

Lazare, Edward, and Paul Leonard. 1992. A Place to Call Home: The Low Income Housing Crisis in 44 Major Metropolitan Areas. Washington, DC: Center on Budget and Policy Priorities.

Leavy, Zad, and Jerome M. Kummer. 1962. "Criminal Abortion: Human Hardship and Unyielding Laws." Southern California Law Review 55:126–46.

Lemert, Charles. Social Things: An Introduction to the Sociological Life. 1997. New York: Rowman & Littlefield.

Lenski, Gerhard. 1966. Power and Privilege. New York: McGraw-Hill.

Lersch, Kim M. 1993. "Current Trends in Police Brutality: An Analysis of Recent Newspaper Accounts." Master's thesis, University of Florida, Gainesville.

Lewin, Tamar. 1997. "Abortion Rate Declined Again in '95, U.S. Says, but Began Rising Last Year." New York Times, national edition. December 5:A10.

Lewit, Eugene M. 1995. "The Direct Costs of Low Birth Weight." Future of Children 5:35–56.

Lieberson, Stanley. 1980. A Piece of the Pie: Blacks and White Immigrants Since 1880. Berkeley: University of California Press.

———. 1992. "Einstein, Renoir, and Greely: Some Thoughts About Evidence in Sociology." American Sociological Review 57:1–15.

Limpson, Lisa. 1997. "Outcomes of Enhanced Prenatal Services for Medicaid-Eligible Women in Public and Private Settings." Public Health Reports 112:122–33.

Lipset, Seymour Martin. 1968. "History and Sociology: Some Methodological Considerations." Pp. 20–58 in S. M. Lipset and Richard Hofstadter (eds.), Sociology and History: Methods. New York: Basic Books.

Loftin, Colin. 1989. "Economic Change and Homicide in Detroit, 1926–1979." Pp. 163–78 in T. R. Gurr (ed.), Violence in America, Vol. 1. Newbury Park, CA: Sage.

Lott, Juanita Tamayo. 1997. "The Limitations of Directive 15." Pp. 72–77 in Chester Hartman (ed.), Double Exposure: Poverty and Race in America. Armonk, NY: M.E. Sharpe.

Luker, Kristin. 1984. Abortion and the Politics of Motherhood. Berkeley: University of California Press.

Lyng, Stephen. 1990. "Edgework: A Social Psychological Analysis of Voluntary Risk-Taking." American Journal of Sociology 95:851–86.

Maier, Norman R.F. 1949. Frustration: The Study of Behavior Without a Goal. New York: McGraw-Hill.

Manlove, Jane. 1997. "Early Motherhood in an Intergenerational Perspective: The Experiences of a British Cohort." Journal of Marriage and Family 59:263–79.

Marsiglio, William. 1993. "Adolescent Males' Orientation Toward Paternity and Contraception." Family Planning Perspectives 25(January/February):22–31.

Massey, Douglas S., and Nancy A. Denton. 1993. American Apartheid: Segregation and the Making of the Underclass. Cambridge: Harvard University Press.

Mattingly, Garrett. 1959. The Armada. Boston: Houghton Mifflin.

McCord, Colin, and Harold P. Freeman. 1994. "Excess Mortality in Harlem." Pp. 35–42 in Peter Conrad and Rochelle Kern (eds.), The Sociology of Health and Illness. New York: St. Martin's Press.

McCormick, Marie C. 1992. "The Health and Developmental Status of Very Low-Birth-Weight Children at School Age." Journal of the American Medical Association. 275:2204–8.

McKeown, Thomas. 1976. The Modern Rise of Population. New York: Academic Press.

McNeil, William H. Plagues and People. New York: Anchor Books, 1976.

Mechanic, David, and David A. Rochefort. 1996. "Comparative Medical Systems." Annual Review of Sociology 22:239–70.

Mellor, William H. 1996. "No Jobs, No Work: Local Restrictions Block the Exits from Welfare." New York Times, national edition. August 31:A12.

Merton, Robert K. 1968a. "Social Structure and Anomie." Pp. 185–215 in R. K. Merton, Social Theory and Social Structure. New York: Free Press.

———. 1968b. Social Theory and Social Structure. New York: Free Press.

———. 1976. Introduction to R. K. Merton and R. A. Nisbet (eds.), Contemporary Social Problems. New York: Harcourt Brace Jovanovich.

Merton, Robert K., and Alice S. Rossi. 1968. "Contributions to the Theory of Reference Group Behavior." Pp. 279–334 in R. K. Merton, Social Theory and Social Structure. New York: Free Press.

Messner, Steven F., and Richard Rosenfeld. 1997. Crime and the American Dream, 2nd edition. Belmont, CA: Wadsworth.

Miller, C. Arden. "Infant Mortality in the U.S." Scientific American 253(July):31–37.

Mills, C. Wright. 1959. The Sociological Imagination. New York: Oxford University Press.

Mitchell, Janet B., and Rezaul K. Khandker. 1995. "Black-White Treatment Differences in Acute Myocardial Infarction." Health Care Financing Review 17:61–70.

Mohr, James C. 1978. Abortion in America: The Origins and Evolution of National Policy. New York: Oxford University Press.

Moore, David W., Frank Newport, and Lydia Said. 1996. "Public Generally Supports a Woman's Right to Abortion." Gallup Poll Monthly 371(August):29–35.

Morgan, Patricia. 1978. "The Legislation of Drug Law: Economic Crisis and Social Control." Journal of Drug Issues 8:53–62.

Morley, Jefferson. 1989. "What Crack Is Like." New Republic (October 2, 1989):12–13.

Morris, Lydia. 1992. "The Social Segregation of the Long-Term Unemployed in Hartlepool." Sociological Review 40:344–69.

Murrell, A. J., I. H. Frieze, and J. L. Frost. 1991. "Aspiring to Careers in Male and Female Dominated Professions: A Study of Black and White College Women." Psychology of Women Quarterly 15:103–26.

Musto, David. 1973. The American Disease: The Origins of Narcotics Control. New Haven, CT: Yale University Press.

_____. 1996. "Alcohol in American History." Scientific American 274(April):78–83.

NACCD (National Advisory Commission on Civil Disorders). 1968. Report of the National Advisory Commission on Civil Disorders. New York: Bantam.

Nadelman, Ethan. 1988. "The Case for Legalization." Public Interest 92(Summer):3–31.

NCHS (National Center for Health Statistics). 1995. "Annual Summary of Births, Marriages, Divorces, and Deaths: United States, 1994." Monthly Vital Statistics Report 44, 2. Washington, DC: U.S. Government Printing Office.

_____. 1996a. "Advance Report of Final Mortality Statistics, 1994." Monthly Vital Statistics Report 45, 3, supp. Hyattsville, MD: U.S. Department of Health and Human Services.

_____. 1996b. "Births and Deaths: United States, 1995." Monthly Vital Statistics Report 45, 3. Hyattsville, MD: U.S. Department of Health and Human Services.

_____. 1996c. "Births, Marriages, and Deaths for 1995." Monthly Vital Statistics Report 45, 4. Hyattsville, MD: U.S. Department of Health and Human Services.

_____. 1996d. "Births, Marriages, Divorces, and Deaths for June, 1996." Monthly Vital Statistics Report 45, 6. Hyattsville, MD: U.S. Department of Health and Human Services.

_____. 1996e. Health, United States, 1995. Hyattsville, MD: U.S. Department of Health and Human Services.

_____. 1996f. "Prenatal Care in the United States, 1980–94." Vital Health Statistics 21, 54. Hyattsville, MD: U.S. Department of Health and Human Services.

_____. 1997a. "Births, Marriages, Divorces, and Deaths for January, 1997." Monthly Vital Statistics Report 46, 1. Hyattsville, MD: U.S. Department of Health and Human Services.

_____. 1997b. "Fertility, Family Planning, and Women's Health: New Data from the 1995 National Survey of Family Growth." Vital Health Statistics 23, 19.

_____. 1997c. "Report of Final Mortality Statistics, 1995." Monthly Vital Statistics Report 45, 11, supp. 2. Hyattsville, MD: U.S. Department of Health and Human Services.

_____. 1997d. "Report of Final Natality Statistics, 1995." Monthly Vital Statistics Report 45, 11, supp. 3. Hyattsville, MD: U.S. Department of Health and Human Services.

NIDA (National Institute on Drug Abuse). 1995. National Household Survey on Drug Abuse: Population Estimates, 1994. Washington, DC: U.S. Government Printing Office.

_____. 1996. National Survey Results on Drug Use: College Students and Young Adults. Washington, DC: U.S. Government Printing Office.

Niemi, Richard G., John Mueller, and Tom W. Smith. 1989. Trends in Public Opinion: A Compendium of Survey Data. New York: Greenwood Press.

NIJ (National Institute of Justice). 1995. Research Preview: Youth Violence, Guns, and Illicit Drug Markets. Washington, DC: U.S. Government Printing Office.

_____. 1996. Victim Costs and Consequences: A New Look. Washington, DC: U.S. Government Printing Office.

Nijboer, Jan. 1995. "Trends in Violence and Homicide in the Netherlands." Pp. 195–210 in Carolyn Block and Richard Block (eds.), Trends, Risks, and Interventions in Lethal Violence: Proceedings of the 3rd Annual Symposium on Homicide Working Group. Washington, DC: U.S. Department of Justice.

Nisbet, Robert A. 1969. Social Change and History, New York: Oxford University Press.

NRCCSA (National Resource Center on Child Sexual Abuse). 1992. The Incidence and Prevalence of Child Sexual Abuse: No Easy Answer. Huntsville, AL: National Resource Center on Child Sexual Abuse.

NTC Publications. 1995. World Drink Trends: International Beverage Alcohol Consumption and Production Trends. Oxfordshire, UK: NTC Publications.

NVC (National Victim Center). 1992. Rape in America: A Report to the Nation. Arlington, VA: National Victim Center.

NYT (New York Times Magazine). 1994. "The Purse Problem." New York Times Magazine. May 29:12.

Ogbu, John U. 1978. Minority Education and Caste: The American System in Cross-Cultural Perspective. New York: Academic Press.

Olds, David L. 1997. "Long-Term Effects of Home Visitation on Maternal Life Course and Child Abuse and Neglect." Journal of the American Medical Association 278:637–43.

Olmstead, Alan. 1975. Threshold: The First Days of Retirement. New York: Harper & Row.

Olshansky, S. Jay, Bruce A. Carnes, and Christine K. Cassel. 1993. "The Aging of the Human Species." Scientific American 291(April):46–52.

Olshansky, S. Jay, Mark A. Rudberg, Bruce A. Carnes, Christine K. Cassel, and Jacob A. Brody. 1991. "Trading Off Longer Life for Worsening Health." Journal of Aging and Health 3:194–216.

ONDCP (Office of National Drug Control Policy). 1994. National Drug Control Strategy: Reclaiming Our Communities from Drugs and Violence. Washington, DC: U.S. Government Printing Office.

O'Neill, Eugene. 1962. Long Day's Journey into Night. New Haven, CT: Yale University Press.

O'Neill, William L. 1972. Women at Work, Including 'The Long Day: The Story of a New York Working Girl, by Dorothy Richardson.' Chicago: Quadrangle Books.

ONS (Office for National Statistics). 1997. Social Trends 27. London: Her Majesty's Stationery Office.

Orfield, Gary. 1997. "Deepening Segregation in American Public Schools." Photocopy. Harvard Project on School Desegregation, Harvard University.

Ornati, Oscar. 1966. Poverty Amidst Affluence. New York: Twentieth Century Fund.

Orshansky, Mollie. 1969. "How Poverty Is Measured." Monthly Labor Review 92(February):12–19.

Oshinsky, David M. 1996. Worse Than Slavery: Parchman Farm and the Ordeal of Jim Crow Justice. New York: Free Press.

Ostrowski, James. 1989. Thinking About Drug Legalization. Washington, DC: Cato Institute.

OTA (Office of Technology Assessment). 1987. Life-Sustaining Technology and the Elderly. Washington, DC: U.S. Government Printing Office.

Page, Walter. 1987. "Water and Health." Pp. 105–38 in Michael R. Greenberg (ed.), Public Health and the Environment: The United States Experience. New York: Guilford Press.

Palmore, Erdman B. 1985. Retirement: Causes and Consequences. New York: Springer.

Panem, Sandra. 1988. The AIDS Bureaucracy. Cambridge: Harvard University Press.

Pappas, Gregory. 1993. "The Increasing Disparity in Mortality Between Socioeconomic Groups in the United States, 1960 and 1986." New England Journal of Medicine 329:103–9.

Patterson, James T. 1986. America's Struggle Against Poverty, 1900–1985. Cambridge: Harvard University Press.

Paulin, Geoffry D., and Elizabeth Dietz. 1995. "Health Insurance Coverage for Families and Children." Monthly Labor Review 118(August):13–23.

Payer, Lynn. 1988. Medicine and Culture: Varieties of Treatment in the United States, England, West Germany, and France. New York: Henry Holt.

Pearlin, Leonard I., E. G. Menaghan, M. A. Lieberman, and J. T. Mullin. 1981. "The Stress Process." Journal of Health and Social Behavior 22:337–56.

Perls, Thomas T. 1995. "The Oldest Old." Scientific American 292(January):70–75.

Perry-Jenkins, Maureen, and Karen Folk. 1994. "Class, Couples, and Conflict: Effects of Division of Labor on Assessments of Marriage in Dual-Earner Families." Journal of Marriage and Family 56:165–80.

Pollan, Michael. 1995. "How Pot Has Grown." New York Times Magazine. February 19:31–38.

Preble, Edward, and John J. Casey, Jr. 1969. "Taking Care of Business—The Heroin Addict's Life on the Street." International Journal of the Addictions 4:145–69.

Presser, Harriet B. 1994. "Employment Schedules Among Dual-Earner Spouses and the Division of Household Labor by Gender." American Sociological Review 59:348–64.

Preston, Richard. 1994. The Hot Zone: A Terrifying True Story. New York: Anchor Books.

Preston, Samuel. 1993. "Demographic Change in the United States, 1970–2050." Pp. in Kenneth G. Manton, Burton H. Singer, and Richard Suzman (eds.), Forecasting the Health of the Elderly Population. New York: Springer.

Quill, Timothy E. 1991. "Death and Dignity: A Case of Individualized Decision-Making." New England Journal of Medicine 324(March 7):691–94.

Rees, P., D. Phillips, and D. Medway. 1995. "The Socioeconomic Geography of Ethnic Groups in Two Northern British Cities." Environment and Planning A 27:557–91.

Reskin, Barbara, and Heidi Hartman. 1986. Women's Work, Men's Work: Sex Segregation on the Job. Washington, DC: National Academy Press.

Reskin, Barbara, and Irene Padavic. 1994. Women and Men at Work. Thousand Oaks, CA: Pine Forge Press.

Reuter, Peter. 1988. "Can the Border Be Sealed?" Public Interest 92(Summer):51–65.

_____. 1992. "Hawks Ascendant: The Punitive Trend of American Drug Policy." Daedalus 121(Summer):15–52.

Reuter, Peter, Robert MacCoun, and Patrick Murphy. 1990. Money from Crime: A Study of the Economics of Drug Dealing in Washington, D.C. Santa Monica, CA: Rand Corporation.

Reves, Randall. 1985. "Declining Fertility in England and Wales as a Major Cause of the Twentieth Century Decline in Mortality." American Journal of Epidemiology 122:112–26.

Riddle, John M., J. Worth Estes, and Josiah C. Russell. 1994. "Birth Control in the Ancient World." Archeology 47:29–35.

Riley, Matilda White, and John W. Riley. 1994. "Structural Lag: Past and Future." Pp. 15–37 in Matilda White Riley, Robert L. Kahn, and Anne Foner (eds.), Age and Structural Lag. New York: John Wiley & Sons.

Rivara, Frederick. 1997. "Alcohol and Illicit Drug Abuse and the Risk of Violent Death in the Home." Journal of the American Medical Association 278:569–75.

Rongy, A. J. 1933. Abortion: Legal and Illegal. New York: Vanguard Press.

Rorabaugh, William J. 1979. The Alcoholic Republic. New York: Oxford University Press.

Rosenberg, Nathan, and L. E. Birdzell, Jr. 1990. "Science, Technology, and the Western Miracle." Scientific American 263(November):42–54.

Rosenthal, Elisabeth. 1996. "Reduced HMO Fees Cause Concern About Patient Care." New York Times, national edition. November 25:1.

_____. 1997. "When Healthier Isn't Cheaper." New York Times, national edition. March 16:1.

Rossi, Alice S., and Peter H. Rossi. 1990. Of Human Bonding: Parent-Child Relations Across the Life-Course. New York: Aldine de Gruyter.

Rossi, Peter H. 1989. Down and Out in America: The Origin of Homelessness. Chicago: University of Chicago Press.

Roth, Jeffrey, and Mark Moore. 1995. Reducing Violent Crimes and Intentional Injuries. National Institute of Justice: Research in Action Series. Washington, DC: U.S. Department of Justice.

Rothman, Ellen K. 1984. Hands and Hearts: A History of Courtship in America. New York: Basic Books.

Ruggles, Patricia. 1990. Drawing the Line: Alternative Poverty Measures and Their Implications for Public Policy. Washington, DC: Urban Institute Press.

Rule, James B. 1978. Insight and Social Betterment. New York: Oxford University Press.

RWJF (Robert Wood Johnson Foundation). 1993. Substance Abuse: The Nation's Number One Health Problem. Princeton, NJ: Robert Wood Johnson Foundation.

Rytina, Nancy F., and Suzanne M. Bianchi. 1984. "Occupational Reclassification and Distribution by Gender." Monthly Labor Review 107(March):11–17.

Saigal, Saroj. 1996. "Self-Perceived Health Status and Health-Related Quality of Life of Extremely Low-Birth-Weight Infants at Adolescence." Journal of the American Medical Association 276:453–59.

SAMHSA (Substance Abuse and Mental Health Services Administration). 1997. Preliminary Results from the 1996 National Household Survey on Drug Abuse. Washington, DC: U.S. Department of Health and Human Services.

Sanderson, Warren. 1979. "Quantitative Aspects of Marriage, Fertility, and Family Limitation in Nineteenth-Century America." Demography 16:339–58.

Sandmeyer, E. C. 1939. The Anti-Chinese Movement in California. Urbana: University of Illinois Press.

Schneider, Beth E. 1991. "Put Up and Shut Up: Workplace Sexual Assaults." Gender and Society 5:533–46.

Schumpeter, Joseph A. 1954. A History of Economic Analysis. New York: Oxford University Press.

Schur, Claudia L. 1995. "Health Care Use by Hispanic Adults: Financial vs. Non-Financial Determinants." Health Care Financing Review 17:71–88.

Searles, Patricia, and Ronald J. Berger (eds.). 1995. Rape and Society. Boulder, CO: Westview Press.

Seccombe, Karen, and Jeffrey W. Dwyer. 1995. "Elder Care as Domestic Labor: A Replication and Test of Competing Theories." Paper, University of Florida.

Sellin, Thorsten. 1980. The Penalty of Death. Beverly Hills, CA: Sage.

Sen, Kasturi. 1994. Aging: Debates on the Demographic Transition and Social Policy. Atlantic Highlands, NJ: Zed Books.

Sewell, Richard. 1975. The Life of Emily Dickinson. New York: Farrar, Straus, and Giroux.

Sgroi, Suzanne (ed.). 1984. Handbook of Clinical Intervention in Child Sexual Abuse. Lexington, MA: D. C. Heath.

Shakespeare, William. 1980. Romeo and Juliet. New York: Methuen.

_____. 1991. Measure for Measure. New York: Cambridge University Press.

Shelley, Louise. 1981. Crime and Modernization. Carbondale: Southern Illinois University Press.

Shenk, Joshua Wolf. 1995. "Why You Can Hate Drugs and Still Want to Legalize Them." Washington Monthly 27(October):32–40.

Shimron, Yonat. 1997. "Baptists Not Ready for Women Pastors." Gainesville (Florida) Sun. July 12:1.

SHNFBN (Second Harvest National Food Bank Network). 1994. 1993 National Research Study. Chicago: Second Harvest National Food Bank Network.

Sieber, Sam. 1981. Fatal Remedies: The Ironies of Social Intervention. New York: Plenum Press.

Simmel, Georg. 1908. "The Web of Group Affiliations." Pp. 65–128 in Georg Simmel, Conflict and the Web of Group Affiliations. New York: Free Press, 1955.

_____. 1918. "Fundamental Problems of Sociology." Pp. 1–40 in Georg Simmel, The Sociology of Georg Simmel. New York: Free Press, 1950.

Singh, Gopal K. 1995. "Infant Mortality in the United States: Trends, Differentials, and Projections, 1950 Through 2010." American Journal of Public Health 85:957–64.

Skolnick, Jerome. 1992. "Rethinking the Drug Problem." Daedalus 121(Summer):133–60.

Smart, Reginald, and Glenn F. Murray. 1982. "Narcotic Drug Abuse in 152 Countries: An Analysis of Social and Economic Conditions as Predictors." Drug and Alcohol Dependence 10:356–75.

_____. 1983. "Drug Abuse and Affluence in Five Countries: A Study of Economic and Health Conditions, 1960–1975." Drug and Alcohol Dependence 11:297–307.

Smeeding, Timothy. 1996. "America's Income Inequality: Where Do We Stand?" Challenge 39:45–54.

_____. 1997. "Financial Poverty in Developed Countries: The Evidence from the LIS." Working Paper 155, Luxembourg Income Study. Syracuse, NY: Syracuse University.

Smith, George Davie. 1996a. "Socioeconomic Differentials in Mortality Risk Among Men Screened for the Multiple Risk Factor Intervention Trial: Black Men." American Journal of Public Health 86:497–504.

_____. 1996b. "Socioeconomic Differentials in Mortality Risk Among Men Screened for the Multiple Risk Factor Intervention Trial: White Men." American Journal of Public Health 86:486–96.

Smith, J. Owens. 1987. The Politics of Racial Inequality. New York: Greenwood Press.

Smith, James A. 1991. The Idea Brokers: Think Tanks and the Rise of the New Policy Elite. New York: Free Press.

Snipp, C. Matthew. 1989. American Indians: The First of This Land. New York: Russell Sage.

Solinger, Ricky. 1994. The Abortionist: One Woman Against the Law. New York: Free Press.

Sontag, Susan. 1978. Illness as Metaphor. New York: Farrar, Straus, and Giroux.

Sophocles. 1972. Oedipus the King. Minneapolis: University of Minnesota Press.

Spector, Malcolm, and John I. Kitsuse. 1987. Constructing Social Problems. New York: Aldine de Gruyter.

Spierenburg, Pieter. 1994. "Faces of Violence: Homicide Trends and Cultural Meanings: Amsterdam, 1431–1816." Journal of Social History 28:701–16.

Spinden, Herbert. 1928. "The Population of Ancient America." Geographical Review 18:640–60.

Stack, Steven. 1987. "Publicized Executions and Homicide, 1950–1980." American Sociological Review 52:532–40.

Starr, Paul. 1982. The Transformation of American Medicine. New York: Basic Books.

Stock, Jacqueline L., Michelle A. Bell, Debra K. Boyer, and Frederick A. Connell. 1997. "Adolescent Pregnancy and Sexual Risk-Taking Among Sexually Abused Girls." Family Planning Perspectives 29:200–203.

Styron, William. 1979. Sophie's Choice. New York: Random House.

Sullivan, Mercer L. 1989. Getting Paid: Youth, Crime, and Work in the Inner City. Ithaca, NY: Cornell University Press.

Syme, S. Leonard. 1994. "The Social Environment and Health." Daedalus 123(Fall):79–86.

Szreter, Simon. 1988. "The Importance of Social Intervention in Britain's Mortality Decline c. 1850–1914: A Reinterpretation of Public Health." Society for the Study of Medicine 1:1–17.

Takaki, Ronald. 1989. Strangers from a Different Shore: A History of Asian Americans. New York: Penguin Books.

Taussig, Frederick. 1936. Abortion: Spontaneous and Induced. St. Louis: Mosby.

Teitelbaum, Michael S. 1975. "The Relevance of Demographic Transition Theory for Developing Countries." Science 188(May):420–25.

Tenner, Edward. 1996. Why Things Bite Back: Technology and the Revenge of Unintended Consequences. New York: Knopf.

Terry, Don. 1992. "Where Even a Grade School Is No Refuge from Gunfire." New York Times, national edition. October 17:1.

Thomas, Dylan. 1988. Collected Poems, 1934–1953. London: J. M. Dent & Sons.

Thomas, William I., and Dorothy Swaine Thomas. 1928. The Child in America. New York: Knopf.

Thompson, W. S. 1929. "Population." American Journal of Sociology 34:959–75.

Tietze, Christopher. 1948. "Abortion as a Cause of Death." Journal of Public Health 38:1434–41.

Tietze, Christopher, and Stanley K. Henshaw. 1986. Induced Abortion: A World Review. New York: Alan Guttmacher Institute.

Toner, Robin. 1996. "Harry and Louise Were Right, Sort Of." New York Times, national edition. November 24:4.

Trussell, James. 1997. "Medical Care Cost Savings from Adolescent Contraceptive Use." Family Planning Perspectives 29:248–54.

Tuchman, Barbara. 1978. A Distant Mirror. New York: Knopf.

Turner, Frederick Jackson. 1920. The Significance of the Frontier in American History. New York: Henry Holt.

Turner, Jonathan H. 1988. A Theory of Social Interaction. Stanford, CA: Stanford University Press.

Turner, Jonathan H., Leonard Beeghley, and Charles Powers. 1995. The Emergence of Sociological Theory, 3rd edition. Belmont, CA: Wadsworth.

Tyson, Jon E. 1994. "Evidence-Based Ethics and the Care of Premature Infants." Future of Children 5:197–213.

USBC (United States Bureau of the Census). 1974. Statistical Abstract, 1974. Washington, DC: U.S. Government Printing Office.

_____. 1975. Historical Statistics of the United States. Washington, DC: U.S. Government Printing Office.

_____. 1992. Statistical Abstract, 1992. Washington, DC: U.S. Government Printing Office.

_____. 1994. Statistical Abstract, 1994. Washington, DC: U.S. Government Printing Office.

_____. 1995a. "Child Support for Custodial Mothers and Fathers, 1991." Current Population Reports, P60-187. Washington, DC: U.S. Government Printing Office.

_____. 1995b. "The Effect of Health Insurance Coverage on Doctor and Hospital Visits: 1990 to 1992." Current Population Reports, P70-44. Washington, DC: U.S. Government Printing Office.

_____. 1995c. Older Workers, Retirement, and Pensions: A Comparative International Chartbook. Washington, DC: U.S. Government Printing Office.

_____. 1995d. "Population Profile of the United States, 1995." Current Population Reports, P23-189. Washington, DC: U.S. Government Printing Office.

_____. 1995e. Statistical Abstract, 1995. Washington, DC: U.S. Government Printing Office.

_____. 1996a. "Health Insurance Coverage: 1995." Current Population Reports, P60-195. Washington, DC: U.S. Government Printing Office.

_____. 1996b. "Money Income in the United States: 1995." Current Population Reports, P60-193. Washington, DC: U.S. Government Printing Office.

_____. 1996c. "65+ in the United States." Current Population Reports, P23-190. Washington, DC: U.S. Government Printing Office.

_____. 1996d. Statistical Abstract, 1996. Washington, DC: U.S. Government Printing Office.

_____. 1996e. "Who Loses Coverage and for How Long?" Current Population Reports, P70-54. Washington, DC: U.S. Government Printing Office.

_____. 1997a. Annual Demographic Survey: March Supplement. Current Population Reports. <http://ferret.bls.census.gov>

_____. 1997b. Poverty in the United States: 1996. Current Population Reports, P60-198. Washington, DC: U.S. Government Printing Office.

USBLS (United States Bureau of Labor Statistics). 1997. Employment and Earnings 44(January). Washington, DC: U.S. Government Printing Office.

USCCR (United States Commission on Civil Rights). 1992. Civil Rights Issues Facing Asian Americans in the 1990s. Washington, DC: U.S. Government Printing Office.

USDA (United States Department of Agriculture). 1994. Tobacco Situation and Outlook Report. Washington, DC: U.S. Government Printing Office.

USDHHS (United States Department of Health and Human Services). 1996. Report to Congress on Out-of-Wedlock Childbearing. Washington, DC: U.S. Government Printing Office.

USDJ (United States Department of Justice). 1995. Drugs and Crime Facts, 1994. Washington, DC: U.S. Government Printing Office.

USDL (United States Department of Labor). 1996. Work Experience of the Population. Washington, DC: U.S. Government Printing Office.

Valliant, George E. 1996. "A Long-Term Follow-up of Male Alcohol Abuse." Archives of General Psychiatry 53:243–50.

van Dijk, Jan J.M. 1990. Experiences of Crime Across the World: Key Findings from the 1989 International Crime Survey. Boston: Kluwer Law and Taxation.

Verbrugge, Lois M. 1989. "The Twain Meet: Empirical Explanations of Sex Differences in Health and Mortality." Journal of Health and Social Behavior 30:282–304.

Vernon, Amelia Wallace. 1993. African Americans at Mars Bluff, South Carolina. Baton Rouge: Louisiana State University Press.

WAB (World Almanac Books). 1995. World Almanac Book of Facts. Mahwah, NJ: World Almanac Books.

Wagner, Ellen J. 1992. Sexual Harassment in the Workplace. New York: AMACOM.

Warner, Roger. 1986. The Invisible Hand: The Marijuana Business. New York: William Morrow.

Weber, Max. 1905. The Protestant Ethic and the Spirit of Capitalism. New York: Scribners, 1958.

_____. 1913. Religion of China. New York: Free Press, 1951.

_____. 1917. Religion of India. New York: Free Press, 1952.

_____. 1918. "Science as a Vocation." Pp. 129–58 in Hans Gerth and C. Wright Mills (eds.), From Max Weber: Essays in Sociology. New York: Oxford University Press, 1947.

_____. 1920. Economy and Society. Totowa, NJ: Bedminster Press, 1968.

_____. 1922. "The Social Psychology of the World's Religions." Pp. 267–301 in Hans Gerth and C. Wright Mills (eds.), From Max Weber: Essays in Sociology. New York: Oxford University Press, 1947.

Welsh-Ovcharov, Bogomila. 1974. Van Gogh in Perspective. Englewood Cliffs, NJ: Prentice-Hall.

Westoff, Charles F. 1988. "Contraceptive Paths Toward a Reduction of Unintended Pregnancy and Abortion." Family Planning Perspectives 20:4–13.

WHO (World Health Organization). 1996. World Health Statistics Annual: 1995. Geneva: World Health Organization.

Wilder, Laura Ingalls. 1953. Little House on the Prairie. New York: Harper & Row.

Wilkinson, Richard G. 1994. "The Epidemiological Transition: From Material Scarcity to Social Disadvantage?" Daedalus 123(Fall):61–79.

_____. 1997. Unhealthy Societies: The Afflictions of Inequality. London: Routledge.

Williams, Bruce B. 1987. Black Workers in an Industrial Suburb: The Struggle Against Discrimination. New Brunswick, NJ: Rutgers University Press.

Williams, Terry M. 1990. The Cocaine Kids: The Inside Story of a Teenage Drug Ring. Reading, MA: Addison-Wesley.

Williamson, John B., and Fred C. Pampel. 1993. Old-Age Security in Comparative Perspective. New York: Oxford University Press.

Wilson, William Julius. 1987. The Truly Disadvantaged: The Inner City, the Underclass, and Public Policy. Chicago: University of Chicago Press.

Winslow, Gerald R., and James W. Walters (eds.). 1993. Facing Limits: Ethics and Health Care for the Elderly. Boulder, CO: Westview Press.

Wolfgang, Marvin, and Franco Ferracuti. 1967. The Subculture of Violence. London: Tavistock.

Wolinsky, Howard, and Tom Brune. 1994. The Serpent and the Staff: The Unhealthy Politics of the American Medical Association. New York: G. P. Putnams Sons.

Woodward, C. Vann. 1966. The Strange Career of Jim Croce. New York: Oxford University Press.

Wren, Christopher. 1997. "Keeping Cocaine Resilient: Low Cost and High Profit." New York Times, national edition. March 4:1.

Wright, Blanche Fisher. 1916. The Real Mother Goose. Chicago: Rand McNally.

Wright, Lawrence. 1997. "One Drop of Blood." Pp. 57–72 in Chester Hartman (ed.), Double Exposure: Poverty and Race in America. Armonk, NY: M.E. Sharpe.

Yeats, William Butler. 1933. Collected Poems. New York: Macmillan.

Zabin, Laurie Schwab, and Sarah C. Hayward. 1993. Adolescent Sexual Behavior and Childbearing. Newbury Park, CA: Sage.

Zelizer, Viviana A. 1985. Pricing the Priceless Child: The Changing Social Value of Children. New York: Basic Books.

_____. 1994. The Social Meaning of Money. New York: Basic Books.

Zimmerman, David. "How About a Self-Destruct Needle?" New York Times, national edition. August 18:A31.

Zola, Emile. 1996. The Dreyfus Affair: "J'accuse" and Other Writings. New Haven, CT: Yale University Press.

Zuravin, Susan J. 1991. "Unplanned Childbearing and Family Size: Their Relationship to Child Neglect and Abuse." Family Planning Perspectives 23:155–61.

Index

Page numbers containing definitions are in bold face

and poverty, 105–107
and racial/ethnic inequality, 82–87
Industrialization, 16, 31, **34**–36, 39,
    63–64, 66, 72, 88, 107–108, 159,
    181, 203, 205
Infant mortality rates, **75**–76, 79, 93,
    180, 181, 191, 192(fig.), 193,
    193(table), 197, 199, 203, 205
    neonatal vs. postneonatal mortality,
    194–195
Inflation, 16, 113–114, 116
Insurance. *See* Health issues, health
    insurance
Interest rates, 116
Irish immigrants, 88
Irving, John, 41

Jacksonville, Florida, 162
Jail. *See* Arrests/convictions
Japan, 192, 193, 194, 212–213, 215
Jefferson, Thomas, 71, 72
Johnson, Andrew, 89, 91
Johnson, Lyndon, 6, 93, 117
Jones, Elise, 40

Kanter, Rosabeth, 61
Kennedy, John, 6
Kolb, Lawrence, 124, 125
Konner, Melvin, 62
Kotlowitz, Alex, 146, 150
Kristoff, Nicholas, 212–213
Kübler-Ross, Elizabeth, 179

Land, 90–91
Land Act of 1820, 91
Lane, Roger, 159
Larkin, Philip, 180, 187
Laws, 89, 112, 113, 161. *See also*
    Change(s), legal changes
Learned helplessness, **54**
Leisure, 176, 177
Liberals, 160
Lieberson, Stanley, 90, 91
Life expectancy, 35, 108, 181, 184,
    192–193, 193(table), 205, 209,
    212, 213, 214

Lifestyles, 8, 9, 15, 63, 109, 111, 137,
    182, 198
Lipset, Seymour Martin, 32
Little House on the Prairie (Wilder), 34
Long Day, The (Richardson), 64
Long Day's Journey into Night
    (O'Neill), 120
Luker, Kristin, 38

McKeown, Thomas, 201, 202, 203–204,
    205
Macroeconomic policy, 109, **113**–114
Making of a Drug Free America
    (Falco), 125
Malaria, 212
Male authority, 50–52, 62, 68
Manufacturing, 115
Marijuana, 123–124, 131, 134, 139, 140
    Campaign Against Marijuana
        Planting (CAMP), 141
    Marijuana Tax Act of 1938, 142
    See also Drugs
Marriage, 6, 18, 22, 29, 33, 44, 50, 61,
    64, 216, 217. *See also* Women,
    employment of married
Massachusetts, 172, 193
Mather, Cotton, 167
Mattingly, Garrett, 42(n7)
Measure for Measure (Shakespeare),
    52–53
Media, 9–10, 40, 44, 66, 128
Medicaid/Medicare, 113, 162,
    172–173, 184, 208
Medical treatment, 201, 204–205, 208,
    209–210, 210(n2), 213, 215. *See
    also* Health issues; Technology,
    medical
Medieval world, 32, 147
Merton, Robert K., 158, 219
Mexico, 139
Middle class, 35, 44, 69, 84, 103,
    110–111, 114, 117, 131, 132, 133,
    146, 200, 209
Military campaigns, 157
Mills, C. Wright, 6, 10
Mississippi, 27, 31
Mitchell, W. Weir, 59